A family business?
The making of an international business élite

JANE MARCEAU
Professor of Public Policy, Australian National University

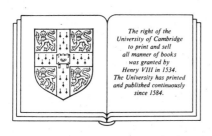

The right of the
University of Cambridge
to print and sell
all manner of books
was granted by
Henry VIII in 1534.
The University has printed
and published continuously
since 1584.

CAMBRIDGE UNIVERSITY PRESS
Cambridge   New York   New Rochelle   Melbourne   Sydney

EDITIONS DE
LA MAISON DES SCIENCES DE L'HOMME
Paris

Publishing by the Press Syndicate of the University of Cambridge
The Pitt Building, Trumpington Street, Cambridge CB2 1RP
32 East 57th Street, New York, NY 10022, USA
10 Stamford Road, Oakleigh, Melbourne 3166, Australia
and Editions de la Maison des Sciences de l'Homme
54 Boulevard Raspail, 75270 Paris Cedex 06

First published 1989

Printed in Great Britain at the University Press, Cambridge

British Library cataloguing in publication data

Marceau, J.F. (Jane F.)
A family business: the making of an
international business élite.
1. Multinational companies. Managers.
Social status
I. Title
305.5′54

Library of Congress cataloguing in publication data

Marceau, Jane.
A family business?: the making of an international business élite
Jane Marceau.
     p.   cm.
Bibliography.
Includes index.
ISBN 0 521 26731 5
1. Business education graduates – Europe.   2. Insead – Students.
3. Business education – Europe.   4. Social classes – Europe.
5. Industry – Social aspects – Europe.   I. Title.
HF1140.M37 1988
331.11′42 – dc19   88-20322

ISBN 0 521 26731 5
ISBN 2 7351 0262 9 (France only)

For Alex, who teased me about this book until I finished it.

For John, who will publish only other authors.

Contents

Tables

Preface

The research on which this book is based grew from an interest in the processes of social and economic change and continuity in Europe. Stemming from an initial concern with education as a mechanism of the reproduction of social inequality, the project developed into a much broader analysis of a three-way relationship: between organisational change in the context of economic shifts, the restructuring of the upper class in Europe and the use of a particular educational credential in the intra-class exclusion strategies developed in response to new conditions. In the light of these combined interests, the arena for the research had to cross national frontiers and include the international aspects of the social restructuring of the business class which are too often neglected by observers looking exclusively at the changing economic base.

This book presents the findings of two studies, carried out between 1973 and 1980. The project as a whole was made possible by two grants, the first from the (then) Social Science Research Council in Britain and the second from the *Commissariat Général du Plan*, through its social and economic research arm, the CORDES, in France.

The study focused on the background, education and careers of students and alumni of the Institut Européen d'Administration des Affaires (INSEAD) coming from twelve national origins. The physical field of the inquiry was as international as the population at the centre of the study. The research was based on archival records held in France, on questionnaires and on interviews carried out in cities across Europe and in the United States, while the results of the survey were analysed in Australia.

A project of this kind demands the time, patience and cooperation of many people, to whom I owe a great debt of appreciation. First and foremost, as the study principally concerned the Institute's students and alumni, I must express my thanks to two successive Deans, Dean Berry and Uwe Kitzinger, and their staff at INSEAD, at Fontainebleau. Without their encouragement and cooperation nothing would have been possible. Students and alumni of the Institute also spent much time answering what must sometimes have seemed excessively personal and occasionally irrelevant questions and talking with considerable patience to the researchers in the study, both indirectly through their replies to the questionnaires and directly in interview. Multinational managers are by definition extremely busy and those concerned frequently spent several hours helping us to understand their complex lives and careers. Thanks, too, must be expressed to their spouses for themselves contributing so much to our understanding of multinational families. I have to apologise to them. My own international career has complicated the production of a promised short report on the study. I hope this book will be some compensation.

The gathering of the data was long and complex and many people assisted with it at different times. They included Marie-Paule Leblond, Ursula Thanheiser, Jane Canva, Janet Massey, and Vincent Delbos. Interviews with alumni were carried out by Bernard Hucher, Nicole Celle, Christine Patte, Clotilde Giry and Pandelis Mitropoulos. Typing and retyping of question-naires was most efficiently and kindly done by Christine Poirot.

In France, the study could not have been carried out at all without the efficient and helpful cooperation of the administrative staff at the Maison des Sciences de l'Homme, who guided me through the intricacies of the spending of French public research monies.

In Australia, my heartfelt thanks must go to Michele Robertson who with the utmost patience not only corrected my naiveties about quantitative research but did all the computing on which the report is based. In Australia, too, my appreciation must also go to four very efficient people, Betty Gamble, Vivien Read, Jill Deck and, above all, Anabel Murray, who deciphered my handwriting and typed against deadlines with great goodwill. The final preparation of the book owes much to their skill.

Finally, I should like to emphasise that the project as a whole could not have been conceived without the intellectual stimulation provided by members of the Centre de Sociologie de l'Education et de la Culture, including particularly Pierre Bourdieu, Monique de Saint Martin, Luc Boltanski and Claude Grignon. Their work provided the framework for my own and they will immediately see the debt mine owes to them. I hope they will not be too displeased with the result. From another perspective, my friend Pascale Gruson was a most helpful and encouraging colleague.

My thanks and appreciation then must go to all these people. Responsibility for shortcomings and errors remains, of course, my own.

1. Introduction

'Le caractère ne suffit plus!' admonished a headline in a business magazine in France some two decades ago. The manager of modern capitalism must add competence to character. Training must be added to innate capacity. The 'natural leader' must rethink his tactics.

By a roundabout route the context and implications of such exhortations provided the stimulus for this book. The book is a contribution to the understanding of a part of that fascinating but slippery subject, social change and continuity in contemporary Europe. It focuses on the business world of Europe, on families, individuals and companies and the interactions between them which lie behind access to top positions in major corporations in the mid to late twentieth century. The context and starting point of the study lie in the major structural alterations which took place in the economic organisations of Europe in the decades after the Second World War. Of especial concern is the internationalisation of economic activity and the rapid growth of giant enterprises often operating across the whole European continent. In contrast to this broad background, the focus of the book is on the operation of some of the micro-mechanisms ensuring European social structural continuities as they relate to recruitment to the senior levels of the business world.

The book describes tactics and procedures developed by members of the business bourgeoisie in twelve countries in Europe as part of 'individualistic exclusion strategies' (Parkin, 1974) for use in the competition for access to coveted positions in the growing European international economy.

Successful exclusion strategies, as Parkin (1974) says, are based on the judicious manipulation of a number of attributes. In the case of the European business bourgeoisie, these attributes include attitudes and values instilled and nurtured within families, possession of credentials gained from valued educational institutions and the willingness to take the risks in the economic arena which lead to the greatest rewards, a willingness supported by the safety net of considerable social and economic capital whose value is in turn enhanced by marriage alliances.

Concentrating on the functioning of the family, in combination with the

1

education system of each country, and on decisions made in the managerial labour market, the book documents the mechanisms which largely ensure that many if not all bourgeois sons continue to enjoy a social and economic position similar to that of their parents. For some sons at least, little of significance has changed. Maintaining that position, however, is not always easy in the new conditions of production which formally separate family position from occupation, for even bourgeois sons must increasingly compete in a market. They must supplement their initial advantages with new weapons in the struggle for advancement, following advice to add 'competence' to 'character'. This book investigates one way in which they increase their chances in the developing European élite labour market.

Taking as a crucible the Institut Européen d'Administration des Affaires (INSEAD), the international business school at Fontainebleau, the book focuses on the experience and decisions of its alumni. The background and the careers of these young men as they move in the expanding sectors of the European economy are taken as a microcosm representing much more general processes of change and conservation in the business fractions of Europe's national bourgeoisies as component groups vie for position in a changing world. The argument is that, despite organisational changes and the formal separation of ownership and control, recruitment to senior positions in European enterprises continues to be a 'family business'. Many of the contenders are from family-owned businesses. But that is not all. Family and marriage continue to play crucial roles, for family capital of many kinds contributes to career success and is in turn reinforced by assets acquired through marriage. Equally important, beliefs developed in families of origin are refined as well as 'modernised' by select educational institutions which create among their students a 'family' of beliefs and orientations. These beliefs concern both the proper management of the economy and the correct ordering of society, present and future. The book emphasises the operation of both aspects of this international 'family business'.

The perspective in the book is on intra- rather than inter-class competition. Even within that perspective, the book suggests the narrow range of the groups competing and the extent to which in most Western European countries the business fraction of the bourgeoisie has managed to keep itself separate from or to dominate other fractions, long ensuring 'business' inheritance of business and linking its members to the liberal professions or to the public sector only in an occasional manner. Economic and other changes in recent years have, however, meant a change in some elements of social practice. In particular, business families have had to modify their methods of economic control and to develop exclusion strategies which maximise accumulation of cultural and social capital as well as the economic capital they traditionally relied on most. The changes in the economy, suggested below in chapter 2, have forced some to reconsider their options. They have had to find new resources for their sons to use in the competition for top positions in the expanding areas of the economy, notably those opened up by the growth of Europe-wide markets and in the companies operating in them, especially in the sectors of banking and finance and new manufactured products such as pharmaceuticals and electronics. High-level business education is one such resource: it limits the competition by redrawing the boundaries of the eligible to compete and, by its well-tailored fit to a niche in the market, highlights to employers the advantages of the qualified.

The 'micro' data presented in the book are the necessary complement to theories and descriptions of macro-level changes in recent European societies. They point to the functioning of the micro-mechanisms operating inside families, inside educational institutions and inside economic organisations and the interactions between these as factors important in the macro results. They constitute an empirical base which can be developed to form a link between the framework of large-scale changes and continuities and the structure of changes open to individuals of achieving or conserving their particular positions and life chances in the societies concerned.

The data used as the basis for the analysis in the book were gathered during two studies over the period 1973 to 1980. Each study used archival research, questionnaires and interviews. The study as a whole covered 2,110 students and alumni of INSEAD. The backgrounds of all 2,110 were gleaned from archival data. Questionnaires covered the careers of 200 French alumni in the first study and 304 of other nationalities in the second. In 1975, 134 French wives replied to questionnaires as did 169 wives of other nationalities in 1980. In 1973–4, sixty French students and twenty of their wives were interviewed. In 1980, 120 alumni of twelve nationalities, working and living in eight of Europe's major cities, were also interviewed, as were 'head-hunting' consultants in London, Brussels, Boston and New York. In the body of the book, the different chapters draw on and bring together data gathered from the diverse parts of the study and the text makes clear which sources of information are being used. Full details of the samples and coverage are given in Appendix A.

The intellectual context

As was said at the beginning, this book is a contribution to that fascinating but slippery subject, social change and continuity in contemporary Europe. The questions which the book addresses derive from long-standing debates among social analysts about the nature and mechanisms of social change in industrial societies. Following a nineteenth-century tradition, some more recent descriptions of modern societies have tried to seize their essential qualities through classification by genre – post-industrial, service, even self-service, or, from a different theoretical stance, 'late', monopoly or financial capitalist. These point the observer's attention towards a particular set of institutions and specific configurations of social arrangements. Such classifications are often said to be of limited use. They tend, for example, to have taxonomic rather than analytical value, although the description of Western European economies as now dominated by financial rather than industrial capitalism would seem apt overall. A second difficulty with such classifications is that they are immediately challenged by new empirical data or descriptions developed by competing theorists which suggest that much remains unaltered (Kumar, 1978).

Some classifications do, however, have their uses as starting points for analysis and one such encapsulates part, at least, of the reality which is relevant here. From the 1930s to the 1970s, in both North America and Europe, there raged a debate about the degree to which key changes in the organisation of the productive base of Western societies had ushered in an era of 'managerial' rather than individual 'bourgeois' capitalism. Initiated by Berle and Means (1932) and developed notably by Burnham (1941) and subsequent writers such as Bell (1961 and 1976) and Galbraith (1971), the managerialist thesis suggested that the organisation of the productive system of modern industrial Western nations and the societies of which it was the base had changed fundamentally with the growth of joint-stock companies, separating ownership from control, and the concomitant rise of the professional manager. In this phase of the system, the apparent controllers of productive organisations, the managers, were thought to be linked only indirectly to capital through employment in a senior executive position in a company owned by a large number of relatively small shareholders or by other corporate investors. In contrast to the situation in earlier phases of European industrial capitalism, in this phase of the system ownership and enterprise had thus been formally separated. Given their indirect link to ownership, these managers, it was argued, would be less concerned with the rights of capital and more with understanding the complexities of running an organisation which included employed 'staff' as an essential component, staff whose rights and status were not simply those of 'hired labour' in the traditional sense. Hence, it was also thought, these 'managerial capitalists' would be more concerned with the long-term performance and endurance of the enterprise they served than with short-term profits, and, indeed, that they might put social responsibility before the making of profits at all. The change in beliefs was felt to be as important as the change in structures.

During the 1970s, interest in issues of corporate management and control was renewed and important empirical studies were carried out in both Europe and North America. Theories were refined and tested with the new data and the data themselves were used to widen the debate to include broader discussion of the determinants and modalities of class formation and transformation in advanced capitalist societies.

This first interpretation of the implication of the changes from family to corporate capitalism was rapidly challenged. First, the data gathered showed conclusively that in their professional lives 'managers' behave in the same way as 'owners' (see, for example, James and Soref, 1981). Data gathered by Pahl and Winkler (1974) indeed found that senior managers were more, not less, profit-oriented than their bosses and they constitute, in Scott's phrase, the 'service' or 'lieutenant' class of capitalism. Moreover, as Useem was able to conclude on the basis of a survey of studies conducted in Britain and the USA, the business community as a whole, including senior managers, was as centrally concerned with profit growth as ever. Managers, moreover, lack public power: when leading corporate controllers enter politics, they do so on behalf of entrepreneurial not managerial interests (Useem, 1984: 27).

Secondly, much evidence now suggests that the whole debate about the separation of ownership and control was misdirected since, for example, top executives and other directors, many of whom hold or have held senior management positions in other companies, hold considerable wealth in shares in the companies they direct – as well as in others. A study by Lewellen of *The Ownership Income of Management* published in 1971 showed that in the USA in the 1960s the senior executives of the country's largest industrial corporations each owned an average of between $1 million and $2 million worth of their respective companies' stock. In terms of market values, these figures represent a threefold to fourfold *increase* in executive ownership since the early 1940s and this degree of ownership surpasses that of the executives of smaller firms, despite the theory that it is in large companies that ownership and control are most distinct (Lewellen, 1971: 11). Moreover, the declared annual income of such executives was three to five times greater than the fixed dollar rewards of salary, cash bonuses, pensions and other items: the difference was income derived from share ownership. Lewellen notes that 'post-tax gains and losses . . . from the mid-1950s on, have expanded to anywhere from $100,000 to $750,000 each year for the typical executive (of the biggest firms). The feeling here is that changes in wealth on that scale should at least begin to sensitise even the most callous professional manager to the shareholder viewpoint' (1971: 85 and 87). By December 1974, according to a study by Herman conducted with the support of the Twentieth Century Fund, the median value of company shares held by officer/directors of the 100 largest American manufacturing companies was $920,000 and this in a period of depressed stock prices (Herman, 1981: 93). In a study of the British business élite in the late 1970s, Fidler also showed the considerable wealth of major corporate directors (1981: 105–8).

It seems, therefore, that those who control also own – and probably vice versa, as Lewellen concludes. Moreover, different forms of corporate control have been identified. Analyses of issues concerning the areas of control by managers as well as of the dynamics of struggle for control within boards themselves, between executive and non-executive directors, have further refined the debate (see for example Pahl and Winkler, 1974 and Herman, 1981). Herman, for example, makes the distinction between literal control and power to constrain (1981: 19) and analyses the differences which occur according to whether there is control through a minority or a majority share-holding.

This new evidence is important for the book because it stresses the similarity of the position of the top executives and directors of joint-stock companies with that of their colleagues, who are more usually considered the business bourgeoisie. At the very top, it seems, ownership and control re-merge, a merger seen in the extent of capital ownership as well as in attitudes, values and policies. The merger is also important because in their choice of successors such owner-controllers will seek people like themselves, judged by the same criteria of profit performance, holding the same tried and trusted outlook, the same commitment to the capitalist ethic. They will seek successors complementary to them in skills, trained in the new techniques of management and with entrepreneurial flair but also adept at the increasingly central task of conducting successful inter-corporate relations and scanning the politico-economic environment. Bourgeois sons with a strong business credential and a wide network of contacts must be strong candidates for the succession.

This re-merger is important, too, for another reason. Over the last few decades, many business-owning families have diversified their wealth holdings so as to make them more secure and have developed portfolios in many other companies (Scott, 1979 and 1982). In some cases they have kept control over the enterprises which were the original source of their wealth – thus, in France, for example, almost half of the 200 biggest firms are still controlled by particular families, whether as majority or minority share-holders (Morin, 1974) – but in others they have sold out and invested capital elsewhere by buying shares. This has meant that many propertied families have become dependent on the decisions of others in the management of their assets. It is in their interests that people like themselves make the crucial decisions. Hence, on the one hand, they have an interest in ensuring that their sons reach those decision-making positions while, on the other, it is in the sons' interest to do so since their patrimony is ultimately at stake.

The result is that both directly through their holdings and indirectly through their sons, and later through their sons' holdings, 'entrepreneurial capitalists' continue to be important in the management of existing corporations and the creation of new ones. To these established entrepreneurial capitalists have been added new families, those of the corporate rich, the 'internal' capitalists, and those with a finance base (Scott, 1982), the financial capitalists first identified by Hilferding (1910). European capitalism thus continues to contain a strong family element and this needs to be remembered in the chapters which follow. The change from family to organisational accumulation is by no means complete.

Within the framework of the same debate about ownership and control, the boundaries of inquiry have been extended to examine the consequences of recent forms of corporate organisation for class formation, reproduction and interaction. First, as the empirical data available on national directors have expanded, so too have the geographical area and the time spectrum covered by the analysis. In particular, Scott (1982) uses directorship and other data to demonstrate the gradual emergence since the turn of the century of an integrated 'business class' in Britain, a process largely completed, he suggests, by the 1950s. This new class has been formed through the gradual building of interlinkages, corporate and familial, between the three previously separate fields of finance, manufacturing and landed wealth. The new 'business class' is both propertied and privileged. Its privileges and its position are both ensured and constrained by the changing conditions of productive organisation. Arising from the new conditions of the monopoly sector and the increased concentration of production, a powerful core of 25,000–50,000 families has emerged, Scott suggests, linked together by education, cultural and economic pursuits and lifestyle. Strategic decisions made by this core, who control the top 1,000 enterprises, determine the conditions for the whole business class who, in turn, determine the conditions of the 'massive social tail' of managers and other professional and technical groups attached to the class through their own position in the productive and political systems.

This newly integrated business class, however, is segmented. The lines of segmentation follow divisions between large and small companies, between sector and sector and by degree of centrality. At the centre, as Useem shows us in Britain and America, are the members of the 'inner circle', described as the 'core' by Scott and the 'inner group' by Zeitlin. These men – and they are mostly men – are particularly charged with two major functions. The first is developing networks of communication between companies, using their positions as outside directors to improve their scanning of business conditions and environments. Their second task is perhaps even more important. This task is the formulation and carriage of the input of business to the political processes and to public policies favourable to corporate enterprise. As the interventionist policies of government have impinged further on business decision-making, whether through regulation or stimulus, so the need for coherent advice from business has come to occupy a greater proportion of management and directorial time. As Useem says, the scale of large companies makes their effective management dependent on continuous monitoring of new developments in government policies, labour relations, international tensions, markets of many kinds, technology and business practices, ranging from stock options to charitable contributions. One of the most important means of keeping abreast of events for senior managers is personal contacts and direct presence (Useem, 1984: 45). These practices, too, lead the analyst back to the examination of kinship, education and informal networks.

Second, investigations have been made into the extent and the functions of formal networks, created through interlocking directorates among major corporations. Studies in most European countries have found quite extensive networks of interlocks between directorates within each national economy. Sophisticated studies such as those reported in Stokman, Ziegler and Scott (1985) using formal network analysis techniques have shown up major groupings of interlocked firms. The precise 'constellations of interest' represented vary from country to country. In some, such as Germany, some banks are central, locking together the direction of financial investments and industrial decision-making. In some, such as France, regional economies rather than national sectors are linked together through corporate interlocks. In Belgium, the holding-company links important industrial and financial groups, some family and some institutionally controlled. Some countries, notably those with the 'Latin' board system, have a high proportion of multiple directors and a high accumulation of positions by industrial directors. Those with a 'German' board system have somewhat fewer.

Most important for this book, moreover, is that the same studies have found an increasingly important *international* network of intercorporate linkages, notably between banks and the major industrial companies across Europe (with American participation in the networks, later joined by the Japanese, as Fennema, 1982, shows) and between national companies and their subsidiaries in other countries. The number of international links, their density and multiplicity, increased over the decade of the 1970s as the international activity of European corporations developed new markets and made new investments, a trend discussed further in chapter 2 below. In Europe, the nations with the greatest rise in the number of international corporate links were France, Switzerland and Germany. As Fennema points out, by 1976 the international corporate élite constituted by the 'big linkers', the persons carrying these important new links, played an important role in cementing national networks into an international whole (1982: 209). Their role, like that of their national counterparts (Fidler, 1981; Useem, 1984) is that of inter-corporate communication, developing policies to deal with common problems and encouraging governments to react favourably to their suggestions. The difference from their national peers is that, like their companies, their operations transcend frontiers and cross the whole of Europe. 'Who' these big linkers are has as yet hardly been investigated at all. This book, while not analysing the current international corporate élite, sheds some light on the processes leading to their emergence. Moreover, many of our respondents work in the companies at the centre of the networks. As true internationals in outlook and experience, they may well be the big linkers of the next generation.

The debate developing within the framework of issues related to the extent and significance of changes in the ownership and control of the major corporations of modern capitalism has thus led on to a consideration of class integration and the political and ideological representation of corporate interests. This integration has been long neglected by analysis and, at international rather than national level, is one of the themes of this book. International integration through people and through common ideas is seen here as going hand in hand with international corporate activities.

A second and major set of changes and continuities also forms the background to the analysis presented in this book. In Europe, from the early 1960s, much attention, both participant and academic, came to focus on the 'modernisation' of European societies seen in the rapidly changing economic structures of many European economies over the period of post-war reconstruction and in modifications to the productive system perceived as linked to the influence of American enterprise expansion and the associated export to Europe of American management methods and corporate structures.

These imported structures and methods were seen by both some observers and some actors, such as politicians, as typical of 'modern' societies and economies, and were welcomed as 'progress', as a step in the 'modernisation' of the 'antiquated' structures and business practices of *patronat* Europe (Servan-Schreiber, 1969). Many even thought, as a variation of the managerialist thesis, that the growth of 'soft' management techniques would herald a reduction in the repressive nature of the internal workings of the enterprise. The *patronat* would be replaced with a more sympathetic system of productive control, technocratically oriented to the proper management of both state and economy.

This second set of beliefs and debates generated a whole literature analysing contemporary movements and exhorting action for the future. The language and concepts used by the 'modernisers' were incorporated into the vocabulary of political parties of many hues and in many countries and became an integral part of the discourse of politicians, public servants and company managers, to an extent which inspired the publication in France in the 1970s by Bourdieu and his colleagues of an 'Encyclopédie de la Technocratie' (1976) which mapped the rhetoric and values of what was seen by many as a whole new economy and society.

Whatever the particular views about the extent, the desirability and the more general consequences of the alterations by the 1960s, it seemed clear to all that much in both economies and societies had indeed changed in significant ways. Individual company size did indeed grow fast, as did the total number of large and giant firms. The internationalisation of productive activity in Europe also grew apace. Corporate structures were redesigned. The ranks of senior managers expanded fast and they acquired new skills in marketing, finance and corporate strategy. Other changes were seen in the rapid introduction of new technology, in the growth of mass markets for consumption products and in rising standards of living and leisure for European populations everywhere.

Other aspects of society also looked different. Mass secondary education had become compulsory and in most European countries the numbers of young people enrolled in tertiary education increased fast. New disciplines, especially in the social sciences, developed and expanded. New professional ideals, credentialled through courses bearing the stamp of higher education, were nailed to the masthead of many organisations and crept into the long-reticent world of business. From these changes grew theses about 'post-industrial' societies with financial capitalism and the service sector as their base.

The social backlash caused by the changes, erupting most dramatically in the street events and violence of May 1968 in France, the economic and political troubles which persisted in many countries and the disaffection of many young people raised in an age of affluence, while they demonstrated that the path forward was not a smooth one did not seriously shake a public sense that change was the order of the day and that the 'modernisation' of the economy and societies of Europe would suffer only temporary setbacks. The near-fatal shock which that view was to receive only came with the oil crisis, which began in 1974.

In the face of change and reaction to it, however, from the late 1960s many European observers began to look more closely at what had and what had not altered in their societies. They saw that while most Europeans were financially better off, not only did poverty still remain in evidence but the structure of societies had changed little. The late 1960s and early 1970s were the heyday among sociologists of a reaction to theses about post-industrial society and of a return amongst both Marxists and Weberians to an interpretation of Western European societies which suggested that while late-twentieth-century capitalism had altered its form it had not changed its nature. Many social institutions previously seen as essentially progressive, as leading towards increases in some form of social equity, were suddenly reinterpreted and emphasis was placed instead on the central role these institutions played in the reproduction over time of the social and economic order of late capitalism. From this perspective, far from acting as an instrument of social change, education in particular came to be seen both in Europe and in America as the prime mechanism of social reproduction (Althusser, 1970; Baudelot and Establet, 1971; Bourdieu, 1970; Bourdieu, 1971; Bowles and Gintis, 1976). Social conservation rather than change came to dominate much academic debate.

Within this discussion, the most influential analysts of the period, whether Marxist or Weberian, emphasised macro-level changes and continuities in economy and society and examined the role of major institutional systems in social reproduction. Some, such as Althusser (1969) and Poulantzas (1974), saw social structures as incapable of explanation through empirical analysis (although Poulantzas did resort to the use of census data for his discussion of the 'middle classes' in France). Even within the Weberian tradition, major analyses of social and economic change or continuity were mostly cast at a high level of generality, while observers with a more empirical slant focused more on very particular aspects of their societies, such as family structure or industrial labour organisation.

These debates and analyses together form the background of the present work. They sketch a framework within which other studies should be undertaken. They invite many and detailed questions about personnel, about mechanisms, about the implications of one set of changes for other areas of economy and society. Pulling together macro-modifications pushes the analyst to investigate further the *micro*-mechanisms of social change and social reproduction and to develop ways of linking these to the macro-level outcomes. In the case of modern European societies, this means first linking changes in the organisation of the productive process and the functioning of other social institutions. But it also means more than that. As was said at the beginning, it also means a focus on the micro-mechanisms which operate inside families and inside selected educational institutions and which influence the allocation of individuals both at entry to and once inside the labour market, that central distributive device so often analysed only or principally at macro-level. These micro-mechanisms in turn need to be understood in relation to their wider context, for they may be conceptualised as elements in strategies which families, individuals and groups develop in the constant battle to maintain or improve position and maximise rewards in an uncertain and continually changing world.

In this battle, some groups, some families and some individuals are better placed to fight successfully. They control, or at least have access to, greater quantities and a wider range of useful resources. They are able to develop strategies whose first effect is to exclude many competitors from access to desirable positions, strategies whose aim, in Parkin's words, is to create and maintain a group of ineligibles (1974).

The major competitors for access to coveted positions in Europe in the 1970s were, of course, largely drawn from a narrow segment of the population. Analysing the strategies developed by the combatants therefore focuses attention on *intra*- rather than *inter*-class relations. A classic form of intra-class skirmishing, these strategies rely on constant redefinition of the characteristics considered essential in the incumbents of high-level positions. In an age that believes in rewarding 'expertise', education plays a crucial role. As Parkin says, the individualistic rules of exclusion characteristic of intra-class battles reach their apogee in credentialism, the use of examinations to control entry to coveted positions. At the same time, other forms of capital must also be used to monopolise chances of entry to the major credentialling institutions. Using such strategies, members of the business bourgeoisie seek to retain the right to nominate their successors in the control of the productive system: in principle singling out specific characteristics of individuals as the criteria of election to these positions, in practice they use the social, cultural and economic power of the family group to maximise the value, both symbolic and practical, of the credentials held. In that way, they ally the full weight of social power to that of educational legitimacy. This book illustrates that process.

In doing so, the book is set within the general framework developed by Bourdieu and his colleagues in their analysis of changes in the productive structure of France which led to the development of a salaried rather than a 'possessory' bourgeoisie and of the role of the education system in the reproduction of the social hierarchy in a situation where bourgeois families could no longer transmit their position directly to their sons but had to develop 'strategies of reconversion' (Bourdieu, Boltanski and de Saint Martin, 1973). That framework serves as the background for the discussion here of family, company and individual decision-making. It generates questions about the role of particular educational institutions, about the way the process of 'reconversion' by bourgeois sons is geared to particularities within the business employment market and about the ways in which families and individuals interact both with the educational institutions crucial to the credentialling process and with the companies which ultimately determine the nature of the managerial labour market. It seeks to show in practice what firms are seeking and the ways in and extent to which the skills encapsulated in new formal credentials interact with, replace or supplement the more traditional qualities sought of senior managers. By doing this, the book seeks to see how effective are these new forms of exclusion strategies and to demonstrate how they interact with more traditional mechanisms to ensure both change and continuity.

The book then has three focuses: family, career paths and beliefs. Discussing these, however, proved to be a particularly complex task, for it involves bringing together individuals, families, firms and a more general socio-economic context. Many issues came to seem to need discussion. In particular, aspects of the stratification debate came to loom large. First, while concentrating on the micro-mechanisms of social change and conservation, the book thus also seeks to widen the arena in which the analysis takes place by extending it to the international stage. For too long, studies of systems of social stratification have referred only to mechanisms operating inside one country or on an imperialistic or colonial basis. In present economic circumstances, this narrow focus neglects a vital section of the system, the links created by a 'local' international productive system and the associated opportunity structure which continually expand the frontiers of the élite labour market and present new opportunities to those in a position to choose as old ones disappear. In earlier times, 'surplus' European sons went to conquer new territories and administer new colonies. Now from the business rather than an administrative or social élite, they go into the international economic arena.

Second, the book seeks to enrich the stratification debate by returning to a theme which interested the early managerialist theorists and whose development looms large in the analysis of the 'inner circle' of modern capitalism by Useem, Scott and others. This theme emphasises family in another sense, that of the attitudes and values held by incumbents and potential incumbents of the most senior positions in European enterprises. It emphasises the development of common frameworks of thought about economic, social and political questions, a framework which binds together members of a group who individually find themselves in diverse social, geographical and professional positions which might otherwise militate against perceptions of common interest. The INSEAD Master of Business Administration (MBA) course seems to develop a set of common frameworks which guide analysis of business and political issues and hence influence the choice of policy answers, for it tends to make some appear self-evident while others are excluded by definition. Especially when loaded with technocratic rhetoric, these frameworks, while using the language of change, become conserving elements by discouraging consideration of all but a narrow range of social and economic innovations at the same time as they exclude 'inexpert' outsiders from an effective share in decision-making by rendering their knowledge illegitimate. Reared in the most traditional sections of the bourgeoisie, nurtured in traditional educational establishments, business-school-trained managers seem mostly to have acquired a new rhetoric with which to express traditional ideas while at the same time rendering those ideas legitimate in a society which has 'change' as a generalised idea on the public agenda.

The growth of the international arena and the common framework for thought developed by business education together have important implications. The creation of a self-conscious international business élite with a sense of *international* rather than national issues as its central concern means that the frame of reference used in business policy decisions and in discussions with public authorities (and trade unions) is fundamentally different from that of national business and public leaders. The stage on which such an élite plays and the economic strategies its members advocate will not have the same boundaries as those of national governments attempting to manage their economies. This difference of focus has become especially important in recent decades as economic management has come to hold the central place in the political agendas and strategies of most European governments, trying to control the economy as the base from which to generate social and ultimately political rewards. The beliefs of the managers of the international economy have thus become of increasing concern to national governments, at the same time as their activities have become harder to control.

These questions are addressed in the book through the beginning of an 'ethnography' of family and educational practices within the business fractions of the bourgeoisie across twelve European countries and through an analysis of the careers of their sons.[1] By the 1980s, many of the young managers concerned, having taken early advantage of the opportunity to acquire a piece of cultural capital with exceptionally high value in the international business market place in the boom years of the 1960s and early 1970s, seemed set ultimately to control large enterprises. While some preferred to move to control smaller enterprises, nevertheless they also often came to occupy positions of influence in national economies. By analysing the career decisions of individual managers, the book examines first the mechanisms by which young people of different European nationalities develop an early interest in a career in business and then take the decision to move on to the international business stage.

Third, and in contrast to the apparent 'inevitability' of the outcome suggested, the analysis focuses on the intricacies of individual strategies for developing the kinds of careers considered appropriate by managers rising in the institutions of international economic life. In particular, the data gathered suggest the inadequacy of the notion of 'career path' as a description of the routes to the top effectively followed by those going fastest on career ladders placed on the international stage. The term career 'path' or even ladder suggests a smooth progression, a track that is enshrined in company organigrams and personnel policies. In practice, it is suggested here, taking maximum advantage of opportunities available requires the constant use of the traditional entrepreneurial skills of risk-taking and flair for locating market gaps. Careers must be cobbled together from a judiciously chosen mix of opportunities, selected from offerings available in diverse companies, sectors and countries, making maximum use of available personal resources derived from different forms of family capital, from possession of specific skills, and from carefully nurtured social and professional networks. Career trajectories leading to senior positions in the international economy are not simple and must overcome many pitfalls: successful strategies are diverse.

The book is also to some extent a work of history and illustrates once again the need for sociological analysis to be located in a specific historical context. Carried out between 1973 and 1980, the study describes a situation in the economies and societies of Europe in the 1960s and 1970s. It focuses on an institution which is itself a result of a particular process of cultural and economic diffusion: from a dominant economy outside its boundaries, the United States of America, Europe after 1945 took over not only multinational companies but also, more gradually, the cultural institutions associated (temporarily at least) with that economy. European patterns of management were slowly adapted to the style and demands of these 'new' and dominant economic institutions whose growth they also imitated, expanding well beyond the national frontiers of their countries of origin. That period of economic expansion slowed down in the late 1970s and 1980s as part of the world recession and the period of expansion of demand for managers with the skills of an MBA may similarly have declined, at least in the manufacturing sector. In different economic circumstances, one may expect different institutions and sets of beliefs to come to the fore and hence new exclusion strategies to be developed. Particularly in times of economic restructuring, new modes of class structuration will eventually emerge. Such changes, however, take time and, once in place, the MBAs concerned will continue to develop their careers in the business market place for many years to come, increasing their importance as they rise in their organisations. As they in turn recruit their juniors, so they will continue to shape company policies and strategies and influence the directions of economic life, since the economic organisations they manage are unlikely to fade from the scene. Their ideas and experiences will continue to be as important as the capital they control through their families and in the course of their professional lives. Their preferences, as seen in their decisions, will continue to influence the strategies their juniors must develop for they will contribute to determining the conditions of action and development, both in the companies they control and beyond at both core and periphery of the capitalism of the year 2000. Thus, for example, as they rise higher some will enter the 'inner circle' of the capitalist class and move major company resources towards broader goals as well as influence both the agenda of public debate and specific decisions made by governments. To the extent that they create a Europe-wide inner circle they will have even greater impact than their 'nationalist' *confrères*. To the extent that they bring to their *confrères'* deliberations and attitudes an internationalist perspective, they will strengthen the integration of national business élites across political frontiers.

To link such macro-level modifications to the micro-mechanisms of change and conservation considered in this book, one must consider the context, the changing economic and enterprise structure in conjunction with a description of the factors leading to the creation of the Business School concerned. The first section of the book, chapter 2, therefore, outlines the reasons why changes in business management practices and organisation were adopted and the consequences for the opportunity structure open to the sons of European national bourgeoisies. The next section, chapter 3, focuses on the social origins and educational trajectories of the students and alumni at the centre of the study. The fourth chapter indicates how individual career choices are made and begins the exploration of the importance of the family in the generation of expectations, motivations and the early career choices made by aspiring managers. The next section, chapters 5 and 6, presents the career paths followed across Europe before and after INSEAD. That discussion focuses on the market 'fit' between hirers' requirements and the ambitions and qualifications of the alumni seeking to move fast to the top and on the major routes they chose to take to reach their goals. The next section has a rather different orientation, focusing on families and their role, through the social, economic and cultural capital which they provide, in the successful pursuit of a high-level business career in Europe. Chapter 8 presents INSEADs as a family in a different sense, one of values, attitudes and orientations. The next chapter assesses the differences and similarities between national and international business élites in Europe, finding the latter both essentially similar to national management personnel and different from them in orientation and outlook. It also looks more closely at the role of origins and connections in the rise to the top.

These last chapters together suggest that, even narrower in origins and educational experiences than national élites, the new international business 'family' has developed a distinctive outlook which will encourage its members to make common cause across national boundaries and to bring to European management new practices while retaining crucial traditional values. The combination may be particularly powerful in the reproduction of business and social structures in Europe, for it creates from kinship and common experiences an extended or parallel 'family' of ideas and orientations which is flexible and forward looking while also socially and economically a 'conserving discourse'. Members of that family, however, despite their origins are, it seems, unlikely to be drawn backwards to the 'new conservative' rhetoric of their national counterparts and thus, perhaps in some ways despite themselves, will remain a relatively progressive force in the business world of Europe. In that sense, while there is much continuity, there is nevertheless some change in the orientations of the 'family business', whose members seem likely to retain their importance in the Europe of the next half century.

2. The creation of a new business Europe: the rise of the multinational firm and its managers

Economic development in Western European countries over the decades after 1945 involved dramatic shifts, summarised in the popular imagination as the 'German miracle', the 'French miracle' and even the 'Italian miracle'. Most European economies enormously increased their productive capacity, through a series of public and private investments in new sources of power, transport, technology, education and the creation of supra-national markets in the European Economic Community (EEC) and the European Free Trade Area (EFTA). Standards of living everywhere in Western Europe rose rapidly in the late 1950s and 1960s and increased incomes themselves generated new economic demands, notably for the rapidly expanding range of consumer goods. The 1950s and 1960s saw greatly altered proportions of the population employed in different sectors of production; increased firm size and a concentration of production into fewer, larger enterprises; the growth of a diversified service sector, including large financial institutions but also many small companies in different areas of the field; and the 'internationalisation' of many activities, in production and in service sectors. While an international focus was not new for some European companies, and by the late nineteenth century large German industrial enterprises were concentrating on overseas markets (Daems, 1980: 6), what was new was the dominance of major markets by transnational corporations and the greatly increased importance of international business.

These changes were accompanied by significant modifications in the relative importance of different productive and service activities and in the internal management structures of business organisations. First, products altered. The products of the first Industrial Revolution, such as textiles, largely produced in small or medium enterprises dominated by single families or groups of family members,[1] gave way to mass-market consumer goods, usually based in the electrical, pharmaceutical, chemical and subsequently electronic industries. Altered product markets led to the closure of many firms and the merging of others, while giant firms grew alongside in the new sectors.

17

A gradual but general restructuring of much of Europe's industry took place, a process accelerated by government policies at home[2] and altered international conditions of production. Changed conditions for manufacturing brought with them new developments in the organisation of financial markets, with the formation of new Europe-wide banking institutions (Renwick, 1985 and Steuber, 1976).

Second, the component elements of the economy, the major companies, changed greatly in size and structure. Many companies grew in size, largely through merger and acquisition. Active merger movements took place, such as those in Germany in the late 1950s and around 1970, notably in food and drink, engineering, metals, textiles and clothing (George and Ward, 1975: 50–1); in the Netherlands, where the number of enterprises acquired or amalgamated in mining, manufacturing and distribution rose from 100 in 1958–61 to nearly 600 in 1966–9; and in the UK. As a consequence, industrial concentration rose markedly, so that by the mid-1970s the largest 100 companies controlled more than half of all manufacturing in the UK and sales in West Germany (de Jong, in Jacquemin and de Jong, 1976: 101).

Increase in company size was particularly spectacular in certain sectors. By the mid 1970s, among the 200 largest companies in the world could be found many which were European rather than American and which were in newly developing sectors. By 1976, for example, among the fifty biggest enterprises in the world could be seen not only the expected European petroleum and motor-car companies but also two French companies, one in glass, chemicals and building materials (Saint-Gobain-Pont-à-Mousson)[3] and one in heavy metals (Schneider). It also included the Italian chemical company Montedison and the British–Dutch Unilever. Two other French companies, both at least partly involved in manufacturing chemicals, appeared in the top hundred: Péchiney-Ugine-Kuhlman and Rhône-Poulenc. In the top twenty was yet another French firm, this time in food, BSN-Gervais-Danone. Others in cement, aeronautics and industrial gas also appeared (*Cahiers Français*, 1979: 5 and 23).

European financial institutions also expanded dramatically and among the world's seven biggest banks in 1976 could be found four which were French and one German. The top thirty included thirteen European banks, notably five German, two British, one Italian and one Dutch as well as the four French (*Cahiers Français*, 1979: 49).

By 1980 the creation of giant enterprises had gone considerably further and far more of the world's largest one hundred companies were European than in 1970. They included Philips and DSM (Dutch), Siemens, Hoechst, Bayer, BASF, Thyssen, Ruhrkohle, Veba, Krupp, Marinesmann, AEG and Telefunken (German), Nestlé (Swiss), ICI (British) and CGE-Thomson (French) (*L'Expansion*, 1980: 142–3). These companies are immediately recognisable as European household names and are especially concentrated in the new sectors of electrical equipment, electronics, pharmaceuticals and chemicals, the quintessential products of late-twentieth-century capitalism.

Some European economies, notably in Germany and France, had proved particularly conducive to the growth of these giant enterprises. By 1970[4], of the world's largest 200 non-American firms, eighty were manufacturing firms headquartered in Europe. Of these, twenty-nine were German and twenty-one French but smaller countries were also represented: nine of the firms were Swedish, seven each Swiss and Italian, six Belgian, five Dutch and one Luxembourgeois. As they grew in size, major firms across Europe also began to change their structures and diversify their activities. Conglomerates, the most diversified and loosely connected companies, began to increase in number in the 1960s, although they were never as common in Europe as in North America. Single-industry firms also formed large groups and some manufacturers, using their enormously increased pool of money resources, moved into the financial markets.

Third, and most important for our thesis here, the internationalisation of company activities simultaneously advanced apace and is one of the outstanding characteristics of the European economy of the last few decades. The European riposte to the 'American challenge' of the early 1960s was well established a decade later. For instance, sixty-four of the giant manufacturing firms mentioned above had enormously increased their international operations, seen both in their volume of exports and the creation or acquisition of foreign manufacturing subsidiaries. As Franko reports, on the eve of the Second World War continental European companies operated approximately 510 foreign manufacturing subsidiaries: by 1971 that number was five times greater (1976: 236). Sixty-four of *Fortune*'s list of the largest non-American companies in 1970 had manufacturing operations in six or more foreign nations while some operated in up to eight more countries. Nine enterprises had more than half of their employees working abroad: these included Swiss, Swedish, Dutch, French and Italian firms. Although it was the American influx of investment to Europe that dominated comment in the press and some academic responses at the time (Servan-Schreiber, 1967), by 1971 the rate of establishment of foreign manufacturing operations of European multinationals was greater than that of American firms and almost five times faster than that of the Japanese.

At the same time, some household-name companies merged or were planning to merge with firms in other countries, thus increasing their transnationality: Ciba-Geigy and Agfa-Gevaert immediately spring to mind. In the 1960s and on into the 1970s, international mergers constituted between 11% and 25% of all mergers in West Germany, the UK, Sweden, the Netherlands, and France (de Jong in Jacquemin and de Jong, 1976: 102). In the finance world, the 1970s saw the emergence of European banking consortia which linked British banks with French and Italian, and German banks with Swiss and Dutch in the scramble to cope with the influx of 'petro-dollars' and the new Euro-dollar market. New financial centres in Paris, Luxemburg, Brussels and elsewhere developed fast in the 1970s (Steuber, 1976). It was the heyday of European multinational expansion, an expansion which continued to intensify, at least until 1976. Multinational interlinks grew apace, sometimes with excessive haste, as the later break-up of firms such as VMF-Fokker and Estel indicated, and by the 1980s governments were stepping in to protect their national interests in crucial fields as the international merger movement accelerated (Fennema and Schiff, 1985).

Most of the expansion, unlike that of the companies' American cousins, remained local, in contiguous European nations. By 1971, eighty-five European multinationals had 781 subsidiaries, around nine each, located within the countries of the EEC. EFTA companies, too, invested within EFTA boundaries, although these firms had on average fewer subsidiaries. Intra-EEC and intra-EFTA investment was particularly high in aluminium, glass, metals, processed foods, and chemicals. Some direct foreign investment also crossed EEC and EFTA borders but remained European. Swiss and Swedish enterprises alone had 202 subsidiaries in the EEC and 131 within EFTA. European multinational expansion was thus essentially European, concentrating its activities and effects in a relatively small geographical area.

The nature of the operations of such giant firms and their potential impact on national economies can be seen in the following newspaper report in 1970:

A lot more is going to be heard about Hoechst and other West German companies in the seventies as Europe's industrial integration movement . . . gains momentum, swinging back the balance of foreign investment from United States hands. Hoechst is paving the way for many who will follow . . . The current rate of long term capital that is being exported is roughly a third of West Germany's annual creation of new capital . . . Bayer alone has over 120 foreign companies . . . The [Hoechst] group . . . has formed in the past year a partnership with France's second biggest [pharmaceutical] firm. Now Reed brings Hoechst to Britain . . . the Common Market has been good for Hoechst – with nearly two thirds of its world turnover now coming from the EEC . . . says Hoechst: 'These bases abroad, consisting of selling and production companies, are an essential prerequisite of the continued growth of the company.'

(*The Times*, 2 January 1970: 19)

While we have emphasised the Europeanisation of Europe's multinational business operations, American direct investment in Europe was of course even more considerable over the period to 1975, with very large numbers of American manufacturing and banking enterprises taking advantage of decreased European regulation and increased individual incomes. Together, large American and European companies were changing the structure of business opportunities in Europe and enormously increasing the international orientations of European enterprise and entrepreneurs.

Managerial careers in movement

By their new orientation and altered structures, companies were also changing the opportunities available to individuals pursuing managerial careers. Greater size, enormously increased trans-frontier activities and, above all, an increasingly competitive and turbulent economic environment encouraged large European firms to modify their structures and to adopt new methods of management, largely following the American model.

Until the 1970s, the operations of most large European enterprises were organised on the lines of a mother–daughter subsidiary relationship and each company was organised along the axes of the major functions involved in the production and selling of its commodities, even when much of this took place outside home-country boundaries. There was only one managerial hierarchy for each function, leading ultimately to the president of the mother company. Reporting procedures were not usually standardised and lines of communication often did not follow the formal chains of command. Problems of coordinating such widespread activities seemed insoluble with functional organisation (Mason, Miller and Weigel, 1981: 353). Worse still for managers geographically far away, no one locally was responsible for all the parts of production and selling operations, rendering local unit coordination difficult (Horovitz, 1980).

In many companies, these structures gradually gave way to new ones, based principally on product or area divisions and the specific recognition of supranationality. Many enterprises adopted 'global' forms of organisation such as world-wide product, area, mixed or matrix structures, joint ventures with local foreign enterprises or holding companies.

These developments had important consequences for managerial careers in Europe. Many offered new opportunities, while some involved reorienting existing careers to take advantage of changed structures. First, and perhaps most important, the adoption of new divisionalised methods created a much more unified European managerial market, for management practices and enterprise structures in different countries began to converge. Thus, for the first time, by the 1970s French corporate structure resembled that of its neighbours, Britain and Germany, for by the beginning of the decade just over half of the largest French, German and British companies had divisionalised structures (Lévy-Leboyer, 1979: 117).

Second, divisonalised structures assign profit responsibility for operating decisions to managers of self-contained business units and push that responsibility further down the line. Success as a divisional manager rather than a functional head thus requires a global approach to the enterprise as a whole and a knowledge of many functions.

Third, within many corporations, divisionalised or not, changes also occurred in the relative importance of different managerial functions. Pushed by the consumer boom and the concentration by many firms on the production of mass-market goods and services, marketing rapidly increased in importance. Large companies also had new internal control needs as well as the need to cope with changing finance markets and investment patterns. Together these needs helped raise the relative status of the financial functions in companies, while the very size and operational complexity of giant firms encouraged the development of long-term corporate plans and new market-sharing and product strategies. In contrast, other functions, such as those of production, were downgraded.

Most important, perhaps, in the context of this book, international operations generated new skill needs, in particular for cultural and political understanding as well as linguistic abilities not previously considered important. These skill needs cut across functions, adding a new dimension to the qualifications considered useful for many posts in major companies, whether divisionalised or not.

Altered size, scale and place of operations, together with lengthening managerial hierarchies, also created for companies a problem of 'managing the managers' and ensuring the acceptability and legitimacy of company activities to public authorities, managers and workers over a wide geographical and culturally varied area. A new *style* of management also came to be needed.

Thus, whether 'strategy followed structure' or vice versa in Europe (Chandler, 1962; Franko, 1976), it seems clear that these changes together entailed many modifications in managerial career paths, creating new opportunities at the same time as they closed off or made less attractive certain existing ones.

The professionalisation of management: business education and the new Europe

At the same time as these changes were occurring, starting in the 1950s, many European private and semi-public bodies such as Chambers of Industry and Commerce were actively seeking to encourage the introduction of American management practices, which they saw both as the key to economic success and the symbol of the existence of a new breed of professional manager. Such proselytisation, together with new demands within firms and the standardisation and formalisation of management procedures across companies, contributed greatly to the professionalisation of 'management' defined as a particular set of skills universally applicable by people suitably trained in formal educational institutions. No longer was a specialist degree, supplemented by experience obtained on the job, seen as sufficient training by Europe's more dynamic companies, who thus altered the value of many of the skills held by aspiring managers. The creation in Europe of graduate business schools on the American model seems to have been an educational response to the objective changes already occurring in the size, structure, operating strategies and environment of the major enterprises developing in Europe in the post-war period (see Whitley, Thomas and Marceau, 1981: chap. 2). At the same time, the existence of credentialled managers trained in these schools could be expected to push companies further in the rationalisation of managerial procedures and to encourage the spread of new practices. For these reasons it would seem that the market for top-level managers began to alter significantly and at an increasing pace.

While business schools offering graduate degrees in business administration or management were created in America in the last decades of the nineteenth century and the first decade of the twentieth, Europe lagged far behind in the academic training of its businessmen until well after 1945. Management education, as distinct from training in commerce, was only introduced to Europe on any significant scale in the late 1950s and 1960s. Private schools came first.[5] INSEAD, the first graduate business school modelled on American lines, opened its doors to its first students in 1959.

A decade later the public and semi-public sector had caught up. Business schools had been established in most countries of Europe and included institutions in London and Manchester in Britain, the Instituto de Estudios Superiores de la Empresa (IESE) in Barcelona, the Centre des Etudes Supérieures des Affaires (CESA) in France and the Interuniversitair Instituut Bedrijfskunde in Delft. Switzerland hosts two major institutions of management education, the Centre d'Etudes Industrielles (CEI) in Geneva and IMÉDÉ at Lausanne, although both for a long time remained oriented to short-course, in-service training for particular companies, such as Nestlé.

The specific circumstances leading to the creation of business schools in different countries varied. In Britain, for example, the schools seemed to be principally the creation of a group of business and university people who took up the ideas of the 'management intellectuals' of earlier decades (Whitley, Thomas and Marceau, 1981: chapter 3). In France, other factors were important. The sponsors of INSEAD were centred on the Paris and International Chambers of Commerce and the European Productivity Agency, groups especially attuned to American methods of business management. As was suggested earlier, these business leaders were convinced that the secret of rapid economic development in European countries lay in the importation of American management techniques. The adoption of these techniques meant education and particularly education in specially designed institutions.

Many European business schools consequently took over from their American forebears the major areas of curriculum and decided to use the teaching methods associated with the most prestigious of them, Harvard Business School. Only little by little did each adapt its specific teaching forms and methods so as to fit better with the local environment. Adopting methods from America, however, did not mean that the schools were international; while some have recently turned towards more particular recognition of the importance of the needs of international business in Europe, they mostly remained focused on their national market.

INSEAD, in contrast, was, and long remained, the only business school in Europe created with a specific commitment to meeting the needs of the *international* manager, operating on a business stage stretching well beyond the national frontiers of headquarter countries. From the beginning, INSEAD, 'School for leading Europeans', as its advertising has often claimed, had a specific commitment to internationalism and more particularly to *European* internationalism.

That commitment to the development of European internationalism had two components. First, the creation of INSEAD was a response to an expressed business need (expressed, at least, by business analysts). One of the hardest things to find then, and it seems still, was the international manager with the complex of skills needed. Even as late as 1974, as an INSEAD brochure advertising one of its in-service training courses pointed out:

One of the problems stemming from the international expansion of corporations is the search for managerial talent to staff positions in foreign operations. The international manager is still a rare asset . . . The successful executive at home might be a failure abroad . . . [skill in international team building] is especially necessary when there is much discussion about the transferability of managment methods . . . when companies have problems developing international managers and adjusting to the changing European environment and when, in the process of building Europe, the number of joint operations between firms of different countries is rising, increasing the complexity of human and organisational problems.

Second, educational institutions nearly always have objectives which are social as well as aiming to provide technical instruction and INSEAD is no exception. Behind the creation of INSEAD lay an idealistic commitment. From the beginning, the Institute was intended, through its own activities and those of its alumni, to contribute in a concrete manner towards the creation of a united Europe. Reflecting the ideas of a decade which in Europe saw the creation of such organisations as the European Iron and Steel Community and subsequently the European Economic Community, then envisaged as an economic union ultimately leading to political linkages, the founders of INSEAD felt that European integration was the key to the solution of the pressing political and economic problems of the time, both at home and abroad.

In a speech in which he put theory into practice by speaking partly in English and partly in German, Posthumus Meyjes, the Dutch first Director General of INSEAD, emphasised the importance of being a committed *European* when welcoming the first participants to the Institute in 1959.

Gentlemen, for the first time in Europe we are assembled here to found an institution for which by many authorities in Europe and by enterprises there is a heavy demand for. We want to form here a small model of Europe, that, by its tri-lingual status and the instructors from over the whole world, should educate you, the participants, to be *Europeans*. To be men who are informed about the problems of other countries too ·beside their own. *Furthermore to be men of co-operation, who by meeting each other will become a family looking into the future*, a common future built by common work and in which personal egoism is not anymore an obstacle. It will depend on you, the first participants and therefore the founders together with us, if we have success or not.

(Emphasis added, spelling and syntax in original)

There has always been at INSEAD a *Weltanschauung* emphasising a mix of business 'need' and an idealistic, ideological, commitment to building a united Europe working within the spirit of the *libre entreprise*.

Refurbishing an image

These ideological issues in business education can be seen as especially important in the political context of the years leading up to the creation of the Institute. In many countries, but perhaps especially in France, the image of *libre entreprise*, both as an organising political and economic principle and as represented in the institutions of business, was in need of major refurbishment. Private business in many places had been discredited through pre-war repression of worker demands and sabotage of reforming governments and through wartime collaboration with reactionary powers. The balance of social power in several major European countries had temporarily shifted. A French observer, Jean Reynaud, long ago pointed to growing post-war social pressures on the *patronat* to find new sources of public legitimacy and to seek new methods of command and influence. As Reynaud said, a concern with efficiency and productivity could be of use in solving both problems of public legitimacy and those of internal command.

It is clear that the rise of opposing social forces leads the *patronat* – and especially the leaders of big business – to seek new methods of action, if need be more publicly defensible to the public authorities . . . In many respects, the concern with technical efficiency provides a respectable argument in discussion with numerous groups (senior public servants, sections of worker trade unions . . .).

(1963: 36)

In spite of massive productivity increases, there remained over several decades a need for business to 'modernise' its image in line with public perceptions about moving towards a more 'modern' society, perceptions dominated by the rhetoric of technocracy in both politics and economy and a generalised belief in the virtue of many aspects of evolutionary social change. Many business organisations, both individual companies and associations of employers, felt the need to emphasise the modernity of their structures and their contribution to the achievement of broadly defined national goals, social as well as economic. As an example of the mood of at least some businessmen, one may cite the change of name of one French employers' association from the *Centre des Jeunes Patrons* to the *Centre des Jeunes Dirigeants d'Entreprise* because of the different connotations of *patron* (bad, old fashioned 'boss') and *dirigeants* (good, modern 'leaders'). When the *Jeunes Patrons'* famous *livre rouge* was issued in 1967 its pages included contributions by 'management and social intellectuals' such as Jacques Delors, Raymond Barre and Bernard Poullain, who advocated a view of the aims of enterprise which linked the legitimacy of enterprise to its participation in and acceptance of broader changes in society, of an economy 'in the service of man' and of rational internal restructuring of enterprises such as to base business authority on competence alone:

> Power can be based only on competence. The *rational organisation of power* can thus only be achieved through a *rational organisation of competences* and responsibilities.
>
> (Quoted in Bernoux, 1974: 54, emphasis added)

While members of the *Jeunes Patrons* undoubtedly represented the intellectual and ideological *avant-garde* of the European *patronat* rather than the broad mass of business owners, none the less the tendency towards support for reform was more widespread. It was frequently felt, especially by rising young executives, that one way of improving a poor public image was by presenting the management of private business enterprise as an efficient, professionalised activity on a par in both status and skill with the established professions of medicine and law (see Whitley, Thomas and Marceau, 1981 on the UK and May, 1974, on Germany). In this, their concerns joined those more specifically focusing on the introduction of new technology and new management practices.

In 'internal public relations', activities concerning potentially conflicting interactions between controllers and subordinates within enterprises, it seems that a new approach was also felt to be needed, involving a new leadership (internal management) style. Taking a perhaps excessively functionalist and somewhat schematic but nevertheless illuminating view, Bourdieu and his colleagues have linked together structural and ideological changes and the reasons which persuaded the traditional *patron* to recycle his internal management methods to match changes outside the enterprise, changes in the whole organisation of production and the mode of appropriation of profit:

> *The personal mode of domination*, preponderant in an earlier state of the economic field (one characterised by the mechanical division of labour between family firms), necessitated agents who had fully internalised traditional models of authority (even military ones) and who were sufficiently well-instructed in the techniques used in the enterprise to be able to mediate between the boss and subordinate personnel

(technicians, foremen, etc.). In contrast, *the structural mode of domination* demands agents capable of carrying out the *external public relations* (with other enterprises, the public administration etc.) which are necessary to the proper conduct of the large, integrated firm and to the maintenance of its dominance over the market and also with carrying out the *internal public relations* by means of which, at least at normal times, order is maintained inside the enterprise. Less and less often equipped with either the institutional insignia (such as decorations) or the natural insignia (such as grey hair and bulging waistlines) of authority, the new leaders of the enterprise, 'young directors' and 'modern bosses', must create new symbols of excellence in order to express the hierarchical position they occupy and the new principles by which that position is legitimated. Here the dominant qualities become aptitude for discussion and negotiation, knowledge of foreign languages, and above all perhaps, the polite and subtle manners which are the opposite in all things of the energy and directness which characterised the older soldier boss (*patron de combat*), at least in his archetypal form. The senior functionary (the modern form of 'diplomat') is substituted for the military officer in the arsenal of social models that business leaders can use as inspiration when constructing the new style of social interaction objectivity necessitated by changes in the structure of the economic field.

(Bourdieu, Boltanski and de Saint Martin, 1973: 80–1; emphasis in original)

It is within this context that the development of the special characteristics of management education at INSEAD and the role proposed for its products in contributing to the creation of a new business Europe must be understood.

Professional managers *par excellence*, the graduates of INSEAD were to be the spearhead in a wider effort to modernise enterprise practices and to link together European nations in a more general movement 'forward'. They, trilingual, quadrilingual, or more, were to contribute to cross-boundary communication. Their language skills were to be enriched by the increased cultural understandings that were taught with them. These personal capacities were to be the essential complement to the hard-nosed business skills of the successful international high-level manager, trained in marketing, finance and corporate planning as well as in the more subtle skills of the creator of new management and leadership styles and novel forms of business organisation. In brief, in their professional, personal and socio-political lives INSEAD graduates were to become over the years what a German newspaper more than a decade later described as 'Die neue Garde von Fontainebleau'.

The public–private connection: politics and the environment of business

With a sharp sense of the unfolding economic and political scene, the founders of INSEAD structured the Institute so that it could reach out towards both private and public sectors of European society and they endowed it with a blend of both social and business objectives. Intended to represent the 'best' of the private sector while also influencing and informing the makers of government policy, it was important for the Institute to be a meeting place of both. As the then Dean said in a speech to new students in the mid 1970s, the Board thus included, by the mid 1970s,

civic leaders, the Paris Chamber of Commerce, members from multi-national corporations, from private finance and from nationalised industries, from academic life, diplomacy, the European Parliament and international public administration.

This mix became of increasingly practical importance once the political limits to European integration became apparent. Further, in the greatly altered politico-economic circumstances of the years after 1973, the generalised commitment to contributing to the creation of a 'new Europe' characteristic of INSEAD's early years had become more specific and reoriented towards the explicit recognition of the importance to the operations of major companies of public policies of many kinds, whether regulatory or stimulatory. As the Dean of the Institute said, in the speech quoted above,

The dominant feature in the firm's environment today is public policy. Every firm has one partner who matters more than its suppliers, more than its customers, even more than its labour force . . . and that is Government.

In Europe, from the 1960s onwards, governments had an enormously enhanced role in shaping the contest of business activities; by the 1970s, they had also learned both to be wary of the power of giant corporations and to act to restrict it. In that situation, companies increasingly came to rely on managers who could negotiate with officials holding a potentially very different set of values and objectives. In short, it had become clear that the skills of 'politics and diplomacy are [as] essential to business as the techniques of science' (INSEAD publicity, 1977). Business schools which claimed to train high-level European managers had to take account of this trend, as an Italian newspaper suggested in the mid 1970s:

qualunque sia la sua importanza, la nosione di efficienza nel management deve integrarsi nell' evoluzione dell' ambiente sociopolitico ed economico che la dieci anni forma l'ogetto di un attenzione sempre crescente nei programmi delle moderne scuole di gestione.

(*Il Giornale*, 23 May 1976)

Creating a multinational executive

Recognising the importance of politics and diplomacy, in creating the multinational executive INSEAD has always paid a great deal of attention both to the specific techniques of management and to personal international skills. More particularly, in training them for the general management positions to which they aspire, the Institute always encourages its students to take a *global* view of the enterprise and its environment, thus including both internal and external elements in assessing every situation demanding a decision.

The curriculum for the Master of Business Administration (MBA) course as a whole has retained the Harvard view of the universality of management techniques and in the late 1970s at INSEAD 'the standard diet of a Business School [was] still with us (staff interview, 1977). The five staple ingredients of the diet remained *finance*, including accounting and financial control, *management sciences, marketing, organisational behaviour* (OB), *strategy and environment*. Courses on *business policy* and, the particular speciality of INSEAD, the *European and international business environments*, explicitly recognise that enterprises operate in an environment including important social and political factors. This is complemented in OB where the young manager has to learn the diplomatic skills and 'leadership' techniques needed for internal public relations, those most closely linked to methods of command and styles of leadership and those whose development has done most to alter the public's perception of the corporate image.

The major teaching methods of the Institute have also remained those used so successfully at Harvard – the case method and group work – while they have been adapted to underline the international context as a working environment. A Harvard Business School brochure has explained the value of the case method:

In the world of business, where every decision must be adapted to a specific situation and where no two situations are identical, it is the ability to analyse, to appreciate trends, to evaluate diverse factors that leads to wise decisions. That is why, from the day of their entry, students at the [Harvard] Business School discuss cases, in other words, descriptions of real situations taken from the business world in which managers act and are responsible for their actions. Each student is repeatedly placed in a position where, as administrator, he must not only evaluate the facts but also act as a responsible person. He is forced to stand up to new situations in which he must measure his intellectual capacities through new combinations of facts, half-facts, opinions and ideas. No book can give him the solution.[6]

Training for international business requires in addition that the manager learn to work in a multinational setting. At INSEAD this is achieved by group work; in particular, the division of each student entry into syndicate groups of six, whose members work together for the whole year, trains people of very different backgrounds to cooperate in decision making, since a syndicate may include a Swiss engineer, a French lawyer, a German economist and mix ages, origins and skills. Together syndicate members battle with the case method to acquire the managerial skills needed for high-level positions and thus learn both to be tolerant of differences of approach and to be flexible in analysis and decision-making, to recognise the crucial elements of situations, which are always new, so as to be able to act appropriately in circumstances of limited knowledge and considerable uncertainty.

A new international business élite?

Through the rigorous education it offers, INSEAD trains young people aspiring to high-level positions in European businesses to acquire and use the technical skills of the financial analyst, corporate strategist or marketeer, while also inculcating the personal manner and appreciation of political issues that will make them especially useful in the modernised, transnational corporations increasingly dominant in Europe in the last decades of the twentieth century. Skilled at foreign investment and in diplomatic negotiations, trained in the subtle variations of different cultural approaches in both business and politics, and able to communicate directly in most of Europe's major languages, the holder of an INSEAD MBA is especially well suited to a career on the international rather than the national stage. In recruiting them, companies acquire young managers able to cross the boundaries of conventional functional divisions, able to take a global view of the enterprise and to operate efficiently in diverse environments. Fulfilling so well the new organisational needs of the European business world, managers thus trained would seem to have followed a strategy particularly appropriate in the race to go far and fast in Europe's larger companies. They may well be the people poised for the recruitment stratum to international boardrooms over the next few decades and hence to the directorial positions which give them a role in the formulation of public policies for both business and the wider community.

This apparently simple match between skills and organisational needs, demand for new skills and supply of appropriate positions, is, however, in practice a highly complex one. Reaching command posts in major enterprises continues to demand the judicious use of resources of all kinds, of economic, social and cultural capital. Investment must be made in a wide variety of social and economic stocks if the aspiring manager is to obtain full value from any one. A portfolio which combines investment in a particular mix of educational, familial, economic and cultural stocks may well be the one that wins where investment in one area alone pays only low dividends. Moreover, much investment in professional lives is high risk. That risk can only be borne with confidence where the capital underlying the operation is sufficient. In these investment strategies, it is *families* as much as individuals that play the game. Families of origin provide the basic resources and make the first crucial decisions. While their role is usurped later by institutional decisions concerning educational achievements, these are themselves replaced in turn by influences from families of marriage (who also provide extra resources of all kinds), from peers and from companies themselves. Playing on the corporate stage, whether national or international, demands flair and contacts, specific skills and more general talents. There are many ladders, but also many snakes. The first steps on the ladders are described in the next chapter.

3. The routes to internationalism: family backgrounds and educational experience

The rhetoric of the decades of the 1960s and 1970s in Europe emphasised the new: new society, new economy, new managers of productive organisations, a new 'class structure', headed by a new bourgeoisie. In contrast, in practice, competition for access to top posts in national enterprises continued to take place within essentially traditional circles. The international business élite of Europe of the late decades of the twentieth century, the people who will control major national and multinational enterprises until at least the year 2000, will, this study suggests, have come from the most traditional sectors of European societies. Their social origins and educational experience will be even more restricted than those of the present controllers of Europe's businesses. While these top managers may be 'new' in the sense of the skills they possess and the outlook they profess, they will in no sense be social or educational *parvenus*. On the contrary, business will continue to lead to business over the generations and the same few élite educational institutions will continue to train and provide credentials for the controllers of tomorrow: the same social forces that have influenced the selection of present business decision-makers will continue to shape the members of the next generations.

Only a very limited range of routes lead to a top-level career in the world of European international business. Family background and family choices continue to determine the likelihood of any individual stepping on to one of these tracks. Families dominate the socio-cultural and geographical environment in which the child who is a future manager is raised, choose the formal education as well as the *éducation* he receives and the values and attitudes which, together with social origins, define and distinguish eligible candidates for a managerial career. Families from the business fraction of the bourgeoisie provide few real choices for their offspring: largely concentrated in the business world, even extended family members provide few competing adult models at the same time as they instil in the young the characteristics likely both to attract them and to make them attractive to a life in business. Moreover, even when the young members are out in the world, their kin do not lose their importance; they continue to play a role in defining and shaping

31

opportunities available and seized upon and to underwrite the risks underlying chances of success in the business arena. Their influences work not only on a national level but are similarly present on the international stage, adapted and expanded as needed. The importance of these influences can be seen particularly on the early paths trodden by aspiring European managers.

Backgrounds and origins

By the time they reached INSEAD, most of the students were between twenty-five and thirty years old. Most were children of the 1930s depression and the Second World War, with only a quarter born after 1945. The majority were single, but 30% were married, with higher proportions of married students among the Dutch, Belgians, French and Scandinavians, and some of these already had children. The great majority in the sample[1] – 99% – were men, leaving only twelve women.

Where then did they start? By which paths, starting from twelve different national points, did they reach INSEAD?

Geographical starting points map fields of recruitment across Europe. International managers holding INSEAD MBAs are overwhelmingly city people, mostly from Europe's major cities. More particularly, chances of working eventually on the European stage are greatly enhanced by birth in a capital city or, if not a capital city, in a major industrial, commercial or administrative centre. To a striking degree, *students at INSEAD are drawn from only a tiny geographical area within each country of origin, frequently encompassing only two or three cities.* For example, almost two-fifths of the Belgians were born in Brussels or Antwerp, while three cities, Madrid, Barcelona and Valencia, saw the birth of most of the Spanish. Half the Austrians came from only two cities, Vienna and Linz, as did just over half of the Scandinavians, whose cities of birth were Stockholm and Oslo. Between half and two-thirds of the Swiss were from only three cities, as were almost half of the Germans. Three cities alone in each country thus accounted for at least a third of the country's representatives at INSEAD and in some cases nearly two-thirds. The Dutch were the exception, for six cities still accounted for less than two-fifths of the Dutch students.

The French show particularly the social importance of birth in the capital city, and even of divisions within it. One-fifth of the 556 in the main French sample born in France were born in the city of Paris, with a further fifth born in immediately adjacent *départements* and 4% in the Paris Basin. Thus, between two-fifths and one-half were born in Paris or its surrounding area. Of those born in the city itself, nearly a quarter were born in one *arrondissement* alone, the expensive *seizième* (16th). A further quarter were born in the other prestigious areas of the city, the 5th, 6th, 7th, 8th, 9th and 17th *arrondissements*. This means that 5% of all the French born in France were born within two or three kilometres of each other at the most, and many within a few hundred metres. Raising the distance to ten kilometres or so included 10% of the French students born in France. As the 5th, 6th and 7th *arrondissements* are contiguous, as are the 16th, 8th, 17th and 9th, the proportions born within a few hundred metres of each other are probably even higher than these figures suggest.

Where the students were not from the capital cities, they were overwhelmingly from the other major commercial and industrial centres of their countries – cities such as Barcelona, Linz, Bergen, Gøteberg, Odense, Antwerp and Munich. Only after these came proportions from the principally administrative or university cities – The Hague, Trøndheim, Malmö and Arhus, Lausanne, Valencia and Salzburg, although Hamburg is an exception. One-fifth of the French born in France were born in the older industrial cities of the *département du Nord* and Alsace.

In descending order again in the different countries were found the provincial cities of Ghent and Liège, Stavanger, Lund, Uppsala, Esbjerg, Basle, Berne, Lucerne, Innsbruck, Hilversum, Utrecht and Eindhoven, Cologne, Frankfurt and Dusseldorf. In the Latin countries, San Sebastian, Bilbao, Saragossa, Naples and Palermo were also represented. In Britain, in contrast to those of continental Europe, towns of birth were essentially the smaller country or university centres rather than the larger, older and less prestigious industrial ones and this difference of birthplace is reflected in the differing social origins of the students.

Even greater geographical concentration emerges where *regions*, rather than individual cities, are the reference point. For instance, two regions in Austria, Holland and Belgium respectively provided half, or more than half, of their students.

The proportions born abroad are also strikingly large. Most nationalities show a quite substantial group born outside their country of nationality – 19% of the Italians, 17% of the Austrians, 15% of the British, 13% of the French and 10% each, approximately, of the Swiss, Dutch and Scandinavians. Many thus began their 'international careers' early.

Birthplace was not the only indication of the extremely limited range of geographical origins. In many cases, sons had spent most of their childhood in the same city, their families' spatial mobility seeming to be limited. There was, however, one important move that frequently took place and that was the move of the family into the *capital city*, thus bringing the sons even closer to the centre of national life. Significantly, if their families of origin had not made this move, the sons themselves frequently did so, particularly in Belgium and France. Thus, while one-fifth of the students born in France were born in the city of Paris and another fifth in its immediate suburbs, by the time they entered INSEAD more than half (53.5%) of their fathers who were resident in France were living in Paris. Moreover, 57% of the French alumni living in

Table 3.1 Region of birth (*cumulative percentages of students admitted*)

Region of birth		British	German	Belgian	Scandinavian	Swiss	Dutch	Austrian	Spanish	Italian	French
Region of capital city[a]		43	14	26.5	43	15	33	42	16	10	36
Capital	+1	53	34	44	52	32	58	55	26.5	20	52
region+other regions	+2	61.5	48	58.5	57	45	67	66	37	25.5	59
	+3	78.5	60	72	60	53	76	72.5	58	31	—
	+4	83.5	70	76	—	61	84	79	63	34	—
N=		331	342	117	164	126	67	62	17	63	627
% sample=		93.5	91	91	87	86	71	90	74	86	95
% abroad		15	7	7	10	10.5	9	17	10.5	19	13

[a] The 'best-known' cities, Berlin and Geneva, were used rather than the true Federal capitals, for the Germans and Swiss

France were themselves living in Paris, with a further 22.5 % nearby in the same three immediately contiguous suburbs as the fathers, making the great majority, four-fifths, of the French living in France immediately before entry to INSEAD, resident in or around Paris and close to their families of origin. Entry to the international arena thus seems first to demand a move towards national centres of power.

Not only does the population considered here tend to live in one city in each country, but they also live in highly selected areas within that city. Of all INSEAD participants living in France, more than half followed their parents' example and lived in the prestigious *quartiers* of Paris: 16.5 % lived in the 16th *arrondissement* alone, and a further 37 % in the 5th, 6th, 7th, 8th, 9th and 17th areas. Two-thirds of the 'Parisians' had thus not only been born but also lived within a very limited area. Spending the early years of childhood in the same locality enormously increases commonality of experience and the likely acquisition of shared attitudes and expectations (de Negroni: 1974) and living close to other family members enormously facilitates continuing contacts as an adult. The importance of this will become clear below.

Social origins: business leads to business

Social mapping complements the geographical and shows an equally limited field of recruitment, making it clear that in Europe in the 1990s and beyond business will continue to be managed by people born and raised in the business world. The young MBA-holders who are potentially candidates for recruitment to leading positions in European business in the next few decades are overwhelmingly from families with close attachments to the business world, attachments frequently of long standing, at least three generations, and of considerable breadth, as seen in the wide range of relatives involved in business and its management. Moreover, the proportions raised not only within the business world but in families from its most senior echelons are striking indeed. Many of these families were part of the 'possessory bourgeoisie' (Bourdieu, Boltanski and de Saint Martin, 1973). *In virtually every country, except Scandinavia, the largest single proportions of INSEAD students were born into families where the father owned, partly or wholly, one or more businesses and usually had an important share in the management of them. These groups, 'Fabrikants' and other 'Unternehmer', 'industriels' and 'impresari', form the possessory 'patronat'* of Europe and their proportions in the families of this youthful population – 19–38 %, according to country – indicate their continuing significance in Europe.

Adding to the possessory *patronat*, the *controllers* of business enterprises, raises the proportions from the *patronat* as a whole to between a third and half.[2] The *présidents-directeurs-généraux*, the chairmen of the board, the directors general, the *administrateurs de société* and their equivalents across

Table 3.2 *Father's occupation (percentages of students admitted)*

Father's occupation	British	German	Belgian	Scandinavian	Swiss	Dutch	Austrian	Spanish	Italian	French
Business owner/independents	26	39	28.5	22	29.5	31	34	19	32	22
PDG, chairman of board, director general	2	2.5	20	4	8	10	2	9.5	7	9
MDs, GMs, *Directeurs*	6	4	1	21	8	23	7	9.5	5	6
Senior management	6	5	3	4	1.5	1	5	—	2	8
Other management	6	3	3	5	3	4	5	5	3	6
Professionals in business	5	9	9	6	11.5	—	8	—	2	8
Total business	51	62.5	64.5	62	61.5	69	61	43	51	59
Senior civil service	8	6	5.5	2	1	1	3	9.5	7	6.5
Army/navy	8	2	5	2	1	1	3	—	2	4
Teaching/cultural/research	8	7	5	8	6	3	2	—	7	4
Doctors and other 'medical'	5	5	5	8	4	8	3	9.5	7	1
Lawyers	3	3.5	2	3.5	2	5.5	3	9.5	7	1
Total non business 'upper-middle class'	32	23.5	22.5	23.5	14	18.5	14	28.5	30	16.5
White-collar and technician	8	3	1	3	5	—	8	—	5	4
Shopkeepers/artisans	2	1	8	4	9	2	3	19	8	5
Manual	2	1	1	—	4	2	2	5	—	2
Farmers/landowners	3	2.5	2	3	3	1	3	—	5	4
Miscellaneous	4	2	3	4	3	5.5	10	5	3	2
Total of other occupations	19	9.5	15	14	24	10.5	26	29	21	17
N=	301	302	109	169	130	90	59	21	59	579
% sample=	85	81	85	91	88	96	85.5	91	81	87.5

Directeurs=top management   GM=general manager   MD=managing director   PDG=*présidents-directeurs-généraux*

Europe formed the families of origin of many of their likely successors. If we include sons with fathers who, as senior managers, are responsible for much enterprise activity, the proportions from important positions in business are raised even further.

In total, half or more of the participants from every nationality, except one, were from high-level business backgrounds. In most countries, their share reached around two-thirds: 69% among the Dutch, 64% among the Belgians, 61–62.5% among the Swiss, Scandinavians and Germans, 59% among the French. Only the British, the Italians and the Spanish are different – and even there half, or almost half, are from these backgrounds.

While in some sense this is perhaps not surprising, since candidates to the Institute themselves frequently described spontaneously the strength of the influence of their families on their career choices, so that 'business leads to business', in comparison with their numbers in their national populations of origin, the proportions here from business families are extremely high. In any national European population, 5–12% are likely to be controlling businesses: here there are 43–69%.

Equally striking, are the concomitantly very low proportions of students provided by other social groups and hence the visible separation of each country's business community from other sectors of the economy and society. Remarkably consistent across the nationalities, with a difference of only 8.5 percentage points between them, and across all three categories of the 'public sector' – senior civil service, army and navy, and teaching, cultural and research pursuits – these low proportions suggest a fundamental separation of worlds, a separation confirmed by studying the occupations of relatives, as we do below, in chapter 7.

Only the British compensate their low proportion from business families with the highest proportion, 24%, from all spheres of the public sector. Britain was followed, but a long way behind, by countries such as Germany, Belgium, Italy and France, with around 15% in public employment. The proportion of military officers was notably low among the Dutch, Swiss, Germans and Italians, as was the proportion of civil servants among the Scandinavians, Swiss and Dutch.

More surprisingly, the traditionally wealthy and prestigious 'liberal professions' of law and medicine also provided a very low proportion students, 13% or less, similar to that of the public sector. There were particularly few lawyers.

The third most striking element to emerge is the truly tiny proportion of participants across Europe from white-collar and manual-worker homes – between 1% and 5%, with none at all from manual-worker homes in Scandinavia or Italy. Shopkeepers did only slightly better. Clearly a function of the pool of candidates rather than the Institute's selection policies,[3] their non-representation reflects the highly socially selective nature of national education systems, at post-secondary and subsequently post-graduate levels. It is also a function of the public perception of avenues to senior positions in European business and the concomitant tendency for qualified young people from the working class to enter the teaching profession or the public service in preference to business for, owing everything to education, they tend to stay within familiar fields or in sectors where educational attainment is given maximum recognition. That is not the case with business, where credentials other than formal education remain important in selection and promotion. Moreover, the location of INSEAD in a foreign country and its use of languages which involve a fourth tongue for many erect further obstacles and reduce the likelihood of white-collar or working-class children either knowing of the Institute or being able to imagine themselves attending it or affording it. The 'internationalism' implicit in attendance at the Institute is also less easy for them to obtain, for their fathers have seldom worked or lived abroad and they have no family connections, the network so important for the students, likely to make them either hear of INSEAD or seek it out.

Students at INSEAD are, therefore, clearly from the upper reaches of their respective national societies. Their origins are indeed even more limited than the categorical analysis suggests for even within these bourgeois groups, there is a perceptible tendency for fathers to be in occupations where they are at the upper levels. There is thus a tendency for the civil servants concerned to be very senior, to be ambassadors rather than consuls, for lawyers to be judges and barristers rather than solicitors, for the doctors to be specialists rather than general practitioners, for the teachers to be working at university rather than at more junior levels, for the military personnel to be generals and admirals (or at least brigadier-generals and rear-admirals) rather than colonels. In social terms, there are greater proportions of aristocrats, or at least families included in such registers as the *Bottin Mondain*, than the general populations of the schools and universities of origin might lead one to expect, even though those institutions are themselves normally 'the reverse of the nation' (Bourdieu and Passeron, 1964, on France). The French as a group show these tendencies particularly clearly, mirroring the conclusions of Girard's study, carried out more than twenty years ago (1961).

There has, moreover, been only a little change over time in the distribution of social origins among INSEAD students. The French, for example, show a very small decline in the overall proportions of those from *patronat* families – from 36.5 % to 34 % in the *promotions* entering the Institute after 1973. Their places were simply taken by the offspring of other businessmen, from salaried senior management positions. *The essential pattern thus remained the same across the first two decades of INSEAD's existence.* Business across Europe looks as though it will continue to lead to business.

Education

Education, both secondary and tertiary, provides the credentials for the move to positions on the rungs of the ladders potentially leading to the top. Born into families ambitious for their future, the young managers of tomorrow are schooled in the best institutions. Across Europe, careful choices are made about place to go and subjects to study. Even at secondary level, the school a young person is educated in is a measure of a number of elements. In part a measure of a child's intellectual attainment, at least where selective systems are still operating, it is also an indicator of social status. In most of Europe not only are some parts of the education system 'better' (academically and socially) than others, but some individual schools stand out. In most of Europe, too, public and private institutions vie with each other for the 'best' pupils. In Britain, private schools as a group are the more prestigious, while in other countries only some private institutions compete successfully for the 'top' pupils. In France, for example, the private Collège Stanislas competes with the public Lycée Janson-de-Sailly, both in intellectual quality and as a symbol of the high status of the parents of its pupils and the Collège Sainte-Geneviève in Versailles is perceived as on a par with the Lycée Louis-le-Grand, the intellectual prestige of the latter (public) matching the social and intellectual selectivity of the former (private). Everywhere, parents who are able to do so choose the best mix of intellectual excellence and social visibility.

Perhaps it is in Britain that the equation between perceived intellectual standard and high fees and hence the high social status of the schools' publics is most perfect. There the social symbolism of and the effective networks created by attendance at one of the most prestigious of the 'public' schools last a lifetime. But Britain is not alone; while it is perhaps in Scandinavia that the fee-paying, private sector of education is least developed, even there the symbolism of attendance at certain schools, even in the public sector, is marked.

In line with the high social origins of the parents, in every country in the study, analysis of the paths sons followed through secondary education indicates attendance by the overwhelming majority in each case at institutions located in the most prestigious parts of the system. Thus, where the country's educational structure and social traditions made it appropriate, maximum use was made by the parents of INSEAD students – who make these decisions – of the private, normally fee-paying institutions. In most countries, these schools also reflect the religious preferences typical of upper-class families in that country – Catholic in Belgium, Calvinist in Geneva. The students, therefore, mostly spent their adolescent years in their respective countries' élite and usually most conservative educational institutions.

The particular kind of institutions chosen differ with each system, it being socially far more acceptable to pass through vocational streams in the Scandinavian and Germanic countries than in the 'Latin' ones, especially France, particularly among families from the business world. The proportion in private schools also varied considerably from country to country. The British, the Belgians, the French and the Spanish made notable use of the private education system, the last three choosing these schools for their religious curriculum (Catholic), as well as their social prestige. Just over a quarter of all the French had been educated exclusively in private schools during their secondary studies and a further 14% had spent part of those years in private schools, with the proportion who spent their special years of preparation for entry to the *grandes écoles* in private schools even higher.

The British, of course, *par excellence*, made use of the private system of education, for 84% had attended independent institutions, the overwhelming majority going to one of the select few known collectively as the 'public schools'. Within these, two-fifths attended one of the nine major schools known as the 'Clarendon Nine' and a further fifth one of the 'well-known' schools such as Haileybury, Oundle, Stowe and Uppingham.[4] The remaining two-fifths had attended a school belonging to the Headmasters' Conference and therefore 'public', but of somewhat lesser renown. It should be noted that many of these, although not on Boyd's list of 'well-known', are nevertheless extremely prestigious and include Wellington, Ampleforth, Christ's Hospital and Lancing College. In sharp contrast, only just over one in ten of the British had attended schools maintained by public funds.

Not only had certain types of education been chosen, but a few schools particularly stood out in each country. One-fifth of all the British (20.5%), or 30% of all the British attending public schools, had been educated at one of only five institutions – Eton, Harrow, Winchester, Ampleforth or Charterhouse – while 7.5% of all the British (11% of all attending public schools) had been to one school alone, Eton College, the most prestigious in Great Britain and possibly the best-known secondary school in the world. The major public schools and Eton in particular have, of course, long been associated with subsequent attendance at the Universities of Oxford and Cambridge and with high-level careers in all sectors of the economy and the public service.

The British, however, were not alone in their use of particular prestigious schools. There were also some clear tendencies in several other countries for certain schools, some public, some private, to provide the nurturing place for the future international business élite. Thus, a fifth of the Belgians had attended one of only five private secondary schools, with 5% at one school alone, St Jean de Berchem, a major Jesuit College in Brussels. Amongst the Swiss educated in Switzerland and declaring their secondary schools, one-fifth had been to one of only three schools: 14% had been to one school alone, the Collège de Genève, with 6% more attending two prestigious private schools also in Geneva. Among the Norwegians, too, almost one-fifth (19.5%) of those declaring their secondary schooling (half the total INSEAD Norwegian population) had been to one prestigious school in Oslo, the Ris Hoyere Skole, while a further 7% each had been to the Frogner school and the Vestheim School and 5% the Katedralskole, all in Oslo. These are publicly maintained high schools but attendance there indicates residence of the students' families in the most prestigious areas of the city of Oslo as well as high academic ability, particularly at the Katedralskole. Two-thirds of the Danes declared their secondary schools. Of these, a quarter had been to one school, the Holte *gymnasium* in Copenhagen. Similarly, two-thirds of the Swedes declared their lower-secondary schools; of these 9% had been to one school, the Sigtma School in Stockholm. Again, these proportions probably result from the geographical propinquity of students' families as well as the aspirations of the parents. The French both chose exclusive private, usually religious, schools and, by residence in exclusive areas of Paris, ensured access to highly prestigious publicly maintained *lycées*, such as Janson-de-Sailly, Pasteur and Carnot. Two-fifths of the French attended one of only six élite schools, some public, some private, at some point during their secondary education, while some had been to two or more as they moved through the different secondary cycles. In secondary schools across Europe, the sons of the business and professional élites acquired a start in life likely to put them well ahead of their fellows when the next choices had to be made.

Higher education

In Western European countries in recent decades, studies have indicated everywhere the existence and persistence over time of close links between the prestige of an institution of higher education and the social origins of the students who attend. Similar relationships can be found between the subject chosen and the students who study it. These relationships remain the same even though nations vary as to which types of institution and which subjects are more prestigious. In France, for example, the engineering *grandes écoles* in Paris hold pride of place while universities fall largely into a poor second position. In Germany and Holland, law and economics are prestigious and socially selective subjects while in Britain the traditions of the classics and humanities retain their attraction for many from cultivated upper-class families. In Switzerland, the study of engineering at Zurich or commerce in Lausanne are appropriate choices for children from privileged backgrounds, while across the border privileged Italian children are doing law.

Choices about the discipline to study at university and the institution at which to study have long been highly important for a future career, but the outlets for particular choices vary across countries and over time. Some choices are directly linked to a professional vocation, others seem vocationally linked but in fact function as a prestigious preparation for a range of careers rather than just one avenue. Others represent an expression of interest in an area but do not bear a direct relationship to the career followed. Medicine is the clearest example of the direct professional preparation, for only a few people trained in medicine subsequently pursue other careers. Law, however, in many European countries, such as Italy, Spain and Germany, is the traditional preparation for a range of high-level careers, in business, in the public service, and, especially in Germany and Scandinavia, in politics. It largely represents a prestigious 'general' tertiary diploma which is the basis for subsequent specialisation. It acts as a 'guarantee', both of the competence and of the social status of the person so trained. In France, too, law holds a similar position but there the education system is geared more towards success in mathematics and to training in engineering. Students at the top *grandes écoles*, while receiving training in engineering, are not all expecting to pursue technical careers; on the contrary, the higher the prestige of the school the less likely the student is to pursue a career in engineering and the more likely he or she is to move out into the public service (especially from the Ecole Polytechnique) or on to careers in management, usually at a high level in private enterprise. In Britain, the study of the classics, closely followed, in certain universities, by the study of modern languages, was for long the educational stream held by employers to be that indicating at the same time the highest intellectual competence and the high social status of the student. The study of the classics in particular was thought to indicate both an ability to deal with complex and abstract questions unrelated to any real experience – and hence was considered an excellent training for the mind as such – and an ability to pursue any career in a disinterested spirit.

The place of crucial subjects and the symbolism attached to them thus vary considerably from country to country, complicating cross-national comparisons. In each country, however, there are always a select few which hold pride of place and which constitute for students a maximum general-education investment in terms of the professional possibilities open. It is largely to those select few that candidates for INSEAD have entrusted their education before entry to the Institute.

Subjects studied at tertiary education levels

Early paths leading to INSEAD are few indeed. Most students had followed only a very select choice of educational trajectories. Two-thirds of their diplomas are covered by only two groups of subjects – engineering with, to a much smaller extent, pure science or mathematics, and economics and commerce. One further subject, law, accounts for another 16 %. Four subjects alone, engineering, economics, commerce and law, form three-quarters of all the first-degree subjects studied by these INSEAD students. Almost 60 % of them are accounted for by only three of these – engineering, commerce and

Table 3.3 Subject of first degree (percentages of students admitted)

Subject studied for first degree	British	German	Belgian	Scandinavian	Swiss	Dutch	Austrian	Spanish	Italian	French	All nationalities
Engineering	15	28	21	23.5	41	20	25	39	38	48	32
Pure mathematics/science	15	7	—	2	7	3	9	—	5.5	5	
Commerce	3	25	46	25[a]	15	5	23	26	25	28	23
Economics (including PPE)	18	13	11	31[a]	10.5	28[b]	6	17	10	5	15
Law (and law politics, etc.)	8	18	12	16.5	17	34	32	17	19	3[c]	16
Arts/language	27	6	10	2	1	6.5	—	—	—	10	7
Other (medicine, social sciences, etc.)	3		—	—	9	—	6	—	1		9.5
Professional qualifications/technician level only	12	3	—	—	0.5	—	—	—	—	—	
N=1,989	354	365	128	185	47	93	69	23	72	653	
% sample=	100	90	100	100	100	99	100	100	99	99	

[a] Economics in Sweden includes 'social economics'
[b] There is some overlap with commerce in Holland because of the existence of 'business economics'
[c] Some students did two first degrees concurrently, especially in France. The 'principal' one recorded was that to which entry was most selective, e.g. political science when law was done with 'Sciences Po'

law. Taking out the few students with a technician-level diploma rather than a degree in commerce and law raises the percentages slightly, underlining even further the importance of these subjects at university-degree level for young people aspiring to enter the multinational business world.

The specific place of each subject in the academic, social and occupational systems and hierarchies of each country varies and hence varies among the population considered here. The concentration in certain subjects in different countries can be clearly seen. The French stand out as engineers. Almost half (48%) of the French had done degrees in engineering. They were closely followed by the Swiss, Italians and Spanish, where two-fifths of each had done engineering. Between a quarter and a third of the Germans had done the same. Next came a range of countries where between a fifth and a quarter had done engineering – Belgium, Scandinavia, Holland and Austria. Britain provides the contrast: only 15% of British students had done engineering, indicating the lower status of this discipline in the hierarchy of prestige in that country.

The relative importance of economics and commerce also varied by country. In most, commerce dominated. Almost half, 46%, of the Belgians had done commerce, dropping to a quarter of the Germans and 28% of the French. Economics was preferred by the Scandinavians. The Austrians, Spanish and Italians showed preferences similar to the Germans while the British followed the Scandinavians, albeit in much lower proportions.

It can be seen then that with one exception *two or three subjects in each country accounted for between a half and two-thirds of all degrees held*. Thus, in Spain, engineering and commerce together dominated (68%), followed closely by Italy (63%), Switzerland (56%), and Germany (53%). In Scandinavia, two-thirds of the students had done either engineering or commerce, while in Holland two-thirds had done either economics or law. In short, in every country except Britain, the educational paths to INSEAD passed along only two or three principal routes. While in many cases these subjects may be seen to have some 'technical' relevance for business administration, it was clear from the applicants' forms and from interviews that they had often chosen to study them for other reasons.

Place of graduation

If the subjects studied for tertiary education were narrow in range, the institutions where the students graduated were equally few in number in almost every country. In two countries, around two-fifths or more of the population concerned had attended only one specific university or equivalent institution; 38% of the Swiss had a degree from the Ecole Polytechnique Fédérale (ETH) in Zurich while 41% of the Belgians were from the Catholic University of Louvain. Proportions graduating from one university in Britain and Austria were only a little lower; just under one-third (32%) of the British

Table 3.4 Proportions in each country graduating from one of only four universities (cumulative percentages of students admitted)[a]

Place of first degree	British	German	Belgian	Scandinavian	Swiss	Dutch	Austrian	Spanish	Italian	French
First university	32	19	41	N[b] 27 S 20 DK 37	38	22	31	22	22	6.5
Second university	60	29	54	N 37 S 31 DK 55	43	36	52	39	37	12.5
Third university	71	38	63	N 46 S 41 DK 65.5	49	48	68	56	45	17.5
Fourth university	77	43	72	N 52 S 48.5 DK 63	53	55	—	65	53	23.5
N=	343	355	127	185	144	92	69	23	73	653
% sample=	97	95	99	100	98	98	97	100	100	99

[a] The proportions are of students with tertiary-level qualifications and refer to first degrees only
[b] DK = Denmark, N = Norway, S = Sweden

students at INSEAD had graduated from Cambridge University and nearly a third of Austrians had attended the University of Vienna. Then came Italy and Spain, where 22% had been respectively to Milan and Barcelona universities and Germany where 19% had graduated from the University of Munich. Only the French emerge here as totally different. Because of the intense competition for entry and the tiny number of places available in élite tertiary institutions for both engineering and commerce in France,[5] the French had spread themselves over a greater number of institutions. In spite of that, 16.5% had been to a recognised élite school, 6.5% to the Ecole Supérieure de Commerce de Paris (ESCP) and 5% to the Ecole Polytechnique in Paris, while 5% had crossed the border and been to the Ecole Polytechnique in Zurich (ETH). These would, of course, be extremely high proportions educated in these schools, if considered in relation to the total population.

In some countries, notably Britain, a second university is of almost equal importance. Thus Oxford follows Cambridge, only a few percentage points behind. Indeed, between them these two universities educated almost two-thirds of the British students at INSEAD. In Switzerland, the University of Geneva followed ETH, but only educated rather less than half as many students (15%).

In Austria, the commercial university in Vienna educated a fifth of INSEAD Austrians and the Escuela Technico Superiore in Madrid 17% of the Spanish. Again, of course, the French stand out as different. The Germans, too, are more dispersed: only 10% went to the second most 'popular' university, Berlin. The low German proportions in each institution are in part accounted for by the propensity of German students to move around from university to university in the course of their long tertiary studies so that their place of graduation is not necessarily the place they began to study in. A massive 37% of Germans had attended more than five institutions and a further 33% five. In contrast, only 5% had completed their studies in one university alone. In Germany, while certain of the universities, usually the older ones have a higher general level of prestige, frequently only specific disciplines are well thought of in a given university and students choose to study in the department headed by a particularly eminent professor and, having learned from him, move on to learn from another. Only in recent years has this begun to change substantially.

Taking each Scandinavian nationality separately shows that the Danes were most likely to be from the Copenhagen School of Commerce and Economics, followed, at a distance, by the University of Copenhagen and the Technical Institute in the same city. Among the Swedes, the University of Lund was predominant, preparing students notably in the field of law and to some extent economics. The School of Economics in Stockholm came next in importance, followed by the Royal Swedish Institute of Technology, also located in Stockholm. The Norwegians, however, had followed a distinctive path; around two-fifths of the Norwegian INSEADs had taken their first degree abroad, a third or so of these in Switzerland, at the Ecole Polytechnique in Zurich and in the commercial school in St Gallen. Most of the Norwegians studying at home (27 %, 41 % of those studying in Norway) went to the Bergen School of Commerce, with a further 10 % at the Trøndheim Institute of Technology and 9 % at Oslo University. In Norway the majority of those in the scientific and technico-engineering fields had studied abroad, while the majority of those in the commercial and economics branches studied at home.

In virtually every country, therefore, only two or three universities trained very substantial proportions of INSEAD participants. Looking across all of Europe, first a very few universities stand out as pre-eminent in the intellectual preparation of the new European business élite – Oxford, Cambridge, Munich, Berlin, the Catholic University in Louvain, the Université Libre de Bruxelles, the Ecole Polytechnique in Zurich and the University of Geneva, Leiden and Amsterdam universities in Holland, both the general and the commercial universities in Vienna, the University of Barcelona and the Escuela Technico Superiore (ETS) in Madrid, the Universities of Milan and Rome, the Ecole Polytechnique ('X') and the Ecole Centrale for French engineers, the Ecole des Hautes Etudes Commerciales (HEC), the Ecole Supérieure des Sciences Economiques et Commerciales (ESSEC) and the Ecole Supérieure de Commerce de Paris (ESCP) for French commercial students, all located in Paris.

This first group of universities is followed by London, Cologne, Liège, Lausanne, Delft, the Technische Hochschule in Vienna, the Commercial University of Bilbao, the Commercial School of St Gallen, and the University of Palermo. These in turn are followed, usually at some distance, by the universities of Manchester, Karlsruhe, Saint Ignatius in Antwerp, Fribourg, Groeningen and Padua, and the ETS in Barcelona. *In all, fewer than forty universities or equivalent institutions out of the hundreds potentially available across the twelve major countries of Europe considered here provide the greatest proportions of the students trained at INSEAD to become the leaders of the next generation of important European and international businesses.*

As may be expected in a post-graduate institute of high international, as well as national, prestige, the student body of INSEAD is exclusive. Very few social and educational tracks lead there from within any given national boundaries. The step on the educational path that leads abroad is taken by an even more socially and educationally restricted group than that which undertakes postgraduate study at home, itself usually only 1 % or less of an age-group. The market within which INSEAD is effectively recruiting is limited indeed.

Table 3.5 Pre-INSEAD international connections, by nationality (percentages of students admitted)

International connections	British	German	Belgian	Scandinavian	Swiss	Dutch	Austrian	Spanish	Italian	French
Born abroad	15	7	7	10	10.5	9	17	10.5	19	13
Father's address abroad	13	7	15	N7[a] S18 DK4.5	8.5	10	10	10	14	6
Secondary education abroad[b]	4	10.5	5	N22 S7 DK3	4	6	13	21	23	6
Tertiary education abroad (1st degree)	4	10	5.5	20 (N=40)	12.5	16	16	9	14	7
Higher degree abroad	12	45	26	34	53	9	7	50[e]	3	54
Travelled outside Europe[c]	61.5 (20.5)	53 (20.5)	54 (27.5)	47 (23)	47 (29)	38 (28)	53.5 (22)	56.5 (38)	46.5 (38)	67 (69.5)
Worked abroad[d] (several places)	43 (15)	37.5 (30)	36 (6)	40 (18.5)	34 (19)	45 (12)	47.5 (24)	40 (—)	36.5 (5)	39 (19)
Own address abroad	26	19	6	42	23	30	41	30	33	13

[a] DK = Denmark, N = Norway, S = Sweden
[b] At least one year
[c] Of percentage with higher degree
[d] All had travelled outside Europe. The percentage in brackets is the proportion of those travelling inside Europe who had spent time in North America
[e] N is only 4

International connections

The year at INSEAD is an important step for all on the road to an international career. Some students, however, had already acquired international connections before entering the Institute. As with their social and educational characteristics, much of that internationalism comes from their families of origin. For many, a father posted abroad or owning a business abroad meant residence outside their country of nationality, often for long periods, including the period of secondary education. For others, internationalism is the more conscious result of the student's own decisions and means periods of study or work abroad as well as extensive private recreational connections acquired before entry to INSEAD.

'Internationalism' measured in these terms varies somewhat from nationality to nationality. Of all the nationalities, the Italians and the British had most frequently been born abroad. They were followed by the Belgians and the Swedish. The British had rarely been educated abroad at secondary level, the alternative of boarding school in the UK being apparently preferred. Only the Norwegians and the Italians had spent part or all of their secondary studies abroad in any considerable proportions and the Norwegians frequently only spent one year abroad. In almost every nationality many more had done their first university degrees abroad, the Norwegians being again outstanding. The French, too, although in much lower proportions, also made use of the international track to the Ecole Polytechnique Fédérale in Zurich. Many more did second and subsequent degrees abroad, notably in the United States, the French having a particular penchant for American Masters' degrees and, to a lesser extent, PhDs. Of those who had spent time living and travelling outside Europe, around a quarter in most cases visited the USA, a proportion rising to nearly two-fifths for the Italians and Spanish and to a very considerable almost 70% for the French. The latter figure in particular must be seen on the context of explicit efforts by business leaders in France during the 1960s to encourage the acceptance of certain American practices in the management of French enterprises and the fascination which all things American held for many young French people, who thought of themselves as 'modern' in the same period.[6]

The chances of going to INSEAD are, as we have seen, notably increased by birth into a family in business. Even within the business world they seem to be further increased by contacts with the world outside the national society acquired through the occupation of the father. Looking through the jobs held and the companies employing the fathers, the observer is struck by the frequency of the names of multinational enterprises, by the frequency of fathers involved in the import–export business or in the foreign departments of banks and other national firms. In many other cases, the fathers are operating companies, their own or other people's, in foreign countries. In the public sector, especially for nationalities such as the British, there is a large proportion of diplomats and army officers, naval captains and fathers involved in international organisations. Among the backgrounds of the British, for example, there appear a shipping executive based in Madrid, the general manager of the European division of a multinational, a director at the Council of Europe, ambassadors, the vice-president of a Canadian firm, executives of major oil companies, based frequently abroad, export managers, and several owners of business interests in different parts of the world. Among the Germans, some families were involved in import and export businesses, one father was the vice-president of an international chemical firm and some others were senior managers in other multinationals. In other countries, even higher proportions of fathers have such contacts through their job, notably in Belgium where a high proportion of fathers were top-level managers, board members, or *administrateurs de société*. Among Belgian fathers in particular are found managers of multinationals, Belgian or with European subsidiaries in Belgium, directors or owners of export firms and consultants to foreign governments. Among the other nationalities, one also finds senior executives and managers from such major international companies as Ciba-Geigy, Mobil, Esso, Liebig, Cockerill, Agfa-Gevaert, MMM, IBM, Krupp, Porsche-Volkswagen, Siemens, ICI, Philips, Fokker, Akzo, Alusuisse, Brown Bovéri, Crédit Suisse, Rhône-Progil, Larousse, Saint Gobain, Thomson, Veuve Clicquot, Air France, Péchiney, Rémy-Martin, CGEE-Alsthom, Alfa-Laval, Honeywell-Bull, UTA, the Norwegian–American line, not to mention the Tramways Company of Shanghai. Many students were thus already the second generation of family members holding high office in the world of international business.

4. Choosing a career: family edicts and school verdicts

Professional inheritance over the generations is now well documented in most Western European countries. It happens in part because the children of the privileged are advantaged by the system of education and the social construction of economic opportunities. It also happens because families build up in their children self-images and values which propel them overwhelmingly in the directions already followed by family members of both older and contemporary generations. These self-images are developed through experiences at home and at school, places which also shape images held of the wider society and its opportunities and rewards. Over the generations, business leads to business in good part because in this shaping process powerful family environments give little indication to their children that anything other than a very narrow range of career possibilities is desirable and hence effectively open to them. Privileged children perhaps receive fewer conflicting messages than do many others for their families both largely control the kind of education each child receives and ensure that a child will mix only or principally with people with similar or related aspirations. For the young of these milieux there are few models of other directions available until relatively late in the decision-making process: children are chosen rather than choose.

The power of the family environment is redefined by the school parents choose, bringing together education and upbringing, or *formation et éducation* in the more eloquent French formulation. The educational institutions through which a child passes in the effectively socially selective educational systems of Western Europe and upper-class family culture influence both the aspiration and ambitions which the child acquires and the self- and world-images developed. Choices made by parents also ensure the accumulation of advantages acquired by passage through each educational institution. In this milieu, families made considerable investments in private education, thought both best academically and morally most likely to reinforce the culture of home and immediate milieu, and which influenced the development of the 'whole' man with appropriate attitudes and values. For most of their sons,

51

through the most formative years of childhood and adolescence, effective access to alternative models was thus extremely limited. It is in this conjunction of experiences inside the intimate arena of the family and the social recognition of privileged educational achievement that the major mechanisms of social reproduction seem to lie. The parents and other members of the families of our respondents inculcated specific values, ambitions and orientations and dominated the choice of the formal educational paths that set the students on the roads into business. Mothers indeed have been shown to be crucial in ensuring maximum achievement by their children in the social contest (quoted Ostrander, in Domhoff, 1980: 76). In their decisions the sons were themselves influenced by their perceptions of the value of specific investments in education and career that provided the greatest returns within an acceptable social, economic and moral framework. In the business world, where economic capital gives extra power to family persuasion, such family attitudes are clearly frequently irresistible.

In complex societies such as those of Europe, choices of educational investments are, however, complex and fraught with the danger of miscalculation as to return and with the risk of unfavourable scholastic verdicts. At secondary level, school performance may be inadequate or subject choice may be mistaken. In particular, not only does the place of certain subjects in the prestige system differ by country but it also has a disconcerting tendency to alter over time, making forward planning of investments a difficult business.

Changes in the opportunities open to holders of tertiary-level diplomas in a particular discipline may be clearly seen over the long term. Law in Scandinavia, for example, used, unofficially at least, to be a prerequisite for entry to the public service and even to politics; that position lasted until the late 1950s or early 1960s after which, little by little, the place of law was taken by economics and 'social economics'. Similar changes took place in Germany. In France, as Bourdieu and his colleagues have suggested, during the boom years of the 1960s and early 1970s holders of diplomas from the most prestigious commercial schools began to displace holders of engineering degrees in the competition for entry to career ladders likely to lead to senior positions in business. In the short term, however, picking winners may be difficult, for while changes in the value of particular credentials are partly linked to economic movements they also vary with the configuration of values expressed in what becomes at any moment the dominant discourse in a given sector.

These changes have very important effects on the choice of educational strategy. They make it difficult for parents, teachers and students to decide which are the most 'blue chip' educational investments. In France, at least during the 1960s, secondary schools continued to push their 'best' pupils towards mathematics and physics and preparation for the engineering *grandes écoles*. This was probably an excellent strategy for those most likely to enter the top few schools but for the others a broadening of interests and an orientation to commercial schools might have been an investment ultimately offering better returns. Choices are made difficult by the long gap between changes at the élite end of the labour market and the views held and advice given by the schools. This lag favours the best-informed, placed in positions in the social structure which allow them access to the latest information and young people from families with members already active in that field. For most, however, even from privileged and alert families, it enhances the chances of mistakes.

For many, the changes in value of particular educational diplomas frequently only become perceptible once they have launched themselves on their careers. They are then able to begin to assess their prospects realistically, to estimate more accurately the speed of attainment of specific ambitions and the likelihood of promotion to any given position in the organisations they have joined and to compare these prospects with those of the holders of other educational qualifications or different professional experience. Many conclude that professional reorientation is necessary and that to make the change they need to make another training investment, notably here at INSEAD.

Both the importance of families in and the difficulties of educational choice are particularly clear in France and emerged in interviews with French students and alumni of the Institute. While the systemic structures and the expected patterns and returns which underlie investments made elsewhere in Europe may be somewhat less well defined than in France, the bases of the decisions are similar in all European countries. In the discussion, it becomes clear how parental wishes, educational verdicts and the structure of available institutions interact to channel young people from privileged families, notably in the business world, into the choices which precede entry to INSEAD and a career on the stage of international enterprise.

In France, as is well known, there is an established hierarchy of prestige among school disciplines, among tertiary institutions and among the special classes that prepare for entry to the high-prestige and highly selective post-secondary establishments. The selection mechanisms of the secondary cycle combine with the perception of the prestige hierarchy to present to both children and parents a clearly defined image of what the 'best' people do, 'best' here being a mixture of academic capability and achievement and socio-economic status. At the time when the students interviewed were making their choices it was clearly understood by all that the 'best' pupils were those gifted at mathematics. They were automatically channelled into the special classes preparing for the selective *grandes écoles* and within these the 'very best' were preparing for the engineering and other science-based schools. Among the schools, those considered 'best' were the generalist rather than the 'specialist' and were for 'physicists' rather than for 'chemists'. Students during the *taupe* (scientific) preparatory years knew that A1 was the best class to be in. They also knew that the chances of entry to *grandes écoles* of their choice were greatest at a select few of the *lycées* and private schools offering preparatory classes. As these schools are themselves selective, the students also knew who had 'failed'. Students not good enough at maths for the scientific *grandes écoles* were conscious of being 'relegated' to the commercial schools and had to bear the ignominy of being taunted by their *taupe* brothers with the name of *épicier* (grocer). Those in the A as opposed to the A1 science classes knew from entry that they were not destined for the most important engineering schools. The sense of relative inferiority is reinforced by the system whereby students with competitive examination (*concours*) grades too low to be admitted to one school find themselves at the school paired with but known to be 'inferior' to it. By the age of twenty most of the French students later at INSEAD, both engineers and *commerçants*, knew where they were publicly perceived to stand in the talent hierarchy, and thus in the labour market. These perceptions were firmly built into their choices.

Crucial decisions about educational *filière* (maths or not maths) were taken partly before the *baccalauréat* and partly immediately after it, the culmination of the influences which had been building up over the preceding years. Here family and school system combined to indicate more or less directly in which specific direction to go. Some choices at this level, notably for commercial education – generally seen as more suitable for some because less 'specialised' than the scientific, mathematics-based training – were made with the aim of 'putting off' final choices, *reculer l'echéance* being a common expression of this desire. Others were negative choices, made essentially because the young person knew that he or she was not good enough at mathematics for the 'best' schools; rather than be second in that field, they preferred to be first in another. Almost all the choices were instrumental rather than expressive and positively directed at acquisition of a specific diploma. In other words, they were usually made with future ambitions in the professional arena in mind rather than any personal interest in the subject matter.

In the development of this instrumental attitude towards subject options, families, especially fathers, themselves frequently engineers, played decisive roles. Thirty-three of the fifty-four male French students interviewed while at INSEAD specifically referred to parental influence on their education choices. In some cases, male members of the family, father or uncles, provided models that the younger generation absorbed as desirable and clung to, on occasions with great tenacity:

Because I had an uncle who was a *Polytechnicien*, I decided at the age of six that I too would go to the Ecole Polytechnique. For fifteen years after that my life had one essential goal: winning the bet that I had with myself. [He made it!]

In other families, the father had expressed precise wishes, in some cases wishes perceived by the sons as amounting to orders. 'My father imposed [this choice] on me', 'my father wanted it', 'I wanted or rather my family wanted for me', 'my father decided on it for me' were frequent responses to questions asking how specific educational decisions had been made. One respondent vividly described how his direction had been chosen:

My father imposed on me – rather, I had a serious problem, and that is that my father imposed my studies on me for a long time because he wanted me to be in his own image and afterwards I was obliged to use a doctorate and INSEAD to reorient myself and change directions because now, at last, I'm able to do as I wish. My father forced me to do the Arts-et-Métiers.[1]

This same interview shows up some of the curiosities of parts of the French education system for, as the student said:

after having done Latin and Greek [the most prestigious track in the early years of secondary education] at a very prestigious Catholic school, Saint-Jean-de-Passy, I found myself in a public technical boarding school in the centre of France learning to make machines work and to file metal, in preparation for entrance to the Ecole des Arts-et-Métiers.

Many other cases, of course, fall between these extremes, advice being more spasmodic or less directional, with the sons little by little assimilating the advice and choosing a direction. Justification for the direction chosen frequently included mention in a more general way of the family milieu in which the child was reared.

The processes for first putting together the choice of maths and the reasons for the selection of a particular educational direction at both secondary and tertiary level, and then the interaction of the school system and parental influences were summarised well by one student:

my father, *one is always very influenced by one's parents*, unless perhaps you have more character than I have, but I know that in the end I did maths because one had to do it but maths in itself has never interested me greatly, *but my father only saw one thing* and that was the *grandes écoles* for engineers. This was because in his view these schools meant that one could progress fast once in industry and . . . I consider that, in one way or another, I was a little bit channelled and that meant that *even if from time to time I wanted to do other things, those wishes were snuffed out by this view of life . . . I got used to the idea of being an engineer . . . for the post that one could then have*. It was also a bit through pride.[2]

Many students had no particular sense of vocation and their rather vague desires and thoughts of other options were fairly quickly smothered. In the absence of that sense of vocation and in the socio-cultural milieu to which so many belonged, it seemed normal to think of education as a means rather than an end. The 'price' of a successful career was recognised to be a few years of boredom and concentrated work on things of no immediate interest.

Where students stood at the end of the secondary educational *cursus* was not, however, always where they wished or expected to stand. Many ultimately found themselves not quite as near the top of the educational tree as they would have liked and as the years of *classes préparatoires* had led them to expect. The interviews revealed that in many cases the students had not been able to enter the higher-education establishment of their first choice and had felt themselves 'relegated' to institutions of lesser prestige. In some cases the sense of failure was acute and had far-reaching effects.

When asked which *concours* they had taken, only ten of the sixty students interviewed declared that they had got the school they wanted or the 'best' school in the *concours* they took. The system of common *concours* for several schools means that students at the Institut Industriel du Nord (IDN) know that they are the *'sous-produits de Centrale'*, as one said, those at Mines de Nancy that they have been rejected by Mines de Paris. The hierarchy of commercial schools is even more salient than that of engineering ones: with HEC clearly at the top, students at ESSEC and ESCP know that they were rejected by HEC. The same is true *a fortiori* for the provincial commercial schools.

Because of the pressures to be 'best' and because of the often acute sense of failure, exacerbated frequently by poor and unimaginative technical teaching, many of the students actively disliked their institutions. One expressed his feelings as follows:

It was absolutely idiotic. It was a bad time but I had to leave with a certificate (*diplôme*). If you don't have one in France, it's really hard . . . I went on with it so I would have a piece of paper.

The students' choices in turn reinforced the system of prestige, for they nearly all said that they took the best (or the only school) they were accepted at, or if they took one they knew to be inferior it was to get out of the 'prison' of the *classes préparatoires* rather than try again. Some, reverting to family as a reference point, particularly those going to Zurich, which is normally after only one year of preparation, said they went to escape from their family milieux. One was actually prevented by his family from attending the school he was accepted at and wished to enter, because it was a specialised school and they did not approve of the career it would have led to.

Choice of career: a limited field

If families influenced a son's education, they seem to have been even more important in the choice of career, and particularly in the decision to enter business. For most sons, indeed, there had been very little real choice: they had selected their career from only a very limited range of options. Most had assumed from an early age that they would enter business management or another business position and considered little else. Only 18 % had thought about entering the public service, politics, an international public organis-

Table 4.1 *Other careers considered, all nationalities*

Other careers considered	All except French		French	
	N	%	N	%
State service, politics, international organisations	203	16 ⎫ 19	68 ⎫ 17	
Army, navy	38	3 ⎭		
Medicine/dentistry/veterinary science	80	6 ⎤ 17	81 ⎤ 33	
Law	135	11 ⎦		
Artistic/cultural/teaching	169	13	84	21
Other business position[a]	642	51	98	24
Total N =	1267		404	

[a] E.g. engineering

ation or the armed forces. As analysis of admission files showed, only 17% of the non-French nationalities had thought of the liberal professions (6% medicine, 11% law), although a third of the French had done so. Teaching or other culturally oriented professions had tempted very few, only 13% non-French and a quarter of the French. The French indeed were rather more undecided, or perhaps more adventurous, than the others, for almost a fifth declared that they had considered several options while none of the other nationalities admitted to such indecision.

The effective career field considered varied somewhat by nationality. The British, perhaps because of the greater proportion with public-sector family origins, stand out as especially likely to have considered entry to the public service, while the Dutch had especially thought of law and medicine. In very few countries had participants considered 'cultural' careers (teaching, artistic or literary pursuits) although Scandinavians and the Austrians had done so somewhat more than others. The Swiss, the Italians and the Spanish all mentioned only business, their only uncertainty being about the position they might hold in it.

Other careers considered also varied by social origins. *Patronat* sons were, as might be expected, most likely to have thought only of business, closely followed by managers' sons, suggesting again the determining influence of the milieu of origin. Public-service sons also followed family tradition in that they first considered the public sphere; in this they joined the sons of doctors and lawyers. Those from humbler backgrounds were more likely to have been divided between law and 'cultural' careers, principally teaching, reflecting perhaps the closer and more clearly apparent relationship between success in these fields and educational qualifications held.

For most students at INSEAD, then, the choice of business as a career had been an obvious one. Hesitations and uncertainties concerned strategies for getting to particular positions within that general field rather than the choice of the field itself. Some choices of position were 'positive', others more 'negative', an escape from specific areas. A few were made for idealistic as well as instrumental reasons. Others expressed moral engagements and feelings of family obligation. Most respondents' decisions indicated a search for a field and a position within it which would satisfy many demands – family wishes, desire for harmonious personal development (*épanouissement*), as well as appropriate social recognition and economic rewards.

The processes at work in choices made were clearly visible in the ways respondents reached their decisions:

Outside business management I never seriously envisaged any other profession. That choice was inspired by the example of several members of my family and immediate circle who, without seeking to drag me down that road, made me understand *objectively* what managing an enterprise was: human contacts, responsibilities, travel.

(Emphasis in original)

The father was often especially influential:

I have to say that I have daily in front of me a businessman who in my eyes enjoys particular prestige – my Father [*sic*].

Family members thus not only provided counsel but also indirectly influenced choices, providing through their own activities models of a desirable career, indicating again the significance of both nuclear and extended family groups.

I never envisaged a profession other than that of banking. My father is a banker. His business brings him into contact with many different people and involves much travelling. I like those things too.

and, as another said:

The example of several members of my family led me to consider a career in business as that seemed to fit well with my tastes because it offers time for reflection and allows me to take initiatives. In addition to that, a business career offers human contacts and very diverse activities.

The son of the owner of a major textile firm indicated the particular pressures on the younger generation:

Brought up in the heart of the family business, a continuously expanding one, I never seriously considered any career but business administration. Filled with enormous admiration for my father, who since I was very young has kept me informed about all his various activities, I always expected to take over from him as as to realise plans and projects that little by little I came to think of as my own.

A few, even though from business families, had none the less hesitated a little and considered going outside the business world. The possibilities they considered, however, indicate how few careers are acceptable in this milieu. In the end, the family structured the choices and then dominated the final decision, either directly through exhortation or indirectly through example and the formation of particular values and conceptions of self:

I never considered any career but business. A career in the law (judge, notary) did interest me a lot but it really remains too exclusively intellectual to fit with my need for concrete results. The profession of architect – interior decorator also corresponds to my tastes. But I chose training for business management, because that career corresponds both to my tastes and my temperament. *Having always lived in an industrial milieu and having been intelligently moulded by my father*, I've always been appreciative of the human and intellectual value of this career which, properly understood, develops the personality and bring out the essential qualities of a man.

For others, medicine was considered as an alternative:

I thought about medicine because I'm interested in the natural sciences and because *I have in my family a number of doctors* who could have counselled and guided me.

This respondent decided against it, however, and in fact prepared for HEC, the top French school of commerce. During his subsequent studies he thought again and envisaged a career in law as a barrister, because 'I was interested in private law'. But that idea was not followed up, both because of family expectations and because of his perception of reduced opportunity in law, a perception probably encouraged by the family:

I abandoned this idea . . . first of all because, *given the position of my father, I would normally be called on to make my career in the business world*. Moreover, the profession of barrister is at present almost overcrowded and offers an uncertain future.

Sometimes, again, a family member was important both in considering and abandoning the idea of particular professional choices:

The example of my elder brothers . . . sometimes influenced me. Because of them I was attracted in turn to medicine and then to public administration, but I finally realised that these careers would not allow me to realise my aspirations . . . Afterwards I thought about a career as an engineer but . . . rather than being the person in the firm who knows how to do something, I prefer to be the one who knows why.

It was the brothers, not the respondent, who deviated from the longer-established family line.

For others not from business families, the traditional family line held strong attractions but *there was not felt to be a future in the field*. This was especially true for those from military families:

The members of my family have always been strongly attracted to the career of arms and I thought . . . of continuing the family tradition (my grandfather was a general in the army . . .) but the changes that have taken place recently in Europe mean that military officers no longer benefit from the same position in society . . . My father, after his military career (brigadier-general), followed a second career in business. I decided to follow the same path.

Finally, some felt that in the choice of a career particular individual interests and aptitudes were not sufficient guides. Rather, the choice should be governed by the possibility of a synthesis between one's job and one's views of life. The managerial positions envisaged were seen as matching the character traits of the respondents which 'naturally' inclined them towards 'leadership' and the 'generalist', 'decision-making' role:

When one is choosing a profession, one can either obey the call of a vocation and go for a liberal or scientific profession such as medicine, following tastes or aptitudes . . . *or one can see the profession chosen not as an end in itself but as the means of harmonising material and spiritual conceptions of life.* It seems to me that business management perfectly fulfils this aspiration and it's for that reason that I followed this branch.

Students thus sought to reconcile social and personality development, values and aspirations nurtured inside the family arena and placed in the context of social and economic opportunities available:

I had thought about a career in law . . . [but] the present status of the legal profession in France is not attractive. I therefore chose business administration because that's the only thing to offer so many possibilities *for taking personal responsibility, for the direction of others, and the more attractive perspectives for personal development* which means that it *matches my personality* over the long term.

In some, the need to lead and dominate was very strong and clearly expressed:

I thought about preparing for St Cyr [the officer-training school] because of an attraction to the career of arms and the desire to play the role of leader [*chef*]. I thought about medicine (my father is a doctor) because that is both technical and human. *In the end, I chose business management* because I'm interested in the economy *and also because being a 'captain of industry' is a superb 'combat sport'*, while I also did not neglect the pecuniary side of this occupation.

Business management, then, as a career seems to be thought to bring rewards on many fronts.

Ambitions and expectations: reaching for the top

Encouraged in this by the milieu in which most had been raised, choosing a career in business is not enough: it has to be a path to the top. These MBAs are ambitious young men, seeking both to satisfy personal values and inclinations and access to the rewards to which they feel their social and economic position entitles them. Most expressed their ambition as aiming 'for the top', for the 'leading positions', usually in important businesses which 'matured' their personalities. When asked specifically (on admission to the Institute) to indicate their career ambitions, almost a third (30%) of the 949 non-French responding said that they would seek a 'leading position' or a 'top-management post'. The French were even more determined to reach powerful posts. Of the 291 who specified their future projects, 82% that said they were aiming at the *direction générale*. More than a third even knew the route they would take, opting for marketing, a technical or a financial function. A further 12% of the French and 10% of the other nationalities also aimed for the top, saying that they would return to head their family's business or that they would create and run their own enterprises.

In line with the factors influencing their career choices, ambitions varied a little by nationality and social origins. The sons of managers in particular favoured a career in a large international company. The same sons were especially likely, with those of the civil service, to say that they were aiming for the top. *Patronat* sons in particular were much less likely to opt for marketing as a suitable route, a choice more likely to be made more by those from non-business related families, who selected a route much publicised in the media at the time. Managers' sons rather frequently chose consulting, another area then also much in the public eye and expanding fast. Those from the less traditional business backgrounds made the less traditional choices.

Some students were quite precise about their career development, and where and what they would achieve in the realisation of their high ambitions:

My career plans are ambitious in that I wish, through a strong attraction for administrative and financial problems, to obtain a decision-making post in a large company. *This kind of post needs great clarity of mind and an aptitude for human contacts at least as much as any particular technical competence.*

Some associated their future success more specifically with the acquisition of a new management style and new management techniques which would allow them to avoid the 'sclerosis' of old-fashioned, local firms of the kind many had been born into. One, for instance, wished to work in a 'dynamic and expanding enterprise using modern techniques (American-style) in their administrative section'. He wished to avoid 'enterprises destined to slow asphyxia, like the traditional textile firms'.

Some drew particularly detailed career maps, indicating geographical location, sector of activity and type of firm as well as function and position to occupy:

I have tried to classify the options that I think I will take in my career. The geographical option is doubtless Europe . . . The choice of economic sector: the private sector in a country of liberal (free enterprise) regime . . . a large company producing capital or consumption goods. Choice of function: administrative or commercial manager [*cadre*].

Others again expressed in interview the beliefs they held about the posts in a firm which were worth having and indicated clearly which were the most suitable and fastest routes to the top. One, for example, chose banking because, as he said:

I said to myself, in the end, even if I don't care for the profession of banker, the training will always be useful.

Once in the bank he had clearly seen that:

The only function, in fact *the* final function, for someone if he wants to pursue a career . . . in business is the financial function. Marketing is OK but it's very rare that the director of marketing becomes president and the only thing that it is amusing to do in a company is to be president, at least I think so.

Moreover, as he said, there are status considerations to bear in mind:

In my view, it's both nobler and more entertaining to sell money than to sell socks.

Aspirations, it should be underlined, included both the position sought and the time at which it would be acquired. These ambitious young men were in a hurry. Not for them the 'slow-burn', slow-climb route to the top. They wanted to get there fast.

Experience in the world of work: detours and disappointments

Decisions about careers take place over a long time, especially during the period in education. Over that time, economic situations alter. The demands of industry and commerce change. The education system fails to keep up with new directions, pushes its 'best' students in inappropriate directions for, as we said earlier, the value of particular diplomas varies over time. Once at work, a degree in engineering or law may seem to have less value than supposed when marketing and commercial skills suddenly command higher salaries and look more like routes to the top. Avenues planned out may suddenly become dead ends as companies merge or restructure and block off promising opportunities. For a multitude of reasons, therefore, early career strategies may need to be revised.

Some strategic revisions arise from work experience which suggests that parental advice may have led in the wrong direction:

doubtless under the influence of my father I came to believe, since I had a certain taste for maths, that I should devote myself to technical activities. As an engineer from Supélec himself, my father fervently desired that his two sons have a scientific training and early on prepared us for the idea. When the hour of choice arrived I opted for an engineering career with such spontaneity that I believed I truly had a vocation.

But, as this candidate went on to say, life in the technical field is not always what it first appears:

rapidly disappointed by the practical reality of this path, I resolved to complement my engineering degree with an economic and social training; at that point I was solicited by my father to enter the glass industry, by my brother to go into the field of organisation and then by my uncle to go towards chemical products. I, in fact, decided to do an MBA.

Another one explained his situation, emphasising both family tradition and the clash between the posts offered and his 'personality', were he to continue with the first choices made:

Family tradition led me towards the steel industry and I thought initially . . . that I would be able to carry out interesting work in that field. But, during my different industry training periods [*stages*] I saw that a simple engineering degree leads instead towards a routine production job . . . This kind of work seemed to me to be totally incompatible with my character and I turned towards the domain of business management which would allow me to stay in the industry . . . and where my character traits would assist me through the breadth of view they had allowed me.

The emphasis both on family and character appeared frequently. Wondering what to do next, many would turn again to the example of other family members:

Being interested in the industrial applications of physics, I had envisaged a career as an engineer . . . [but I saw] that several engineers in my family, having obtained a complementary training, left their technical functions to move into positions in business where they found more personal development and fulfilment.

Once within the world of work, various experiences persuaded these ambitious young managers that they would do well to reconsider their strategies. Virtually all the students interviewed during their year at INSEAD had already had some professional experience. They had, therefore, had the opportunity to savour the reality of the relative salary figures for the graduates of different schools published annually by the French business journal, *L'Expansion*, and other European management journals. They could, further, see from the same data that passage through INSEAD raised the salary scale way above that of the major engineering and *a fortiori* the major commercial schools. In France, the salary range in 1974–5 for Polytechnique graduates was between 43,000 fr. and 54,000 fr. per year – that of INSEAD graduates 52,000 fr. to 75,000 fr. with the other French graduate business school, the Institut Supérieur des Affaires, in the range of 58,000 fr. to 60,000 fr. To ambitious men, this must give pause for thought.

But there are other factors perhaps more important than salary and these are responsibility and promotion to high places, which may be expressed differently as power. As the interviews showed, the students themselves often emphasised power (expressed as responsibility) as vitally important in the jobs they wished to have, for it was part of the image of a business career which they had internalised and seemed to fit well with their own 'character'. In practice, in contrast, their experience of business life had tended to suggest slow-promotion paths, with, in France at least, privileges and responsible posts given to men of other educational backgrounds, perhaps 'relegation' for respondents to the more technical side of the enterprise concerned.

The reasons for this professional dissatisfaction were varied, but several themes were frequent. The French said 'I began to be blocked in', 'the firm is very small – one has soon done the rounds', the 'jobs were too limited and repetitive' and often too purely technical, such as computer jobs which 'became boring', particularly in the case of large firms. Frequently, too, there were problems of human relationships, as when the 'boss' changed and his replacement was difficult. The changing economic circumstances, which meant slower expansion in the companies or mergers between firms and therefore no new posts or promotions, also had their effect. Some in fact had been sacked with other employees. Many interviews revealed these preoccupations.

Some expressed their problems in a general way. One, for example (an engineer) explained that he had chosen to go to a business school because:

The market for engineers has weakened, there is less need for them, . . . or at least, companies have noticed that engineers are not polymaths, and it's not necessarily from an engineer that one can make a good manager.

In France, in particular, some of the reasons for INSEAD were clearly perceived as related to the inadequate power on the élite managerial labour market of the educational qualifications acquired earlier. Some, when interviewed, specifically attributed their lack of promotion and success directly to the fact that their previous diplomas did not fit with the high-level recruitment policies of the firms concerned. One began abruptly: 'The first statement to make, the first thing to realise, is that I just had to make a change.' The market for the product he was selling had reached saturation point and he had also run up against problems of diploma value:

I finally came to realise . . . that people set a lot of store by their credentials . . . and with the INSEAD credential one is OK . . . in firms some people don't take much notice . . . of credentials but . . . when it's a question of recruitment to an important post, the mafias, even if people won't admit it [came into play]. I saw that at R. where ENA and X are very well placed, Arts-et-Métiers too, HEC much less and us not at all well.

INSEAD, however, will compensate. The student continued by saying:

And as soon as I was accepted at INSEAD, at R. truly I saw a red carpet rolled out in front of me. I had conversations with people that before I had only briefly glimpsed . . . and then I talked to them for an hour and [they were] very, very friendly, real acquaintances. Perhaps they had told themselves that in four or five years I would be their competitor . . . and so I have a medium term objective . . . it's that really I felt I was lacking something which could stand up against all those HEC, all those accountants, and even against all those Doctors of Economics.

Another student linked together both his feelings of disappointment over the school he had attended and the recruitment patterns in firms. He mentioned the internal mechanisms which mean that once one had been declared the best, to the best more is given, thus increasing the effective gap:

I noticed that I needed a supplement . . . I have to say that in France people are obsessed by the level of a credential and that . . . it's rather painful, it means that when one fails to get accepted at a *grande école*, one finds oneself afterwards, not quite in a state of inferiority but with a feeling that one has not done as the others have done, that one is idiotic and stupid. It is nevertheless certain that the difficulty of the entry examination does operate a certain selection and I don't claim to have the mathematical intelligence of my *polytechnicien* colleagues . . . but I do believe that what makes the difference afterwards is the difference in training in the schools themselves. There's no doubt that in the French *grandes écoles* . . . people inculcate students . . . with a way of seeing things which allows them afterwards to behave differently in the milieu they go into. There's no doubt . . . that from the moment you tell someone that he is a leader, that he's made to take responsibilities, he behaves differently from someone to whom that has not been said . . . and that, I believe, is important. So afterwards, someone who's a graduate of a *grande école* in France is very often . . . quickly drawn into decision-making, he is sent quickly round all the firm's sections, he is trained rapidly etc., there's a whole phenomenon there which puts all the others into an inferior position. I think that in that situation, the only solution is to defend oneself and to act.

And that is why he went to INSEAD.

In thinking about going to INSEAD and obtaining an MBA, family members often continued to be important, either directly or indirectly. Some students indeed had first heard of the Institute from relatives (4%). Others followed family examples. In one case, for instance, going to INSEAD fitted into a formula already tried by siblings and which provided the opportunity to fit together satisfactorily both ambitions and personal tastes and character traits. As the candidate went on:

Moulded by these contacts [with the family] and having spent two years specialising in . . . the economics of the enterprise . . . *INSEAD will allow me to gain access to . . . a career that fulfils the tastes inspired by my family milieu and is in accord with my character*, as I am more a man of analysis and coordination than research.

Sometimes, indeed, the family continued to advise on choices and specifically counselled business education as a means of acquiring these extra dimensions of business training and hence better chances of access to 'appropriate' positions:

I have been able to observe . . . *and the counsels of my father have persuaded me* that technical competence needs to be allied with competence in [proper] methods of management if *one wished to accede to the posts with the greatest responsibilities*

and even more directly:

My mother wanted me to spend two years at Harvard Business School but for a variety of reasons I preferred INSEAD

and:

My father made me promise, after my studies, to gain admission to INSEAD.

Escape from the family business

Given their attachment to family and to business, one could expect most to return home to the family firm after their first degree, to take up their place, at least where the business was successful enough to absorb new generations. In practice few did, for the problems arising where members of a family work together, especially when not only fathers but also uncles and cousins are also active in the business, are legion. Some sons may also be insufficiently qualified for, as one respondent said:

[I come] from a family where several generations of business owners (*chefs d'entreprise*) have followed on from each other . . . But in this same family, there's no question of dynasty and thus of automatic succession whatever the type or level of training received.

Others felt the need to establish themselves, for personal as well as professional reasons, independently of their families, in spite of the long exposure to the values of both family and enterprise and the daily links between them observed as a child. In some cases, that very closeness is too much:

The nature of the profession of my father . . . means that there are particular links between his professional activities and his family life . . . These links no doubt explain why I have always had a great interest in the world of commerce and business and why for a long time I expected to have a position in the wool trade. But after a lot of reflection, I abandoned that path, reckoning that it was important for my internal equilibrium to exercise a profession where success would not depend on the inheritance I had received.

For yet others, the values of their world of origin seemed too restrictive as they gained experience of the world outside. They witnessed sometimes the decline of the world into which they had been born and felt that they must gain more strength and knowledge in the world beyond before perhaps one day being able to do something positive both for their families of origin and for the whole region in which they grew up. One student highlighted such feelings and indicated the deep changes taking place in traditional manufacturing areas:

I come from an industrial family which is half from the *Nord* (father) and half from *Tourcoing* (mother) but I was brought up in boarding school . . . so, without being moulded by it, I shared in the progressive decline of this world of great families. That was a spectacle that was very painful but also instructive as it taught me not to be too regional, nor too sure of my name, but much more absolute and complete through myself than through my name. This experience of returning from time to time to a milieu that my distance allowed me to judge more objectively, helped me to understand better the value of work, of the family, of moral ideas, of prudence in business . . . But I also discovered *a certain lack of culture, a certain retrograde regionalism, certain outmoded conceptions of family businesses, a certain incompetence among the protected and privileged fils de famille* ['*boys of good family*']. These things I criticise in nuances but I am happy to be aware of them because I can correct myself, avoid falling into a given biassed view, and perhaps one day I will be able to assist my milieu, in an evolution that will avoid destruction of its present patrimony.

An international future: necessity and ideal

Many students were thus seeking at INSEAD a credential allowing them to step out in new directions and to rise faster in corporate hierarchies. They also sought a means of harmonising in their new careers what they saw as their own personalities and their quite traditional value systems acquired from families of origin with effective opportunities on the labour market. To these considerations, they also added those of status in the society and the remuneration that could enable them to maintain a lifestyle appropriate to a bourgeois position.

Stepping on to the international stage was perceived by many students at one and the same time as a personal, a company and even a national necessity. In their eyes to be international and, especially, European was to show that one understood the 'necessities' of 'modern' economic life and the need for individual companies to take advantage of the new opportunities offered by a united Europe. At the same time, such a reorientation clearly offered a wider stage for professional activity, especially perhaps in the marketing and financial field. INSEAD, of course, situated at the crossroads of Europe and depicting itself specifically as an internationally (and European) oriented institution, with its mix of languages, nationalities and teaching staff and materials, stood out as ideally suited to the needs of someone with this orientation.

An interest in the Institute embraced many strands, ambitions and values. For some, INSEAD is the consecration of the new European ideal and study there has both idealistic and practical elements. Others emphasise that an INSEAD MBA opens up new career possibilities in companies operating not on a national but on a European scale. Some can see quite precisely the development of their careers on the European stage, indicating that they wish to 'have an administrative and commercial career in a company of a size appropriate to the Common Market', or saying that 'within the framework of the Common Market, I would like to be responsible for the commercial representation of a firm abroad', or again that 'I should like to participate in the top management of a commercial, industrial or banking company with a European orientation or even more international activity.'

For others, the values and politics lying behind the unification of Europe were important. INSEAD allows the student to feel that he or she personally has contributed to the creation on the ground of the European idea. Some said simply:

I am a convinced European. I wish to think Europe, see problems as a European.

I have a very active sympathy for all that can contribute to the creation of a united Europe . . . INSEAD has a dual duty: to train men for business and to prepare them for a European mission.

Some had clearly thought long and deeply about the situation and the way in which their own careers could be fitted into the idealism underlying the creation of 'Europe', for only then could 'personality' and 'position' be made fully consonant:

I wish to confront commercial or psychological problems rather than purely administrative or financial ones. Selling such and such a product rather than another means less to me than does the ambiance in which I work and the responsibility I'm given. The feeling of efficiency *vis-à-vis* a clientele or my Country [*sic*], freedom to act or not in harmony with my rhythm and temperament and the possibility of sharing in a good activity, these are the points that are particularly dear to me, especially when joined to contacts with very diverse men and countries, something which has always greatly attracted me. *I believe deeply in Europe as a primordial condition of the survival of the civilisation that we have created and that we must go on developing.*

The search for an 'appropriate' career means bringing together attitudes, values, ideas and marketable skills in a complex and continually changing environment. Families push and pull, advise and command. But their edicts combine with school verdicts and labour market demands in ways which can lead to confusion. While young people absorb values and attitudes which suggest that a high-level business career is the *only* professional avenue in which to combine successfully personal character traits and talents which fit them only for leadership roles and the desire for an appropriate place in the social and economic structures of their countries, it is only in the labour market that they can test the reality of their choices. Experience there leads many on the route to INSEAD. For some the Institute fits into a well-planned and defined career path. Others, disappointed with earlier rewards, are seeking to realise their ambitions through a change of orientation or to establish themselves in senior positions faster than would be possible without an MBA. Yet others are still seeking their path forward, trying to orient themselves in an unfamiliar world. Many are searching for a more satisfactory way to fit together personal ideals and effective careers, their personal desires and the internalised wishes of those around them. They enter the Institute with ideas and aspirations in various stages of achievement, with varying degrees of success and failure behind them. At entry to INSEAD, however, they all have high expectations about what the Institute will do for their professional lives.

5. Careers across Europe

Ambitious at the outset, young managers sought in their MBAs a credential they associated with a rapid route to the top in business. While in theory there are many possible paths to controlling positions in major companies, in practice only a few tracks give access even to the springboards from which to make the final jump. Even among these tracks some lead upwards more swiftly and surely than others. As we have seen, the early life of Europe's young managers is often one where family and educational experiences generate certainties about their future in terms of goals to aim for, means to achieve them and the directions to take in business and personal lives. In contrast, these certainties are equally often sorely tested during the early years in the professional arena. Brought up to feel themselves leaders by virtue of character, training and background, many find disappointing and disorienting the realities of the junior positions, technical jobs and slow-burn career paths which they are offered with their only formal credential, their first degree. American management techniques and the expanding international opportunities which their possession seems to make possible are greatly tempting.

Careers, these young men find, in companies operating in a turbulent world, are not simple. Even in expanding markets, individuals, like companies, must learn to take advantage of new opportunities, to cut losses, to change direction. In these years, ambitious young entrants to the managerial labour market must learn to be wary of potential dead ends while they develop more effective tactics for taking better advantage of future opportunities. Rather than stepping directly on to a fast track upwards, many find they must spend a period of 'milling about', of getting a 'first foot' rather than a sure one in the search for the rapid professional rewards young people from privileged backgrounds are early taught to expect as their entitlement. Brought up to be leaders, many spend some time seeking the appropriate troops to command and the directions in which to lead them.

Data gathered through the questionnaires, on which this chapter is based, suggest that there are two points during these early years at which aspiring managers feel the need to change direction by taking a year out to invest in an INSEAD MBA. The first is very soon after entering jobs in business, only one or two years into professional life. This is particularly true of the European continental nationalities. Except for the British, the majority had worked only one year or less, with a second peak after two years. Between half and two-thirds of the remaining nationalities had worked one year or less. They were followed by a quarter to a fifth from Germany, Belgium, Switzerland, Italy and Scandinavia who had had two years of professional life. For many, then, two years is a turning point. After three or four years of work, people in all the countries seemed less inclined to look to the MBA as a way forward. In contrast, five years again constitutes an important decision point, especially for the British, who seem to persevere longer with the fruits of their initial credentials and decisions, but also for the others. Their perseverance may be related to their first degrees – the arts-educated British finding themselves in an early career market rather different from that of their engineering and commercially trained continental cousins, while their upbringing in non-business families may also have imbued them with different expectations. With time, however, all have felt the need to make a change. Observation and discussion with friends, colleagues and superiors suggest INSEAD as the key to expanded possibilities or even faster ascent.

During these early years, half the respondents had already sampled the offerings of more than one employer, including a third who had investigated possibilities with three or more. A third had stayed only one year or less in their first and last firms, and the remaining two-thirds two years or less. Their growing dissatisfaction with their proposed careers can be seen in the shorter periods spent in each subsequent firm.

Where then had they been placed in the economic life of Europe? How had they prepared their moves into their own transnational operations? Some, of course, had early acquired international connections through multinational kinship networks or birth and education abroad. Others had to make a start during their working lives and many had already tested the international business waters before going to INSEAD. In part this early internationalis-ation is a function of the size and type of companies and the industrial sectors they originally chose to join.

The 'ideal-typical' student at INSEAD had held a job immediately before entry to INSEAD and had done so in a large, public, multinational or foreign company, outside his country of origin, but in Europe, in a finance, marketing or general management position in a firm in the service sector. The many exceptions to this general picture of the starts made in their professional lives underline the complexities of choosing career paths at the same time as they emphasise the amount of professional experimentation that characterises the first years after entry to the labour market.

The service sector dominated initial choices. Rather more than half 55 %

Table 5.1 Sector of professional experience before INSEAD, by nationality (percentages of respondents)

Sector	British	German	Belgian	Scandinavian	Swiss	Dutch	Austrian	Spanish	Italian	French	Average (all nationalities)
Primary	2	11	7	9	3	8	—	—	4	4	6
Secondary	43	62	28	34.5	38	38	46	64	43	49	47
Tertiary	47	13	45	51	46.5	43	44	36	41	40	37
Combination	7	14	20.5	5	12	10	10	—	49	7	10
N=	277	358	83	138	99	60	39	14	49	375	1,492

Data from files

and 56% in first and last firms, had worked in that sector. Almost all the rest were in manufacturing, with only a handful in the primary sector, mostly associated with mining and oil. Within the service sector, banking and the financial area are clearly dominant, early on as well as later.

Ambitious young men choosing a career in business generally consider a large firm to offer the best possibilities and the majority began their careers in Europe's largest companies. More than half (52%) had started in firms employing more than a thousand people and an additional 9.5% in giant firms of 10,000 or more, with a fifth in firms of between 2,000 and 10,000.

They also tended to stay there: proportions remaining in large firms in their last, as in their first firm before INSEAD were virtually identical, although the anonymity of life in such large organisations may eventually have contributed to the need felt to move elsewhere, or to acquire additional cultural capital valuable in the effort to make a mark and distinguish oneself from the numerous otherwise similarly qualified competitors at the same level. In spite of their university degrees, most students began in very junior positions, entering their first jobs in their first firms as trainees in a modified kind of 'apprenticeship'. The others were more or less evenly divided between staff and line positions. By their last job in the first company a good deal of change had occurred. While 28% were still in trainee positions, a considerable proportion, two-fifths, had obtained line posts, there being only a small increase in staff positions. The 'management-training' course inside companies thus seems to remain a major induction mechanism for those who will later hold line posts and most had acquired more senior posts before leaving for INSEAD, with more than half in line and a third in staff posts. For the line managers, a desire to accelerate promotion further up may have been essential in the decision to enter INSEAD. For the third in staff posts, the MBA may seem the best mechanism for making the often difficult transition to a line position.

Some also wished to find a way to move functions, for many had become aware of the differential career chances offered, especially as between production and finance or marketing. Around a fifth before INSEAD had already moved into the 'modern' functions of finance and marketing, and between a quarter and a third were already in 'general management', although the term is somewhat ambiguous. Making these transitions, they had moved out of production and management services and consulting. In terms of positions held, the biggest increase was among those occupying 'combination roles', such as personal assistant to a senior figure or liaison officer between functions. These are often excellent positions for gaining insight into the functioning of the organisation as a whole, or at least a major part of it, as they involve easier access to a range of persons and information and a global view of the enterprise not available even to senior management in highly specialist areas. Being in such positions gave them a view of where the best futures lay,

Table 5.2 *Place of professional experience before INSEAD, all nationalities (percentages of respondents)*

Place of professional experience	British	German	Belgian	Scandinavian	Swiss	Dutch	Austrian	Spanish	Italian	French
Home country only	58	63	61	58	68	55	44.5	60	63	61
Europe	19	6	14	24.5	11	28	27.5	40	19	—
Outside Europe	4	4	9	8	4	8	2.5	—	8	—
Combination	19	28	15.5	10	17	9	22.5	—	10	39
N =	274	358	84	143	99	65	38	15	52	360

Data from files

but also showed them that they did not have the tools they needed to move fast up the ladder.

Not all had gone straight to the international arena. For many, the realisation that the international card was an important one to play came only gradually. Half had begun in companies owned and operated in their country of origin. A further quarter worked at home but in multinationals based in that country, thus taking a small step into the international arena. Only a quarter first joined foreign companies. By their second firm, however, many more worked internationally, both in home-based or other multinationals, notably French and American firms. In their last firm before INSEAD many more not only worked for foreign companies but had begun to work abroad, so that while in their first firms more than two-thirds worked at home, by the last firm almost half were abroad. Most worked principally in Europe, only 6% having gone as far as North America. Many indeed had converged on France, increasing their chances both of hearing of INSEAD and of having adequate French for entry. At entry to INSEAD, therefore, the students were already principally a European-oriented population.

Some nationalities were more likely than others to have moved into the international arena. The Austrians were most likely to have worked outside Austria and the most likely to have combined working in Europe with experience elsewhere. They were followed by the Dutch, the British and the Scandinavians. In contrast, the Swiss were the most likely to stay at home. For many, then, the year at INSEAD was their first experience of working in an international environment.

In their attempts to find the right position students had tried a wide range of alternatives. Some tried moving firms. Some had moved both sector and functions. Others had tried working overseas. Paths chosen in the search for that coveted position varied by nationality. Some stuck more to one sector. Two-thirds of the Germans and the Spanish and half the French had worked only in manufacturing. Others concentrated on the tertiary sector: between two-fifths and half of the British, Swiss, Belgians, Dutch, Austrians and Scandinavians had worked only in service industries, while a third of the French had done so. Given their low proportion with technical backgrounds, the British, although in the majority in the service industries, were also surprisingly well represented in manufacturing (43%) and, like the Italians, divided almost equally between the two. In contrast, some moved sectors, including one-fifth of the Belgians and 14% of the Germans who had tried both. The tendency of the vast majority of each nationality to work in only one sector suggests that they had found difficulty in moving from sector to sector, even where they had wished to do so.

Particular combinations of choices of direction owed much to the influence of background, social and educational as well as nationality, and to the particular combinations of these. Class origins helped to correct career errors early; social background particularly influenced the length of the period before the decision to enter INSEAD. *Patronat* sons were noticeably younger and thus earlier acquired the career benefits of the MBA. Access to informal career counselling clearly helped most *patronat* sons, who, in contrast to others, had been advised about INSEAD by family and friends.

Class origins affected career paths, notably the choice of economic sector in which to work. Sons of business owners were concentrated in manufacturing (50%), with a third in the service sector and 12% with experience in both. They were followed in their choice of manufacturing by the sons of senior managers and those of the lowest prestige group. In contrast, the sons of the 'non-business' group were noticeably more likely to have gained their work experience exclusively in the tertiary sector.

These differences may be linked to educational credentials, which also affected the number of years INSEAD participants had worked before entering INSEAD. Lawyers, in particular, went early, with just over half entering the Institute almost immediately on graduation. This proportion dropped somewhat among holders of degrees in commerce and economics and much further for engineers (a third), declining to a quarter for holders of arts and other degrees. Diplomas held also affected place of work. Least likely to have worked abroad were those with law and arts degrees, these credentials perhaps being especially closely linked to a particular national system, the one of law, the other of culture. Most likely to have worked abroad were engineers and the holders of commercial diplomas – perhaps the most portable qualifications, giving access to business activity of many kinds. Finally, the number of years taken to realise that they needed a means of making a new start or of speeding faster along a chosen path varied by nationality as well as by social origin.

The MBA at work

Motivated at entry to INSEAD by a desire for 'career reorientation', widened career opportunities and an interest in the international, new MBAs step back again after graduation into a highly complex professional arena. As their INSEAD year draws to an end, they devote much time to searching the labour market for the 'right' position, which by the day of graduation most feel they have found, either via the formal mechanisms of the placement service, through newspaper advertisements or by using their informal networks of well-placed friends and family.

The results of that search show both continuation and change, both an accentuation of trends already present and moves in new directions. As careers develop over time, the weight of early influences, education and first job choices, diminishes and is replaced by the 'track record' which a manager makes for himself. Some of the shifts which the MBA ultimately makes possible only become visible as careers develop, for acquisition of the new credential does not end career changes. In some cases, rather, it strengthens the likelihood of moving around. Analysis of the ways in which people choose where to go makes apparent a series of specific career strategies. Over a period of years important trends emerge. These are seen in movements:

towards working in European companies and out of American ones;

towards entering smaller companies and leaving large ones;

towards services and away from manufacturing;

towards the 'newer' sectors within manufacturing, such as electricals, electronics and pharmaceuticals;

away from marketing and finance towards general management functions;

consequently, away from staff and towards line positions;

towards a division of the MBA population into those moving to work 'at home' after some years abroad and the true multinationals who remain indefinitely on the international stage.

Several major changes in overall orientation can be seen on graduation. The first big division is between manufacturing and the service sector, notably banking and finance. Within manufacturing there is a further important divergence, between the traditional areas such as textiles and mechanical engineering and the 'new' sectors such as pharmaceuticals and electronics, perceived in the 1970s as at the forefront of technological progress and usually producing for a mass market. Of the twenty-five business sectors classified on the INSEAD scheme,[1] twelve lost members after MBA graduation and eight gained members. The single biggest area, banking, insurance and finance, retained a fifth of respondents both before and after graduation. Manufacturing was a net loser of graduates, while consulting gained considerably. Within manufacturing, the more traditional areas lost out to the newer ones. There was thus a clear move towards the expanding sectors singled out by observers, both academic, such as Bourdieu, and economic, such as the journal *L'Expansion*, as the sectors of greatest managerial opportunities in the 1960s and 1970s.

Equally, INSEAD provided the occasion for many to move both function and type of position held. The sector gaining most MBAs was marketing. Conscious of the newly important place of marketing in company activities and hierarchies, many graduates joined marketing areas (which they created) so that marketing doubled its share, rising from 15 % to 30 % of all posts held. In contrast, only a few more entered finance and corporate planning after INSEAD than before. Production remained clearly out of favour. That decision to enter the fashionable marketing area may ultimately have cost them dear.

Analysis of functions entered by MBAs shows that INSEAD by no means wiped away the effects of earlier career choices. Paths followed varied according to where one had been before. Thus, while some entered different functions, many returned to familiar ground. Marketing, in particular, retained many: half of those there before entering INSEAD returned, while only 17% moved out to enter corporate planning and 12.5% each general management and consulting. Of all those previously in finance, a third, the biggest single proportion, returned. A further 29% went into a finance-related area, corporate planning, and only a fifth or less into general management or consulting. Interestingly, those earlier in general management seemed to be most willing or to find it easiest to change, for only a quarter returned, while the most common destination of the others was marketing (35%) followed far behind by consulting and management services. Early career decisions thus seem to count still on re-entry to the labour market after INSEAD. Moreover, it seems that some paths rarely or never cross; even an MBA seldom leads financiers into consulting or marketeers into finance.

In spite of its rhetoric, INSEAD cannot, it seems, create instant generalists, or even make 'generalists' within any given function, at least not in large companies. Some of the difficulties of moving across business areas seem to be due to the difference in the kind of training and track record established by a financier acquiring his experience in a banking institution or in a financial function in a manufacturing company, as was the case with nearly half of those in finance before INSEAD. Similarly, general management experience in banking or consulting companies, the place where experience in that field was acquired by around a quarter of the MBAs before INSEAD, may not afterwards be considered suitable for similar positions in manufacturing companies, which have very different sets of problems, and vice versa. Not all the new posts were high level and many people found, to their chagrin, that the MBA was not always a direct route into line management. On the contrary, *fewer* people were in line positions in their first firms after INSEAD (42%) than before (52%) and hence more were in staff posts.

Before stepping firmly on to the road to the top, therefore, many other moves need to be made. The way forward and upward is a good deal trickier and more ill defined than business-school rhetoric and emphasis on general management would suggest. In part, the difficulty of entering line positions may be due to the enormous size of the firms in which new MBAs so often choose to work; 13% went into companies with more than 50,000 employees and 31% into those with 10,000 or more. Such companies are unlikely to trust the young with major managerial responsibilities. Other strategies must be preferred by those wishing to go fast, for instance, trading off major economic influence in the future for lesser power at an early stage. The competition for positions further up the hierarchy is enormous in the larger enterprises but some nevertheless feel it worth the wait and the uncertainty. In any event, many took the opportunity offered by an INSEAD MBA to move into or confirm their interest in an international arena. Many more entered foreign firms than were in them before, although proportions working outside their home countries rose only slightly.

The next stage: fields of ambition and competition

Some sectors of the economies of Europe are especially attractive to MBAs, who choose them as their preferred fields of ambition and as arenas for the competition for recognition in the European business world. Within these fields, they spread across Europe in diverse directions, juggling the rewards to be obtained from their skills and talents with the constraints and opportunities provided by the market in different countries and companies and the demands on and returns from investment in their private lives. Strategies adopted vary by nationality, by class origin and by educational trajectory; paths developed crossed and criss-crossed countries, companies and position, interacting with hirers' requirements and opportunities perceived. From the confusion of individual choices some patterns begin to emerge and these are traced as background to the analysis of the fast tracks that follow. They show the complexities of career decisions, the factors that must be matched and the trade-offs made.

(a) Sector and company

The sector of employment is in part determined by the nationality of the firm selected. The place of company nationality in the strategies which MBAs adopt for career advancement varies both with the nationality of the INSEAD graduates concerned and over time, according to the year in which the MBA was obtained and the number of years its holder had been out and working in business, as well as with the number of moves made between companies.

Where, then, did they go? A first move in many strategies was placement in an American company. In their first firms, the biggest single proportion of respondents entered American banks and consulting companies (45%). Indeed, American companies were the most probable first destination in all sectors, except services and mining and petroleum: of all those who entered traditional manufacturing companies,[2] a third went to American companies, followed by 26% who went to multinationals belonging to their country of origin and 25% to their own national firms.

Those who entered companies in the 'new manufacturing' sector were even more likely to enter US enterprises – nearly two-fifths (39%). They were followed far behind (24.5%) in that sector by proportions choosing firms of their own countries, notably local multinationals (18%). In contrast, of all

Table 5.3 *Sector, five firms after INSEAD (percentages of respondents)*

Sector of activity	First	Second	Third	Fourth	Fifth[a]
Electrical, electronics, computing	7	7	12	17.5	31
Banking, insurance, finance[b]	19	22	16	15	15
Consulting	14	11	11	17.5	15
Metals and mining	5	1	—	2.5	—
Chemicals, plastics, rubber	8	6	4	2.5	—
Petroleum	4	3	2	5	15
Pharmaceuticals	4	4	4	5	—
Energy, electricity, gas, coal	1	—	2	—	—
Mechanical engineering	5	5	3	5	—
Automobiles	4	2	1	—	—
Aeronautics and shipbuilding	1	1	—	—	—
Textiles and clothing	3	2	2	2.5	—
Food, drink, tobacco	3	4	5	5	—
Cosmetics and toiletries	3	3	2	2.5	—
Timber, paper, packaging	2	4	—	—	—
Other products	6	7	8	2.5	—
Building, property, real estate, civil engineering	3	4	6	5	8
Travel, transport, tourism	1	3	1	—	—
Commerce, trade, retailing	2	3	2	2.5	—
Printing, publishing, TV, journalism	1	3	3	2.5	—
Advertising and PR	—	2	—	2.5	—
Government, Civil Service, army, etc.	2	—	4	—	8
Teaching and research	1	2	2	2.5	—
Conglomerates	1	3	6	—	—
Other services	2	2	3	2.5	—
N=	302	189	99	40	13

[a] Fifth, or last firm if the respondent had worked in more than five. Numbers in the group are tiny and are given simply for information in the following tables
[b] Includes chartered accountants
The nomenclature is that used by INSEAD
Data in this and all subsequent tables in this chapter are from the 1979 questionnaire survey. For this reason, unless otherwise stated the French are not included, as the earlier survey focused less on careers

those entering the miscellaneous services sector, essentially more local activities, 80 % went into their own national firms.

A second element in many career strategies is a further move – this time *away* from American companies. In some sectors, by entry to second firms there were already big moves away from American companies. In particular, in banking and consulting, where by far the biggest single group had entered American firms, a big drop occurred. Similarly, in the significant area of new manufacturing, proportions in American companies fell by a third between first and second firms, in favour of European multinationals based in the MBA-holders' own countries, although in traditional manufacturing there was little change from the first firm. Many, thus, as they change firms also change their orientation, from looking towards the USA to taking a European perspective. Only in mining and petroleum was there a reverse movement, with the proportion in American firms rising to 37.5% and that in local multinationals dropping to a quarter and this was because of the structure of those particular sectors.

Similarly divergent trends can be seen in third firms, and, as far as can be seen from the small numbers, in fourth and subsequent firms. *These differences indicate that choice of sector effectively means a choice of different international routes. Some, a minority, lead outwards from Europe, while most are intra-European, leading essentially to a European business orientation.*

Paths chosen through opting for a particular sector also varied with the nationality of the INSEAD participant. There are, however, a number of clusters, with some trends apparent over changes of firm, while ultimately a number of contrasting paths appear.

In their first firm, the *British* more than any other nationality *entered banking and consulting* (43%) and more of the British entered that sector than any other, the proportion only dropping in moves to third firms.[3] In the proportion first entering banking, the British were followed by the Scandinavians and the Swiss, while the Germans only joined them in their second firm.

In their first firm, the *Germans* tended to put a major group (35%) into *traditional manufacturing activities*, following still, perhaps, the legacy of their engineering education and their *patronat* origins. The biggest contingent of the *Swiss* (34%), however, in spite of their engineering backgrounds, and perhaps following their country's well-known traditions, *entered banking and consulting* straightaway, although more, 44%, entered manufacturing if the 'new' and 'traditional' fields are taken together.

In the movements between sectors as people moved firms, *one trend is striking*. In their first firm, only the Dutch entered the miscellaneous and service sectors in any numbers (14%). However, in second and subsequent firms those sectors received considerable proportions of recruits from among the Scandinavians (16% in the second and 25% in the third firm), the Swiss (18% in the second and 27% in third firm) and the Belgians (12.5% in second firms). *If one single trend emerges, it is the increasing tendency among several of the major nationalities to enter the miscellaneous and service sectors, to the detriment of the others. This means a fairly rapid spreading out of MBAs across a wide variety of companies and kinds of activity.*

The tendency to diversify the sectors and companies in which they work is often accompanied by a change in size of firm chosen. When they entered the labour market after obtaining their MBA, INSEAD alumni enormously increased their tendency to work in large or very large companies. Nearly two-thirds (62%) entered companies employing more than 2,000 people, including

Table 5.4 *Sector in first three firms entered after INSEAD, by nationality (percentages of respondents)*

Nationality	Banking/ consulting			Traditional manufacturing			New manufacturing			Metals/ petroleum 1[a]	Service/ miscellaneous 1[a]
	1	2	3	1	2	3	1	2	3		
British	43	43	26	21	25	17	16	9	22	—	—
German	27.5	43	32	35	23	24	12	18	20	13	—
Scandinavian	33	26	12.5	24	32	19	17	13	31	—	—
Swiss	34	21	27	22	18	—	22	36	33	—	—
Belgian[a]	23	12.5	—	35.5	50	—	23	12.5	—	—	—
Dutch[a]	29	29	—	29	29	—	—	—	—	—	14

[a] Numbers too small to count in three firms

Table 5.5 *Number of employees in five firms after INSEAD (percentages of respondents)*

Number of employees	First firm	Second firm	Third firm	Fourth firm	Fifth firm
Fewer than 50	12	18	25	33	60
50–199	10	18	18	18	—
200–499	13	12	13	5	10
500–999	6	5	4	10	—
1,000–1,999	9	9	9.5	10	10
2,000–9,999	20	18	10.5	10	10
10,000–49,999	18	14	14	8	10
More than 50,000	13	6	6	5	—
N =	298	187	95	39	10

31 % in firms of more than 10,000 and 13 % in giant firms of more than 50,000. The present study, in common with my earlier one on the French alumni of INSEAD, Whitley and Thomas' (1977) study of London and Manchester MBAs and Egon Zehnder's study (1975b) study of European MBAs from both INSEAD and other business schools, showed a marked trend for people, as their career developed, to move out from these large firms in favour of smaller ones. Thus, while only 35 % of MBAs entered firms employing fewer than 200 people in their first firms, by their second firm almost half (48 %) chose these much smaller companies and 56 % did so when they moved to their third firm.[4] The trend seems to continue in fourth and fifth firms. It seems, then, that many INSEAD alumni little by little remove themselves from the competition for the very top in large firms. To some extent this move may be linked with the other tendencies noted, that is, the move away from American companies and towards working at home, and the move away from public companies towards private ones.

While noting the trend, however, it should none the less be emphasised that *many MBAs do prefer big business*; two-fifths, 40 % or so, of alumni in their *third* firms were still in companies employing between 1,000 and 50,000 people, including 20 % in firms of more than 10,000, and many of the smaller firms may well be subsidiaries. Firms employing between 1,000 and 10,000 people are still large by European standards; even if not all are in the top 500 companies of some countries, many would be in others. If MBAs reach the top in these they will be running companies of considerable importance to the European economy, and of particular importance to the economies of the smaller countries of Europe and beyond.

Although it is not wholly clear from the data whether the firms concerned are subsidiaries or independent, 35 % declared that they had first entered firms

Table 5.6 *Turnover of five firms after INSEAD (percentages of respondents)*

Turnover $	First firm	Second firm	Third firm	Fourth firm	Fifth firm
Less than $100,000	4	7	10	3	9
100,000–499,000	4	5	6	17	—
500,000–999,000	3	2	5	11	18
1–9 million	14	21	19	23	27
10–99 million	19	23	21	17	9
100–499 million	19	15	17.5	14	18
500–1,000 million	9	10	7.5	6	—
More than 1,000 million	28	17	14	9	18
N=	231	149	80		11

of fewer than 500 employees. This would seem to suggest a basic division in the orientations MBAs had chosen. Many of the small companies, however, are likely to be consultants and from those it is still possible to move to much larger enterprises.

In building this picture of career paths across Europe, it is useful to take another view, that of the proportions of jobs in a sector taken by different national groups. Thus, for example, in banking, of all the MBAs working in that sector, one third (32%) were British, 20% were German, 14% were Scandinavian and 14% Swiss. Similarly, in traditional manufacturing, 20% were German, 19% were British, 13% Belgian, 12% Scandinavian and 11% Swiss. In new manufacturing, 24.5% were British, 18% Swiss, 16% German, 14% Scandinavian. In other words, of all the opportunities open to INSEAD MBAs in the banking field, one-third had been taken by the British, while a maximum of only a fifth had gone to any one of the other nationalities. This is important because it may refer to hirers' preferences and hence career chances. Bankers and consultants seem to prefer the less 'specialised' education of the British (a group perhaps particularly favoured by the American banks for their native English speaking and their City of London traditions) to the more 'manufacturing-marked' Germans and others. In contrast, the British were a less popular choice by, and perhaps offered themselves less often to, traditional manufacturers, who preferred the more technically appropriate educational backgrounds of the Germans. The 'new' manufacturers, however, again preferred the British, perhaps because the companies focused less on production than marketing and hence less on technical engineering skills.

The opportunities available to MBAs also varied quite considerably even over short periods of time and this variation suggests again the difficulties of long-term career decision-making. Among those graduating in the early years of INSEAD, there was a greater propensity to enter traditional manufacturing and such areas as metals and petroleum. In later years, however, in line, perhaps, with perceptions of expanding opportunities in the financial arena and the 'new' industries, larger proportions of young MBAs moved towards banking and consulting and the newer high-technology, consumer-oriented manufacturing sectors – pharmaceuticals, cosmetics and electronics. That change results both from students' preferences and perceptions of the market and from a change in demand – bankers and consultants in particular were the employers most in evidence on campus at INSEAD in the 1970s as manufacturing was hit by the recession.

Indeed, by 1981 there were almost 600 INSEAD MBAs working in the financial sector, spread over 282 banks and insurance companies. In some of these institutions, INSEAD graduates are now concentrated in considerable numbers. By 1981 Morgan Guaranty had 35, First National Chicago Bank had 21, and Citibank 27. Paribas had 22, of all nationalities, though mostly French; the Crédit Swisse had 10, all Swiss. The Chase Manhattan, the Banque Nationale de Paris, and the Banque d'Indochine had 12 or 13 each, while American Express had 10.

Ambitious young managers, moreover, have to be prepared to move sectors several times in the course of a career. There is a consistent movement *towards* banking and consulting in *second* firms over all the years, except for the period 1965–9, while, equally visible, in contrast, is a move *away* from those sectors where *third* firms are concerned, and an associated move *towards* a miscellaneous service group of firms. This may suggest that, after a number of years in what might be termed the 'major' MBA-employing sectors, as the competition for the smaller available number of senior jobs increases, some people move off to colonise new territories or to be the MBA-in-a-senior-position in smaller firms in more varied areas of activity.

These trends are also visible in the paths followed by different cohorts of graduates. Almost all years show a fairly strong division between traditional manufacturing firms and banking and consulting, which maintains itself over time, with some variations according to the period in which the MBA was obtained. Table 5.7 compares paths followed by different groups of MBAs. In particular, the table shows both the likely sector divisions and a *process of 'spreading out' over time as people perceive new opportunities*. Thus, of the group graduating in 1959–64, a quarter entered banking and consulting in their first firms, a proportion which rose slightly in second firms, but dropped to 13 % in third firms. Similarly, of the same group of graduates, 28 % entered traditional manufacturing in their first firm, a proportion dropping to 23 % and then 13 % in second and subsequent companies. In contrast, a much larger proportion, 47 %, entered the miscellaneous and service categories.

In contrast to the first MBAs, the second group, those graduating between 1965 and 1969, increased their representation in banking and consulting between the second and third firms. Table 5.7 also shows, for instance, that

Table 5.7 *Sector entered, first three firms, by year MBA (percentages of respondents)*

Firms	Banking/ consultancy			Traditional manufacturing			New manufacturing			Metals/oil			Services/ miscellaneous		
	1	2	3	1	2	3	1	2	3	1	2	3	1	2	3
Year MBA:															
1959–64	24	27	13	28	23	13	—	—	20	24	—	—	—	27	47
1965–69	32	25.5	31	35	38	20	—	21	21	14	—	—	—	—	13
1970–74	31	34	29	26	20	18	—	19	26	9.5	—	—	—	—	13
1975–79	38	41.5	27	24.5	24	18	19	12	18	5	—	—	—	—	27

there was noticeably heavier representation of banking and consulting among those graduating in most recent years, especially in second firms entered. By the third firm, however, *more than a quarter even of that last group was spread out over the miscellaneous and service areas,* a proportion even greater than that in new manufacturing and equalling those in banking and consulting. The 'spreading out' thus started early and similar changes continued with each cohort over the period.

In summary, after the earliest group, 1960–4, there was in each group of years some *rise* in the proportions entering *new manufacturing* in their first firm. In the later periods, there was an especial *drop* in numbers entering traditional manufacturing spheres and a consistent drop in metals and petroleum, while, in contrast, *banking and consulting* continued to *increase*. By the second firm, there continued to be a rise in that latter sector, except for the 1965–9 group who, in contrast to all the others, found their biggest group still in manufacturing. New manufacturing *gained* recruits in the second firm over all periods except the last, suggesting perhaps an MBA saturation in that sector with a consequent reduction in opportunities for rapid production there. By the third firm, in almost all cohort groups, there was considerable movement and a good deal of spreading out into firms in a great variety of sectors, a trend especially noticeable for the most recent MBA group and perhaps linked to the increasing familiarity of companies with the skills of the MBAs and to possibly greater competition in the traditional fields of INSEAD MBAs from MBAs trained elsewhere. So, by the time of the survey in 1979, INSEADs had spread well beyond their traditional strongholds and were colonising new areas: from the training bastions of large firms, marketing and finance functions, banking, consulting and mass-market manufacturing, they had moved out to a wide variety of sectors, to smaller firms and to positions of much greater responsibility. Following changing market opportunities, those rising towards the new international business élite spread ever further afield.

(b) Functional areas

The biggest groups of INSEAD MBAs were recruited to two functions in their first firm; half the graduates entered positions in just two areas – marketing (38 %) and finance (21 %) – those most associated with the 'new' managerial functions.

Taking the trends over five firms, however, suggests other patterns, indicating considerable movement out of finance and marketing and into general management posts, as can be seen in Table 5.8. The closeness of proportional changes between marketing, finance and general management, the relative stability in numbers in other functions, together with the acknowledged low likelihood of people moving from finance or marketing

Table 5.8 *Functional area, five firms after INSEAD (percentages of respondents)*

Functional area[a]	First firm	Second firm	Third firm	Fourth firm	Fifth firm
Finance	21	18	18	13.5	9
Marketing	30	22	19	19	9
Production	2	3	1	5	—
Corporate planning	8	4	3	3	—
Personnel	8	2	5	—	—
Management services	2	4	6	8	9
External consulting	6	10	13	8	18
Other/general management	20	36	34	43	54.5
N=	279	179	94	37	11

[a] Excluded here are 15 people who went into positions such as teaching, which could not be classified into functional area

into production or personnel, *suggest that marketing and finance may be the functions that offer the best chance of entering general management positions, at least where people who are prepared to change firms are concerned.* This is confirmed by studies of other managers. An article in *L'Expansion* in June 1977, for instance, showed that one in four of the directors general of France's biggest firms had held commercial posts, one in seven production posts and one in ten financial posts (Beaudeux, 1977: 151). A much earlier study of business-school graduates in different European countries suggested a similar pattern. It showed that the majority of managers in the *direction générale* had been drawn from marketing (27%), finance (24%) and other general management functions (19%) (see Sarton, 1968: 459–60). This was at the high point of the demand for marketing in Europe.

The specific functions chosen varied over time and the differing proportions entering each one suggest the link between opportunities offered in the market and the different economic periods outlined in chapter 1. In the early 1960s, more than half, 58%, of each cohort of MBAs went into marketing and a fifth into finance. By the late 1960s, this had dropped slightly, with a third entering marketing and 13% finance. By the early 1970s, in contrast, there was a sharp reversal, with less than a quarter choosing marketing, while finance rose, also to a quarter. By the late 1970s the position had stabilised, with just over a quarter in marketing and a fifth in finance. Put differently, of all those entering finance over the two decades of the 1960s and 1970s, nearly half did so in the early 1970s. The same proportions were also found among those entering corporate planning and consulting, while marketing showed the reverse pattern. In times of recession, financial skills may count for more.

Positions chosen as starting points on the race to the top varied considerably by nationality, as different nationalities perceived opportunities differently and chose different functions as their first preferences. Some were considerably more likely to enter marketing in their first firms than were others. That function was most favoured by the Belgians (55%) and the British (32%) in their first jobs. They were followed only at some distance by the Scandinavians (27%) and the Germans (23%) while the Swiss barely entered marketing at all (12.5%). Entry to finance similarly varied; 24% of the Dutch and 22.5% of the British chose finance, as did 20% of the Swiss and the Scandinavians, whereas hardly any interest in finance was shown by the Germans and Belgians.

In general management, the Swiss came out by far the best. Almost half the Swiss entered general management positions immediately after INSEAD while only a third of the next most successful, the Germans and Scandinavians, gained such positions. Much further behind still came the Belgians (16%), the British (15.5%) and the Dutch (9.5%).

As far as the other areas were concerned, the Dutch (10%), the British (15.5%) and the Germans (14.5%) were the most likely to enter consulting jobs and the Dutch (14%) and the British (11%) corporate planning careers. The Belgians, the Swiss and the Scandinavians entered management services more than did the others.

Starting points, however, still allowed much subsequent changing around. The links between nationality and function chosen were very largely lost by the second firm. In general management, for instance, the Swiss in their second firms appear last, not first, in proportional terms, overtaken by the British and Scandinavians, while more Swiss were in marketing. By the second firm, there were more British in finance than in marketing, a reverse of the position in first firms. In third and subsequent companies no particular links at all between national origins and function appeared on the career paths followed. The spreading out process thus affected functions as well as sectors.

The functional area selected in first firms not only varied with the nationality of the participant but with the nationality of the enterprise joined. Those who chose marketing and finance, for instance, had a much greater likelihood of entering American companies than any other kind, respectively 39% and 41%, whereas only a quarter in each case went to multinationals belonging to the participants' countries of origin. Consulting here stood out even further; two-thirds entered American consulting companies, while almost no one joined European-based multinationals, the remainder largely staying at home in national enterprises.

In contrast, while the consultants spread themselves across national boundaries, by far the greatest proportions of MBAs achieving general management positions in their first firms did so in national companies of their country of origin (48 %), followed by only 22 % in 'home' multinationals. Hardly any one obtained such coveted positions in other European companies and only 18 % achieved them in American ones.

These trends are clearly related to the size of firm chosen: the large American enterprises are far more likely to see young MBAs as suitable for staff positions, while smaller national firms are prepared to take on the generalist skills of the MBA while still young. The trade-off in this for the manager is that early general management success in a small firm is the end of the road, for it effectively eliminates him from the competition for top jobs in larger corporations. At least, one move remains very hard to make, that from a small to a large business. Thus, while in the later years of the 1970s some Europe-wide firms gave earlier line responsibility to those rising through marketing, for early access to general management positions these ambitious young men had to choose smaller national firms in their country of origin and remain there, effectively excluding themselves from major roles on the international stage.

A good deal of this flux and uncertainty over choice of direction to take results from the tensions between high ambitions and the constraints on the range of opportunities which result from previous educational qualifications and career paths. The slate of the past, as we saw, is by no means wiped clean by acquisition of an MBA. The labour market on graduation is far more limited in the opportunities available to candidates of different earlier backgrounds than many expect. This in part explains the continuing searches seen in mobility between companies, countries and functions as a career progresses. Many of the complex links between nationality of manager and firm and function chosen are related to educational qualifications. In the first firm, in particular, a very close relationship even after the MBA can be seen between subject of first degree and function entered. In those firms, marketing was the only real 'catch-all' category, absorbing around a third of all those with commercial, economics or other non-science-based degrees. About 60 % of people with commercial qualifications entered staff positions in finance and marketing, a move in which they were closely followed by economists. In contrast, economists and commercial graduates seeking general management positions were much less successful than engineers and lawyers in obtaining them in their first firms. Very few of the latter went into corporate planning or management services.

Some changes, however, can be arranged: after those in general management, the biggest group of engineers went into marketing, indicating that it is possible to move from the 'heavy science' disciplines to positions more commercially oriented. Lawyers have even more choices. One-quarter of the lawyers who did not go into general management went into finance and a further fifth to marketing. The range of avenues possible for any discipline may in part be due to the place it holds in the national educational system of

Table 5.9 *Salaries, five firms after INSEAD (percentages of respondents)*

Salaries in $	First firm	Second firm	Third firm	Fourth firm	Fifth firm
Less than 15,000	22	11	11	8.5	—
15–20,000	14	8	9	10	—
20–25,000	12	13	4	13	31
25–35,000	20	23	18	26	23
35–50,000	18.5	18	18	10	—
50–75,000	7.5	19	20	18	31
75–100,000	5	6	12	15	8
100–250,000	1	3	5	—	8
More than 250,000[a]	—	—	2	—	—
N=	292	181	93	39	13

[a] One person earned $500,000 in his sixth firm

the holder as well as to the effects of an MBA training, for in some countries lawyers and in others top engineering graduates (as judged by place of training) would be considered by employers to be generalists rather than legal or industrial specialists.

By the second firm, however, a breakthrough occurs: the professional track record a person has established seems to begin to count as much as education discipline and the links become greatly attenuated. In particular, MBAs from non-engineering backgrounds, notably economics, attain general management positions in their second and subsequent firms in much higher proportions than in their first. By the third firm, competition from the engineers increases again, for the latter have not only regained but increased their dominance in the field of general management.

The spoils of position

The keenness of demand for the skills of the international MBA is illustrated by the rewards which firms are prepared to pay. Salaries, even for young MBAs, are high, many very high indeed when compared either to salaries for 'equivalent' qualifications held by people working in other sectors (public administration or universities) and to those received by non-MBA managers in similar countries at similar periods of time. In France, especially, an INSEAD MBA commands a salary premium even beyond that of the Ecole Polytechnique and the postgraduate Institut Supérieur des Affaires.

Some salaries indeed were extraordinarily high by any standards, as can be seen in Table 5.9. At the very top of the salary range was one star person earning between $500,000 and $1 million in his sixth firm at the time of the study. Below him, but still firmly at the top of the range were the people earning, *in or before 1979*, between $100,000 and $250,000. Salaries increased with time and progression through a number of firms, but already in their first firms 9% of MBAs earned more than $50,000, with a further 18.5% between $35,000 and $50,000. The proportions in these categories steadily increased: in second firms, 28% of the sample earned more than $50,000, as did 39% in their third firms, 33% in fourth firms (a slight drop back) and 47% in fifth ones. More recent graduates are, of course, more likely to earn higher salaries in their early firms. Of those graduating in 1970–4 and 1975–9, 11%–13% earned more than $50,000 in their first companies, exceptionally high salaries for the time, although, of course, still far below those of America's chief executives in the 1960s, reported by Herman (1981) and Lewellen (1971) – a gap which only serves to underline further future possibilities for the MBAs.

Salaries in first firms also varied by sector and on the whole were best in banking. Of those who earned more than $50,000 in their first firms, nearly half (43%) were in banking, where two fifths earned between $25,000 and $50,000, but a further 16% earned between $50,000 and a $100,000. The latter were almost matched by rewards to people in new manufacturing (13%) and 10% of those in the more traditional areas, although in the latter most earned between $25,000 and $50,000, suggesting that salaries in traditional manufacture were often particularly low. This may reflect, however, greater proportions of respondents entering the sector some years ago, when salaries were lower.

In second firms, banking paid fewer very high salaries than did new manufacturing. In the latter nearly one-third (29%) of respondents earned between $50,000 and $100,000 and 5% more than $100,000, while the proportions earning less than $50,000 dropped considerably, perhaps because in new manufacturing the essential MBA skills of marketing are of greater importance. In banking, too, in second firms, one-fifth earned between $50,000 and $100,000, as compared to a quarter in the traditional manufacturing area and in other services. Indeed, services come very much to the fore here as providers of high salaries, for in them a third earned between $50,000 and $100,000 and 5% more than $100,000. The salaries paid there are perhaps a key to their increasing attraction for MBAs.

Thus, by their second firms, 40% of respondents earned, before 1979, between $25,000 and $50,000. As these proportions include people entering those companies up to seventeen or eighteen years before the survey, the average figure there at the time of the study was much higher and some salaries are now very high indeed.

These high rewards can be seen in the fact that, by their third firms, a very large proportion (40%) earned more than $100,000 and 8% more than $250,000. Again allowing for the great range of years over which people entered the companies, the proportions in that category at the time of study under- rather than over-estimate the average salary received. Some sectors continued to offer better rewards than others. More than two-fifths of those in new manufacturing (43 %) and banking (41 %) in their third firms earned more than $100,000. This is double the proportion earning such salaries in traditional manufacturing. The numbers in other sectors in third firms are too small to be significant but, for interest's sake, five people out of nine in services earned more than $100,000, as did all those in oil.

Salaries received also varied with nationality. In their first firms the British did the worst, with the Italians. The Belgians, in contrast, did particularly well, followed by the Swiss and the Dutch. Thus, of the British, only 37 % earned more than $25,000 in their first firms while 67 % of the Belgians did so, including 38 % who earned more than $50,000 in their first companies. Of the Swiss, two-thirds earned more than $25,000, including 27 % who earned over $100,000. As they went on in their careers, some nationalities indeed seemed to do increasingly well.[5]

These differences in remuneration seem to result from particular combinations of credentials, track records and choice of country, sector and firm. A study by Michel Carré, entitled 'Paying the price for "blue chip" managers', published in *European Business* in late 1971, pointed out that INSEAD graduates in the UK did badly in salary terms in relation to those in other European countries, notably Germany. In some countries, too, career structures seem to be different, paying INSEAD graduates low salaries in the early years but allowing them to catch up or even to earn much more later on, as in Belgium, for instance. Switzerland is rather similar to Belgium and career structures and salaries in both may be linked to the fact that more MBAs there worked in the many multinational firms headquartered in those countries.

Salaries paid are normally linked to the size of the employing company and the posts held. While in first firms there seems to be little relationship between salaries offered and the size of the company, measured in terms of numbers of employees, in second firms higher salaries were clearly paid by the larger companies. This finding accords with a study by *Le Point* of French companies with a turnover of more or less than 100 m francs (1978: 77). In third firms, in contrast, it seemed to be small companies that paid relatively better, reflecting the higher-level, decision-making line posts given there to MBAs. Salary *ranges* for the same positions seem to be narrower in larger firms (Hornyold-Strickland and Weskamp, 1977: 7), perhaps because of their bureaucratically organised company structures, with more formalised personnel systems; while in smaller firms there may be closer links between the salaries paid to senior managers and the profitability of the enterprise and salaries may be fixed much more on a one-off basis.

In contrast, there were no clear links between educational qualifications obtained before INSEAD and salaries received over time, although this connection may vary by nationality, for Hornyold-Strickland and Weskamp showed that German INSEADs who also held doctorates comprised 75 % of all the highest salary earners (1977: 9).

In first firms, it also paid to work abroad in particular countries. Working outside home frontiers but in a European country was financially especially rewarding, as was a period in the Far East or in several countries, but again this relationship was attenuated in second and subsequent firms. Variations may also occur because the bases companies use for salary calculations vary. Thus, in France, forms tend to pay the person rather than the position, rewarding 'age, antecedents, contacts (*relations*)' (*Le Point*, 1977: 74).

Salaries, then, for most MBAs were not only remarkably high by almost anyone's standards but particularly high for the decades in question. Only a very small fraction of any European population earned even $25,000 in the 1970s, much less in the 1960s. The proportion recorded here as earning $100,000 or more put their holders into a tiny group of Europe's top salary earners. *Their position is particularly striking when it is remembered how few respondents at the time of the survey had even reached forty years of age.*

Their salaries can be compared, for instance, to those who held the top posts in the biggest companies, French and multinational, operating in France two years after this study, in 1981. At that time, the average salary for the *Présidents-Directeurs-Généraux* (PDG) running companies with a turnover in France of 10–20 billion francs was approximately 1 million francs or $200,000 at the 1981 exchange rate. In these companies, the *directeurs financiers* and *directeurs commerciaux* were earning approximately $110,000. In somewhat smaller but still very large companies, with a turnover of 1–5 billion francs, the PDGs were earning $150,000 while most of the functional *directeurs* (marketing, etc.) received around $80,000. The latter figures, high as they are, were almost certainly matched and exceeded by large proportions of INSEADs by 1981, for 80 % of all managers sampled in the study quoted in *L'Expansion* still earned less, and usually much less, than $40,000 (Beaudeux, 1981: 97–129).

Earning such incomes is important to future chances for many reasons. First of all, it allows relatively young managers to maintain a lifestyle that is socially desirable and professionally rewarding even over the period of heaviest family responsibilities. Second, it also allows them to accumulate quite considerable quantities of capital, augmented by the capital inherited from families of origin and brought to the couple at marriage and afterwards by their wives. This capital enables them, on the one hand, to take the career risks which make even greater professional success more likely and, on the other hand, to invest in their own enterprises, thus increasing both income and capital further. Third, possession of such wealth will also contribute to ensuring both that their children will be able to find 'suitable' positions in Europe beyond the year 2000 and that the structure of capital ownership does not alter as much as the change to 'managerial capitalism' may seem to imply.

The importance of economic capital to careers is discussed again in a later chapter.

Strategies for advancement: mobility and the international card

Mobility is part of many managers' strategies for taking maximum advantage of the opportunities of the labour market and particularly is often seen as the strategy *par excellence* of the MBA (Hughes, 1977).

Mobility means different things. Some moves are between companies, others between kind of job or sector and yet others between countries or even continents. Some moves mean success, while others indicate disillusion. Some moves are more frequent at certain stages of a career or among those working in a given professional arena. At each point individuals have to judge whether mobility is going to pay – in salaries, promotion opportunities and speed of ascent, in degree of job challenge and personal satisfaction. Some major jumps in a career, whether sideways or upwards, may in turn be followed by periods of consolidation of gains and relative stability.

Mobility *per se* does not characterise INSEAD MBAs as strongly as some observers have suggested (Hughes, 1977), as Tables 5.10 and 5.11 show. Two-thirds of respondents had not moved at all. While many of these were more recent graduates, 111 respondents had been in one firm for up to fifteen years. Two-fifths had spent at least six years in one of the firms they had been in before moving on and 3 % eleven years or more, while eighty-four respondents were still in their second companies. Even among those who had left INSEAD sixteen to twenty years before, 40 % had not worked in more than two companies. Many thus seem to be choosing the 'slow-burn' or 'loyalty' way up the ladder.

The same figures, of course, also indicate considerable inter-company mobility, for one-third had worked in three firms or more and two-thirds in at least two. This rather suggests that the road to the top is seen to lead through a series of organisations rather than one alone or even two, for few of the MBAs had yet reached the age of forty.

Inter-company mobility strategies varied between nationalities. The Ger-. mans and the Swiss were particularly stable, staying longest in first and second firms, although this stability may be more apparent than real, reflecting mainly the smaller number of long-standing graduates from those countries in the sample.

Mobility as a strategy also varied across functions. Respondents already in general management, having fulfilled their immediate ambitions, were the most stable. Of that group, half had been in one firm only, and a further quarter in two firms only, followed by 16 % in three, 7 % in four and 3 % in five enterprises. It is not clear whether this means that 'loyalty' helps in obtaining general management positions, that holding such posts gives greater job

Table 5.10 *Years worked in each of five firms after INSEAD (percentages of respondents)*

Number of years worked	First firm	Second firm	Third firm	Fourth firm	Fifth firm
Less than one	8	13	15.5	28	25
1	14	10	17.5	5	—
2	24	23	20	18	8
3	13	16	20	20.5	17
4	10	11	12	8	17
5	6	7	6	8	8
6–10	19	16	8	10	25
More than 10	6	4	1	3	—
N =	302	189	97	39	12

Table 5.11 *Percentage of respondents still in each of six firms, by years since MBA*

Years since MBA	N	First firm	Second firm	Third firm	Fourth firm	Fifth firm	Sixth firm
1–5	98	58	31	11	—	—	—
6–10	116	32	35	19	14	2	—
11–15	65	26	20	35	9	9	1.5
16–20	25	8	32	25	30	6	—

satisfaction so that mobility seems less desirable, or that people reaching those positions while still young find it harder to move to equivalent ones elsewhere. Finance managers were also relatively stable, for 34 % in those areas were still in either their first or second firms, with a further quarter in their third. Those in marketing were rather more mobile, while consultants were much more likely to change companies, perhaps using their contacts to find interesting new jobs (see chapter 9).

Does mobility then seem to pay as a career strategy? Much depends on the objectives. Stability may be a better tactic if promotion means the rapid attainment of a general management position. Two firms seems to be the optimum number here, for, of all those working in only two companies, half held general management posts, whereas of those who had been in three, only a third held similar positions, with similar proportions in four firms or only one firm.[6]

It seems, however, that in the search for rapid promotion it is less the *amount* of mobility that is significant than the *kind* of movement undertaken.

The mobility that really pays, as suggested by the career paths of many of the most successful, is one that involves two elements. The first is the opportunity for the manager to indicate clearly his worth, and particularly his direct financial worth, to the enterprise. The second is preparedness to take risks, often considerable ones, in the entrepreneurial pursuit of opportunities to demonstrate that worth. *It is not thus mobility on its own, although that may increase salaries, but mobility linked to a challenge–success career path that gives the highest rate of return.* We explore this further in a later chapter.

Playing the international card

In the struggle to maximise prospects and minimise competition from other aspiring young managers, the international card, a card INSEAD MBAs are almost uniquely well qualified to play, may be a winner. Europe, *par excellence*, would seem to be the arena for play, with excursions for a time into other areas of the world. And play that card most respondents did; it was used at different times and in different ways, but almost always proved an ace in the competitive game. Ability to choose jobs across national boundaries enormously increases the range of possibilities open, while the demands which such transnationality makes limit the field of competitors. Once they play that card, INSEADs effectively move themselves into an advantageous position in a labour market narrow in numbers of immediate openings but unlimited in career prospects for the future. Few others can compete there so well.

It is little wonder, then, that two-thirds of all respondents first joined companies not belonging to their country of origin (see Table 5.12). Some joined American firms, sometimes operating in Europe and sometimes outside, but many entered European multinational enterprises, circulating in their professional lives around Europe.

Some nationalities were particularly likely to take advantage of their international training. The Belgians, perhaps influenced by the range of foreign companies headquartered in Brussels in the late 1960s and 1970s, were especially likely to join non-Belgian firms. Almost as many Dutch (71 %) and Italians (70 %) followed the same route, closely followed by the Germans (69 %), the British (68 %) and the Scandinavians (67 %). Even among the Swiss, the most 'stay at home' in their choices, more than half first chose non-Swiss firms.

First steps into careers after INSEAD for most alumni involve transnationality, the experience of working outside one's own national environment, adapting to the culture, language and management practices of firms owned and controlled from elsewhere, or at least working at home in a foreign-owned firm. Early in their careers it is clear that INSEAD graduates already see themselves as well suited to developing top-flight careers on the international, and particularly European, professional stage. They learn early on to think

Table 5.12 *Nationality of firm, five firms after INSEAD (percentages of respondents)*

Nationality	First firm	Second firm	Third firm	Fourth firm	Fifth firm
Own country's national firm	27	32	35	46	46
Own country's multinational	22	19	15	16	9
American firm	34	29	22	11	9
European multinational	17	20	8	27	36
N=	280	172	88	37	11

Table 5.13 *Place principally worked, five firms after INSEAD (percentages of respondents)*

Place worked	First firm	Second firm	Third firm	Fourth firm	Fifth firm
Home country	53	61	65	66	54
Abroad	47	37.5	35	34	39
50–50	1	2	—	—	8
N=	304	192	100	41	13

transnationally and to weigh the advantages and disadvantages for them of entering manufacturing in Italy, banking in Scandinavia or consulting in Germany. In doing this, they also learn about management practices, product markets, career opportunities over many companies, industries and countries, acquiring on the way the *pifomètre* necessary to sense the need for a change of direction and future strategy at the same time as they evaluate immediate concrete possibilities.

After this early experience, divergences occur. Some groups, as they change companies, remain abroad and develop long-term careers either outside their countries of origin or in 'foreign' firms. With each change of firm the Dutch and the Belgians in particular increased their representation in foreign or multinational enterprises so that all of those moving to a third employer chose foreign companies.

There are several types of transnational career. One choice is to become the 'true transnational', spending a whole professional life outside one's country of origin, working probably for a foreign firm. The most extreme 'transnational' will be working for a foreign firm operating in a third country, for instance a Belgian working for a Swiss bank in London or an Italian for a

Swedish firm in Paris. The other, in sharp contrast, takes advantage of the initial period 'abroad' to acquire high-level positions in a national company or a European multinational headquartered at 'home', a choice frequently made by the French. In between come those who work in foreign companies but at home, as the Belgians and Dutch increasingly did. Later in their careers, these may become the majority. By their second and third firms, between half and two-thirds of the British, Scandinavians and Germans were still working in multinationals, although many had moved back to their home countries.

The extent of foreign experience acquired in diverse ways is considerable. At the time of the study, just over a third, 122 of the 304 in the sample, were working abroad. Of those in their first firm, forty-nine were abroad (44% of all those in their first firm at the time). Of that forty-nine, forty-two (86%) were working in Europe (including five still in France after INSEAD), although a high proportion (59%) were working for American companies. For most, the place of work was always essentially Europe. Almost half (48%) worked outside their home countries in their first firms, of whom three-quarters remained in Europe. Later, however, there could be seen some tendency to move beyond European boundaries and to colonise the USA, for if many MBAs begin their careers as local European managers for American enterprises, later they may challenge the Americans on their home ground in the USA. For most, however, as they change company the focus becomes increasingly European.

By 1979, several different geographical and professional paths had been trodden across Europe. Choice of paths to follow varied by nationality and over time: in their first firm after INSEAD, the British were especially likely to be working in France, the Swiss to be in the USA and Switzerland, the Italians and Scandinavians to be in other European countries and the Middle East. By their second firm, more Swiss, more British and more Germans were likely to be in the USA, with even more British in France, a trend strengthened in third companies. Standing in some contrast to these are the third or so of respondents who after an initial period of 'foreign' experience move not only back behind their countries' frontiers but also into nationally owned and operated enterprises. This last may be the strategy for reaching the top at a young age which works best. People choosing the transnational route may have to wait longer, but the rewards in terms of power may be greater.

Approaching the summit

Assessing where the majority of respondents had reached in their efforts to climb to the top in company hierarchies is difficult. Questionnaires can give only a very approximate picture and interviews with alumni revealed a wide variety both in positions held and in the significance of those posts in relation to company structures. Moreover, career paths are, of course, affected by other elements of company organisational structures. While, as we have seen, there has generally been a tendency in Europe for companies to move towards a divisionalised structure, many national differences remain. In the mid 1970s, Horovitz (1980) could still report that many companies in Britain remained holding companies in which a small central staff oversaw twenty to fifty subsidiaries, each headed by a managing director and with its own products, brands and markets and the necessary resources to operate. Decisions about any subsidiary's activity were still largely taken at that level, while the central company shaped group policy. In German firms, in contrast, although half the companies Horovitz studied were organised as large divisions, half were functionally structured and the top management team was composed of functional specialists, even at division level, with little authority delegated. In France, too, many companies remained functionally organised but with little committee management, with chief executives delegating little and retaining many final decisions when conflict between functional areas arose (Horovitz, 1980: 54–70). Such differences in company organisation mean differences in the structure and organisation of boards of directors and hence, too, of the power held by the incumbents of any particular position.

The data gathered, however, do give some indication of position reached and suggest that this was frequently high. By their second firm, two thirds or more of the respondents were occupying positions very near the top of functions and divisions and some were near to or on the boards of the subsidiary companies in which so many worked. Some indeed were approaching the recruitment stratum to the main board. In the first case, many were already in positions such as head of function and division and member of the board of the subsidiary, or immediately below them or one position further below these. In the case of the main boards, many respondents were immediately below the boards or one position further below.

Who, then, in social, educational and national terms had climbed highest up the ladders and which were the routes upwards, both in terms of characteristics of the job and those of the companies? Forty-five people were selected as those in the sample apparently doing best. These were respondents who were functional heads or above, were heads of divisions, were on the boards of subsidiaries or the boards of main companies or one place below any of these. The top people included some chief executive officers.

Access to these positions seemed to vary relatively little by nationality, except that the British seemed to do badly. Of all those in the most successful group, a large proportion (29%) were Germans. Taking the proportion in the MBAs' national population of origin in the sample as the base, however, reduces that predominance: 18.5% of all Germans held those posts, 18% of all Swiss, 20% of the Belgians, 15% of the Scandinavians and 14% of the Dutch. Only 8% of the British, however, had obtained them.[7]

As an educational preparation, *acquisition of a degree in commerce seemed to pay best* overall in the mid 1970s. One-third of all those who held commercial degrees, in contrast with the 11 % they represented in the whole sample, had reached the positions considered here. This compares with a fifth of the engineers (20.5 %) and rather fewer of the lawyers (17 %). Although engineers represent more than one-third of the forty-five, they are less well represented than their proportion in the total group of respondents would suggest. The economists and those with arts or social science degrees did notably badly – respectively only 5 % and 9 % achieving top posts. Those with more than one degree did well (17 %), especially those with American postgraduate qualifications, but here the numbers are small. These figures seem to support Bourdieu's contention that, in the new era of mass market and financial capitalism, the new opportunities are mainly open to those trained in commerce rather than engineering or law.

Of the forty-five, *the largest single proportion worked in companies in the new manufacturing sector (29 %)*. In this case, they also did best in proportion to the category of origin, for more than a quarter (26 %) of all those who pursued their careers in new manufacturing, entering the sector in their first firm, had by the time of the study obtained positions qualifying them for inclusion in the forty-five. Service and other miscellaneous industries also did well, but the numbers are small. In contrast, in banking and consulting companies, which might be thought a specifically appropriate MBA field, people seemed to do less well. Although 22 % of the sub-group were in these companies, in consulting, for example, the successful (partners) only represented 10 % of the whole category of origin. Those in traditional manufacturing did even worse – 13 % of the sub-sample but only 7 % of the category of origin. This suggests greater openness in new areas to those with new credentials while also indicating that MBAs have not replaced the traditonal 'mafias' in the older fields.

Size of firm chosen may also be important in the path to the top. Studying the successful seemed to suggest that it was *useful to join as a first firm a company that was medium to large sized*, employing between 1,000 and 10,000 people. Those thus beginning their careers only represented 15.5 % of the forty-five, but constituted two-fifths (41 %) of their group of origin. Those joining giant firms (10,000–50,000) also did considerably less well, as did those in very small firms (below 200 employees) and small to medium enterprises (200–1,000 workers).

The *function* which provides the best route to the top cannot be clearly distinguished because of the high proportion in general management positions from their first firm onwards. *Of those who were not in general management positions, those in finance posts did best, well ahead of marketing and others.* The respondent quoted above who expressed his belief that finance was *the* function for those aiming for the top seems to find considerable support here.

Looking now at nationality of current firms shows that more than two-fifths (42%) of the forty-five were in enterprises belonging to their own country and working essentially within those national boundaries. These included two people who owned the companies they worked in. In relation to the whole group in national firms, they did quite well (being 25% of the group of origin) but *not nearly as well as those who worked in European multinational companies. This suggests that the best choice for the ambitious is indeed a European multinational company.*

In contrast, working in the home country was clearly a help in reaching the top positions, even though working in a European company was at a premium as well. While only just over half of the original sample worked at home in their first firm, by the time of the study two-thirds of those in the top forty-five were working in their country of origin, most having returned from abroad. The thirty found in these positions working at home represented 18.5% of their category of origin, as opposed to 10.5% of those working abroad. *In some senses, therefore, working at home after a period abroad but remaining in a European-oriented company was an especially good strategy for approaching the summit while still young.* This fits well with other evidence that transnational companies entrust functional posts, especially in marketing, to non-nationals, but reserve places at the summit for candidates from the home country (Mason, Miller and Weigel, 1981: 366–7).

Reaching the top

The survey revealed twenty-one people who could be considered as having reached the top in that they were on the boards of subsidiary companies or even on the main boards of their firms, or as having reached the immediate recruitment stratum for those jobs, in that they were currently one place below.

The twenty-one were composed of four Swiss, three British, four Germans, four Belgians, three Scandinavians, one Dutch, one Spaniard and one Italian. Discounting the last two nationalities because of tiny sample numbers in the survey, the figures suggest that the Belgians have done proportionately best, followed by the Swiss and the Scandinavians and the British, themselves followed by the Germans. The Belgians seem to have adopted most frequently the winning combinations – a commercial degree (a good basis for a financial post, itself the best springboard to top management), financial experience and an early career at 'home' but in a foreign owned European multinational.

More generally, however, it is a hard task to attempt to pick a career path as 'ideal typical' of an INSEAD MBA. A rough picture would suggest that he (or one of the few women) first enters an American firm, working in Europe probably, in banking or 'new' manufacturing, occupying a position in a large company in a marketing or financial function. He subsequently moves to a smaller firm, probably a European one, working again in a similar function. Little by little, and sometimes with big steps, by moving on and being constantly alert for opportunities, he reaches general management positions, probably in firms somewhat smaller and geographically much nearer home. By that time, too, he may well have left the tracks frequented by many other MBA competitors and joined a company in a service industry where few MBAs have preceded him. In this way, new companies and sectors are constantly being 'colonised' and the potential influence and network of internationally minded MBAs spread over ever wider fields, both within countries and across the whole arena of European business.

Career tracks thus show enormous variety. There is no obvious single route to the top. Engineers, lawyers and commerce graduates start on different routes and move sideways by function, sector, firm size and nationality to different degrees and at different times in their careers. They leapfrog over each other, cut corners by taking risks, juggle their relative advantages and handicaps, their education and track record in highly complex ways, their ambitions interacting with the demands of hirers in the market, to weave a web of tracks upwards and sideways, that cross national boundaries, mix cultures and overcome barriers of distance and language. Their paths bring them to join other INSEAD MBAs at certain times and then diverge from them at others.

How then do these tracks get woven? What are the choices? How are they made? In which ways does the international managerial labour market operate? In the next chapter we look more closely at individual strategies and their interactions with company requirements.

6. Escalator or roller-coaster? Moving on and flying high in the businesses of Europe

During the boom time of Europe, in the 1960s and into the 1970s, the European executive emerged as a new and distinctive breed, flying high and blazing a trail across Europe in the search of the challenges and successes which would lead him on a rapid route to the top. Such, at least, is the public image. Writing appropriately in British Airways *High Life* magazine, Robert Heller remarked that:

American companies, after a string of disasters with American managers in Europe began to recruit Europeans. The obvious candidates were those who had studied at American business schools. The quintessential 'mobile executive' thus became the Harvard Business School man who (to quote an actual career pattern) left his *alma mater* to work for an American bank in his home town, Paris, then liaised for an American aluminium company with the French management of a new plant in Africa; departed to run a French subsidiary of another American multinational; next joined an ancient European company in a state of disrepair; and finally, having repaired the ruin, moved on yet again – and all before reaching the age which an earlier breed of managers would have considered that of discretion. Companies first sought Europeans business-school trained but with experience in American companies. Later, after the American challenge faded, the European executive . . . has emerged in brighter colours and greater and greater numbers.

(Heller, 1977: 33)

Many of the most successful INSEAD MBAs followed career paths strikingly similar to that described by Heller.

Confident that they were indeed a favoured generation, INSEAD MBAs, the European executives *par excellence*, were ambitious indeed. Expressing at entry to the Institute a wish for high office in business, by the time of the survey they felt that these positions seemed almost within reach. More than half expected by 1990 to be the owners of or partners in companies, including family businesses, to be members of the board of directors of firms large and small, to hold president, chairman or chief executive officer positions or, more modestly, to be senior vice-presidents or to hold other top management positions.[1]

104

Just as class origins impelled divergences in direction in early careers, so ambitions continued to be affected by social background. Respondents from *patronat* and top-management families expressed notably higher ambitions for their 1990 posts. Taking a broader group, to include fathers in the liberal professions and the senior echelons of the public service, showed that more than half expected to have reached the top of their trees by 1990. In contrast, only two-fifths of those who had started from less advantaged beginnings had the same expectations. Social backgrounds affected the sectors chosen as fields of competition for the next decade as they did those selected earlier in careers. Public-sector scions chose consulting and small companies and showed least interest in the financial, banking and manufacturing fields. Manufacturing was chosen by the lower social groups, but they rejected new technology and the risks associated with a future made up of a decade of experiment with a variety of different sectors or sizes of company. They mostly preferred the escalators, the slow-burn way upwards on tracks leading through the big businesses seen as 'safe' and offering promotions by small steps in a well-established hierarchy. The challenge–success obstacle race, in which moves must be made not only upwards but downwards and across, in which one must face the excitement of the risks of transnational movements from enterprise to enterprise, function to function, position to position, the risks which are the keys to the high salaries and top posts coveted by the true high-flyers, was not for them. Challenge–success careers were largely the prerogative of those whose backgrounds encouraged confidence and provided a safety net in case of the disasters that occasionally occurred. Possession of that confidence largely indicates business background rather than other élite group member-ship, for while inter-group differences are subtle and mediated by the *éducation* common to upper-class families across Europe, by the early education at élite institutions received by many and the polishing received during training for the MBA, they nevertheless show clearly enough that sons from the business world have greater chances of the 'seagull' career, flying high and pouncing on opportunities, which characterises those most success-ful before the age of forty.

These differences, however, only appear with time. In the early stages of their careers after INSEAD there remains much sorting out to do, more testing of the waters, more extensive searching for the tracks and the niches that offer the best rewards, that best satisfy present and fuel future ambitions. Almost every one during these years was ready to move on, considering any given job only as the period between the last and the next, in the same company and country or different ones, for, given such high demands, the 'right' jobs are not easy to find. European MBAs, with a credential promising access to the whole European stage as their privileged arena, play for high stakes. For them, careers are seldom straightforward ladders; they involve searching and being sought in a game where the rules are not explicit, the opportunities unpredictable and the rewards various.

Table 6.1 *Means of hearing of job in three firms (percentages of respondents)*

How heard of job	First firm		Second firm		Third firm	
Business school placement service	42		4		2	
Press/notice	10		19		19	
Friends/alumni of INSEAD	6		11.5		6	
Other friends	6	} 20	11	} 28.5	6	} 18
Parents/other relatives	8		6		6	
Chance personal contacts	15		32		35	
Invited to apply[a]	13.5		13		20	
Changed jobs in same company	—		1		1	
Created own business/other[b]	—		1		1	
N=	303		191		99	

[a] In reality, 'invited to apply' is largely covered by 'chance personal contacts', 'friends/alumni of INSEAD' and 'parents/other relatives'.
[b] 'Other' includes returning to the company who had sponsored the respondent at INSEAD.

In their search for appropriate positions, they bring to play an arsenal of techniques, information and contacts, use formal and informal channels of communication and take advantage of networks, both professional and familial. They constantly seek to 'internalise' external labour markets through the use of 'chance' contacts which are in reality highly structured by past experiences, social, professional and educational, and to which access is severely restricted. While INSEAD's placement service is usually, but by no means always, a means to a first job, after that the informal managerial labour market never ceases to grow in importance as careers progress, as parents, relatives, and professional contacts provide information on opportunities and pass on expressions of interest by candidates for ever better positions. While many search long and hard for their first jobs under INSEAD's auspices (between seven and forty-five job interviews), in later years their personal reputations and positions become crucial to each subsequent step. Later, too, many create their own jobs, either inside an existing firm (Granovetter, 1974: 14 and 65–7) or by founding their own enterprises, as a fifth had done by 1979 – notably in consulting and financial and other services, for the success of Egon Zehnder stands as an enticing model.

In the early years, searches have to be made with only a relatively limited set of tools. Resources available then include, principally, contacts made through family and educational institutions and information gleaned from formal labour-market mechanisms. All are used. Which are predominant depends on local and national circumstances. In some countries, such as Spain, where INSEAD is less well known, previous places of education overshadow the Institute as a credential and continue to provide the means of contact between employer and potential employee. As a Spaniard who had graduated in law and business management from a major Jesuit university in Spain declared:

I got into C. through the contact that my old University had established. It's a University that is very well-known and highly prestigious in Spain. For getting into the company, my INSEAD qualification played no role. It was my early training that was determinant.

Another used INSEAD only indirectly as a means of finding his first job:

I needed a much more high-powered training. I discovered that what really interested me was finance. In 1961 the choice was easy. One of the professors of finance who worked in the bank and whom I admired a lot persuaded me to accept the offer made by that bank. The idea of working with him suited me well.

The rather limited tools of search in the early years may mean that mistakes of orientation are made and that prople are not protected against having to move on because of changes in company personnel or in enterprise structure and policies in the areas they have chosen: Promising careers may suddenly come to a dead end. Many lack the experience to judge what the realities of a company or sector are until they have joined. Personnel changes and company internal politics may suddenly alter the work environment and hence the use which an MBA can make of his skills.

I left M.N. because the staff changed. Before I left I looked after foreign investments in Belgium which was very interesting. The man who was my direct superior in the hierarchy was great and very active. He left the firm to become a politician and from one day to the next the department was taken back by the traditional side of the bank. So, after this man left I had only two alternatives – rejoin the traditional side of the bank or leave. I chose the second option and, through replying to an advertisement, I left for Antwerp.

(Belgian, 1966, British bank in Brussels)[2]

Not everyone was seeking the same combination of job characteristics. In particular, some sought *potential* in a post while others preferred security; some emphasised job location, while yet others saw salary as primordial in cases where trade-offs had to be made. On graduation, career choices had often to be made with only very limited knowledge of the European managerial labour market and these frequently needed to be modified.

Moving on

By the time people changed companies, looking for second jobs, some of the consequences of these choices were becoming clear. In making their new choices, some were changing direction because they had been offered something positively attractive while some moved rather for negative reasons, leaving because of current disappointments and because they were *still* searching for the place to feel at home. Some were moving by conviction, others by necessity. Most involved more steps on paths leading across Europe.

Some alumni took a number of years to find the niche they were seeking and moved between sectors and types of company several times. Sometimes the kind of work was right but other aspects of a particular position were unsatisfactory. Thus one Swede interviewed, working for a Latin-American company in Brussels at the time of interview, had first joined an American manufacturing company 'through INSEAD and through friends'. After two unsatisfactory years he had moved to a consulting firm 'which I joined through my personal contacts. I had friends in New York who worked there.'

He explained his subsequent movements as follows. He was ambitious and entrepreneurial and was also very interested in working in a certain wealthy Latin-American country. That ambition was thwarted, but he received other offers:

I joined M.X. (the consulting firm) for two reasons. One: this firm is the equivalent of God in the minds of MBAs. Two: when I joined it was understood that they were going to open an office in . . . and that I would be part of that. That office never saw the light of day and so I went to Germany, to Dusseldorf. Over the two years I was there, I carried out all sorts of studies. I only stayed two years for a variety of reasons. One: when I saw that the opening of the new office was never going to happen or at least not happen at once, I lost all interest in the field. Two: with three colleagues, we decided to set up our own consulting company to assist client companies who wanted to invest in a particular field. Three: I happened to meet the Director of D. who encouraged my idea but who also offered me a place in his own company. He invited me to his country to visit. After two years I left M.X. and with my friends we tried to set up our own firm. After three months it was clear it was not going to work – problems of people. So I got back into contact with the Director of D. who made the same offer to me. He also tripled my salary. I accepted.

One motivation for going to INSEAD is the desire to change the sector of activity in which a respondent was previously involved. Sometimes this strategy works at the first try, sometimes it does not. Even in consulting companies, previous qualifications and experience may determine the sector of operations to which a new recruit is allocated: 'As an engineer, I was given responsibility for heavy industry and I couldn't get to change sector' (Belgian, 1969).

Sometimes problems arise because over time companies change their policies; sometimes posts that look promising from the outside are much less so once a person is in the job, when they find, in the words used by many, that they are not 'at ease', that they are 'under-utilised' or that 'the job does not correspond at all either to my tastes or to my capacities'.

The following case illustrates the sometimes quite considerable changes that have to be made before the right place is found. The respondent faced a combination of company retraction, blocking access to promotion, and the disappointment involved in an 'uninteresting job'. First, he worked for an American multinational operating in his native Spain, but once there he discovered that:

> The mother-company was more and more pulling out its investment in Spain. I could see that in that company the way forward was rather blocked up so I moved to a bank.

But then he found that a bank was not right for him either:

> I only stayed six months; the banking world is not for me. The structure is too hierarchical, too closed and I couldn't even use my languages or my skills. The work climate didn't interest me. I think it's the same in all banks. I don't believe that big banks can accept independent work teams which means that possibilities of action are always limited. Moreover, *there's no element of risk*. After six months, I began to look elsewhere and I found a job at E. in Spain and then in Paris. I found it through personal contacts, friends that knew about it . . . Moreover, in 1968 that company was recruiting a lot.

> (Spaniard, 1962, working in the European division of an American company in France)

Problems with the closed and hierarchical nature of management in many companies were referred to again and again and were perhaps the chief reason for a person saying that 'banking is not for me' or 'industry does not suit me'. INSEADs generally perceive themselves as dynamic and as possessing valuable and immediately usable general management skills. Where these qualities cannot be used, many become disillusioned, not only with their present company but with the sector as a whole, including firms of different size and type. All complainants manifested irritation at what were seen as unnecessary and stifling procedures, whether these concerned direct decision-making processes or the influences which seemed to weigh most heavily on the decisions taken.

One respondent, having tried and been unhappy in consulting, moved on to a bank, but that was not successful either.

> I left banking because it didn't suit me. At present bankers are like public servants, bureaucrats: they whisper among themselves, they're all starchy and narrow-minded in their suits . . . Moreover, I don't like the mentality: at the moment, banks are lending to big clients just because they're big and won't lend to little ones just because they're small . . . Finally, bankers don't like contacts with people.

He had, therefore, moved on, changing sector completely by going to take over a small manufacturing company where he felt very much more content.

> I like my job a lot because I am in contact with everybody. I too gossip when bankers invite me to lunch. And then when I want to I can also go down to the canteen to talk to the unions.

> (Belgian, 1966, Belgian firm in Brussels)

Many, as ambitious as they describe themselves, seek to move on to companies where they feel that their entrepreneurial talents will be given greater room to develop.

My new job was much better both because of the level of responsibility that it offered me and because of the *freedom it gave me to undertake new activities.* There is no one between me and the top management [*direction*]. It's a group containing 3,000 people, a holding company, a family firm. The job was also better paid. But that wasn't my main motive for taking it, I can distinguish between my taste for money and the means of obtaining it. I wouldn't do just anything: speculation, for instance, I don't like.

(French, 1974)

Salary was thus one reason for the respondent feeling more satisfied, but other factors also counted: the area of work was socially and morally acceptable as well as interesting and he was largely independent, an aspect of his new position which was especially appreciated after a spell in a large American bank, even one recognised as '*the* most aristocratic American bank'.

Others moved because they wanted the power to decide rather than advise and had grown tired of the frustrations of being in a staff job.

In 1976, I wanted a change. Three years in a staff position is good because you make a lot of contacts but three years is enough, because staff roles mean that you're always proposing, never deciding. *I wanted to take decisions, have responsibilities to exercise and I wanted more independence.*

(French, 1974, director general of an industrial company in Paris)

Management styles mattered, too, in the decisions to move on. Some respondents felt too European for companies 'managed in a very American manner' and were unhappy even though they had interesting jobs.

It wasn't the life for me . . . Professionally speaking, it was very interesting. I was only 26 or 27 years old and there I was in the Board rooms in international companies. And what's more, whenever I spoke people listened to me! And I did have useful things to say . . . two years earlier [before INSEAD and HBS] that would have been inconceivable. At that time people were almost kicking me in the shins in the corridors! But the management style was very American and, in a European context, that made me ill at ease.

(British, 1975, merchant bank, London)

Some, in searching the market, found after a time that only one sector really suited them, because only that one would offer the scope for entrepreneurship and the independence that many sought. Perceptions about the suitability of positions offered by companies owed much to respondents' perceptions of their own individual personal characteristics and of the way in which these would fit, or would be shaped to fit, with the structures and mentalities of the activities concerned. Some people preferred banking, 'nobler and more amusing', as well as 'more dynamic', feeling that industry was mostly led by 'men without ideas' and, worse, that industrial firms were very hierarchical, thus limiting the opportunities available to more entrepreneurial newcomers. This seemed to be particularly true of the UK.

In France perhaps industry has higher status than in England. French industry is small but has a better reputation. In England, in industry it's rigid, the sector has no flexibility, you have to spend ages getting anything done. Everybody with any spirit avoids industry . . . and goes into other sectors.

(Englishman, 1973, working in a French bank in London)

Those in banking also distinguished between kinds of bank. Many, for instance, felt that, in common with industry, the clearing banks and their non-British equivalents were much too hierarchical. In contrast, merchant banks provided plenty of scope. The person quoted above went on to say:

In banking, on the other hand, I would never work in the clearing banks, unless a really interesting opportunity came up. They're hierarchical companies where you can get stuck . . . Merchant banks are quite different . . . they're much more a sector for the young . . . The hierarchy is much less in existence. It's conservative of course, but there are lots of opportunities in merchant banking.

Experience inside companies, however, differed and other respondents felt the reverse; to them industry offered more than banking:

In all cases, in banks and insurance companies, work is much more routinised than elsewhere. There's very little room for innovations. On the other hand, in industry things move. There are a lot more possibilities, big new markets, especially since the energy crisis. One can really earn oneself a lot of money.

As some distinguished clearing from merchant banks, so others distinguished between industrial sectors. Product counted; some did not wish to work with 'dead matter', so that only certain kinds of industry or services would be acceptable.

I myself, for example, I could never work in heavy industry. I don't like dead matter. Music, wine, that's different, they're techniques, they're living. There are not the same constraints on production either. Consumption is different too.

This respondent, in the last part of the quotation, also indicated a reason for avoiding industry – dealing with production problems – which seems to be important in the decisions of many INSEADs not to enter that field. In terms of the prestige of different sectors, indeed, little seems to have changed since the 1950s, when Lewis and Stewart wrote that the aircraft industry and chemicals had high prestige in Britain while oil was like entering the Foreign Service. Manufacturing of consumer goods, in contrast, was to be avoided (Lewis and Stewart, 1958 and 1961: 68–9).

Promotion prospects were important. Many felt that there were certain stages in life, and indeed certain ages, when crucial decisions about careers had to be made or all was lost.

It's true that in a consulting firm we're more flexible than in any other kind of enterprise: in other types of company everything is played before the age of 45 – after that, it's all over. After 45 years of age, you're working for your pension – it's only before then that you can work for your career.

(Dutch, 1971, American consulting firm in Paris)

I'm 37 years old. It's before 40 that you have to make the jump to the next post up.[3] After 40 you suffer from a handicap . . . For that reason, even if all was going well in export I wouldn't stay. For three reasons: one, path blocked at the next stage [places taken by *Polytechniciens*]; two, competition is intense and here prestige goes to the technically trained and I'm considered to be commercial; three, in two years I will have been nine years in the Group. If I don't leave here soon I'll retire here! So what I need now is a good kick in the pants to prevent me going to sleep, to force me to go off and breathe different air.

(French, 1974, American multinational, Paris, interviewed 1973 and 1980)

And the future? 'My objective at 40 years? To be a generalist, to be out of commercial management . . . But I don't have a precise career plan. I'm going to look around, reply to advertisements.' Thus, in subsequent decades as much as in the first, careers are a continuous searching, looking around for opportunities. Even where managers are quite happy in the job, the sector or the kind of company they are in, 'if something interesting' offers itself they will change completely. Few are firmly committed to a type of company or sector of activity; they remain open to all opportunities, at least in their own minds.

A few, but a very few, were frankly disappointed with what they had been able to achieve so far. They felt that their talents were unrecognised and that they had come into the market at the wrong time. 'It was easier between 1960 and 1970. Now there are too many Directors.' Some who leave are not searching for new appointments but go because they are pushed by mergers or policy and structural changes in their company and by the closing off of their imagined career paths. As one respondent said, the situation in his company was:

catastrophic where the managers are concerned. There was a total merger of managers at the higher levels of the company – existing staff had been simply added together at all levels and especially at the level of top management. Without that merger, I should by now be much higher up. There's now a big gap between us and INSEADs who joined the bank earlier. Those who joined two years before us had the time to climb . . . I won't climb much more now.

These, so dissatisfied, however, were few. Most felt that, although it certainly was harder to get ahead quickly in the present climate of recession, there were still opportunities available to those who knew where to look and how to play the game.

Most, in contrast, move because they receive attractive offers, emanating from many different sources. Many offers were channelled through personal relationships and contacts made independently of the current post, going back again to family positions and educational itineraries. These informal information channels were especially useful for jobs in the country of origin, often in companies which were 'going international' and felt in need of the technical or financial skills of the MBA. A classic example of this 'reactivated contact' (Granovetter, 1974: 76) and the importance of friends from the same educational institutions is seen below: 'I left X.H. because a friend came to see if I was interested (in joining the bank. The contact with the bank I made through an old university friend.'

Most, however, received offers because of contacts made through their current jobs. Some sectors are especially propitious for establishing such relationships. Consulting in particular is widely considered as the trampoline from which to move to a plum senior or top managerial post elsewhere and for many it effectively operates as such:

Then I got two more years of additional training at M. When I left, I was contacted with a proposition to join W., [a well-known British merchant bank] . . . I joined as an assistant-director [*sous-directeur*].

(Belgian, 1966, British bank in Brussels)

Banking also plays a very similar role. In banks, both national and international, and in certain functions especially, contacts can be established by an individual with a wide range of companies and conversely the performance of the potential employee can be assessed 'in safety' by the client company subsequently making an employment offer. This mechanism was especially useful for jumping to extremely senior positions. Thus, as one French alumnus of the early days of INSEAD said:

I joined this company through my *relations* (personal contacts). *One of my clients introduced me.* I joined as Director for Paris. After several years I became the associate of the *Président-Directeur-Général* (Chief Executive officer).

(French, 1960)

and another:

I had a proposition from the company . . . *who knew me because it was a client of the bank.*

(French, 1974)

Links between companies may also offer opportunities:

I found my job through contacts. P. is the mother-company of the firm where I worked. *By chance I happened to have personal contacts with the other company.*

Yet other possibilities are sought out in more formal ways. 'Headhunters', executive search companies, play an important role in these labour markets, to the extent that it was sometimes said that they followed the careers of INSEAD graduates particularly carefully so as to build up a pool of possible people to propose to clients. As one Frenchman said,

In my whole life I have never looked for a job. People have always come to me with propositions. At M. a headhunter contacted me.

(1961)

For his second job, another respondent said that he 'knew someone', but for his third he had been:

recruited by a headhunter for a private bank which belonged to a manufacturing company and which was seeking to stimulate further investments.

(German, 1965, director of a British firm in London)

For those 'pushed out' by pressures in their firm, personnel changes around them are important because many work in very small management teams. Frustration with present problems may combine with attractive offers to encourage a move to a post with a higher salary or a more international working *milieu*. A job by invitation does not necessarily mean a series of similar moves or a more brilliant career but it is a major means of changing tracks. As one respondent who left a bank to join an insurance company explained, the firm where he had first worked

was a consortium bank, the atmosphere was always very tense, quarrels were permanent. One of the directors general left because of that and went to join B. He suggested that I join the new team as an assistant director [*sous-directeur*]. *I accepted the offer in spite of the lower position that it meant taking.* Why? (1) Because the situation is politically calmer here. (2) The group has wider international coverage. (3) My salary went up 50 %. I have been here seven years and have not changed jobs at all. My function is very specific. I am responsible for finance for the ships belonging to the Group . . . *So, over the last seven years it has been the responsibility involved in the post that has increased: I moved up with that increase, not by changing.*

Some people use their contacts to change sectors or functions when they change jobs and to move on to tracks they had not earlier intended to follow, as in the following example:

I arrived in advertising accidentally. Over the last three years I spent at G. I got interested in the publicity for our products. So for those three years I worked closely with the advertising agencies. Then I decided to make the jump and go to the other side of the fence.

(Belgian, 1963, managing director of the Belgian division of an American company)

When asked about the roads to the top, there were almost as many opinions as respondents. Some voted for functions, some spoke in organisation terms, of divisions and subsidiaries, or geographically, working at home or abroad. Thus, for instance one said:

If you are going to be in banking, you *have* to go to the USA. In general, it's better to begin in headquarters and finish up in subsidiaries. It's much easier to do it that way than the other way round. An exception to that rule might be to begin in the regional or divisional headquarters [*sous-centrales*] of a very large multinational.

In this the opinions of MBAs themselves were reinforced by those of 'headhunters', who in some cases also added a caveat:

Routes to the top are very varied. It can be useful to go through a subsidiary but that depends on the distance of the subsidiary from the parent company. In the States subsidiaries are frequently a dead end. Routes to US Boards are various but usually go straight through the parent company.

(Interview with Egon Zehnder consulting group, Brussels 1977)

Some respondents emphasised pitfalls, indicating that some paths were not routes to anywhere, for job titles are often misleading, frequently subject to inflation and may serve as substitutes for promotion, and reminded us that some tracks which look promising turn out to be dead ends. Those seeking top positions in Europe must leave American firms young, they said, because hierarchies, management procedures, and recruitment practices are different. In general, people must not stay too long in the same post. For instance, personal assistants, one respondent advised, should not stay long, but rather they should get active in production or, more especially, in sales. Overall,

People should stay five to six years as functional experts and then ask to be transferred to another function. Also international moves and training periods are crucial.

(Same interview with Egon Zehnder, Brussels, 1977)

MBAs are usually relatively well able to make the appropriate moves for, as, a French observer has remarked, new MBAs, American and European, are frequently recruited by fast-growing enterprises who give them responsible posts, allowing them to develop new products, to instigate new budget control procedures or long-term planning and information systems, to make studies of acquisitions and to suggest the creation of new companies, often putting that suggestion into effect (Dougier, 1970: 65). Similarly, Jacques Maison-rouge, himself then only forty-five years of age and already the French president of IBM World Trade, could emphasise that many companies employing MBAs gave 'them a chance very early in a career and [could] . . . motivate them by increasing responsibilities' (quoted Dougier, 1970: 63).

The fast tracks: flying high by taking risks

One respondent, a highly successful one, summed up the best route to the top:

The fast tracks?
Where functions are concerned:

marketing *used* to be;
export today and certainly tomorrow still;
finance and the social in the future perhaps.
Where sectors are concerned:
electronics;
information technology;
new energies.
In general, *the international above all.*

The emphasis here then, within firms, is on a few functions and on sectors at the forefront of technological progress. What can also be seen, however, is that changes occur over time in the routes to the top. Marketing, for instance, is referred to as belonging to the past, perhaps to the consumer boom of the 1960s. In less propitious periods, finance and external relations will clearly come to the fore and industries using new technology must be the most flexible and most likely to change, for what means success today may not do so tomorrow. Where things change, the risks of mistakes are greater but the rewards of success may be higher. Finance was cited by many more: 'all sections which are customer related, marketing or which deal directly with finance', 'fast tracks are the financial and trade departments', 'business development in banks and financial management in general'.

Taking a chance

But, while sectors and functions are important, it is *risk* which is the recurring theme. Even in banking, marketing was mentioned as the fast track by several people not because of the importance of selling but because of the risk involved in product development. The fast tracks seem to consist, as one person summed it up, in 'all the positions where you are most exposed'.

This view of the importance of risk has been confirmed by others. It was publicly stated by a multinational chemical company quoted in the London Business School MBA brochure, 1979, p. 27, whose spokesman said:

In our view, business graduates should be looking for a fairly exposed position of responsibility in marketing, technical management or industrial relations soon after they join us. These are the fields in which reputations are earned. At least in our case it is a fallacy to think that there is a quick route to the top through corporate or financial planning.

The recurring themes of 'risk' and 'exposure' give us a clue about where the secret really does lie. It seems to lie in the translation of 'responsibility' into 'profit'. Finding the path to the top means searching around for the right position in which to use entrepreneurial talents to get the results which will make the entrepreneurs themselves noticed by the top management of the firm. Getting themselves noticed in this way means that the ambitious have to take considerable risks. Respondents again and again described how often it was necessary to drop salary, to begin again in a different sector, firm or country or to accept a job at a lower level in the enterprise in order to jump upwards once their worth could be seen in concrete financial results. The need to do this could indeed arise not once but several times within the space of a few years, as many discovered. Disillusioned with his early opportunities, one respondent explained that he realised that he constantly had to increase his range of skills, move company, country and sector, decreasing and then raising his salary as he went.

Then I decided to change and I joined a private German bank in Frankfurt. I chose banking because I didn't know anything about finance and I wanted to diversify my skills. As I was joining a sector I hardly knew anything about, I couldn't ask for a salary equivalent to the one I had had at C. I chose to return to Europe [from the USA] and [after a few years in the bank] I joined my present company as a member of the Executive Board (*Comité de Direction*). Joining that company for me was yet another career conversion and once again I joined it at a lower salary than the one I had before. I stayed for three years as a member of the top management team and then on 8 February 1980 I became the Chief Executive Officer (*Président Directeur Général*) of the firm. Its the Board of Directors that chose me for that position. G. is a big company: in Belgium 6,000 workers, in Holland 1,000 and others in Spain.

(Belgian, 1963; Belgian firm, Brussels)

This see-saw progression, a strategy of *reculer pour mieux sauter*, involves many elements: learning new skills (finance), working overseas (USA, then Germany), in a foreign company (German bank), trading off salary against the increased chances of achieving a top management position. The opportunity to show one's worth in this manner may be found inside a company, by moving to take over a division or subsidiary, or it may mean moving out to a new company.

Skill in finance is crucial in many successful risk-taking strategies, as is the ability to relate good financial management to other aspects of the organisation of the enterprise. Success in that sphere may offer the opportunity to be the visible hand running another area of activity. Not only are financial results important in establishing credibility, but the positions that are used to gain them, such as assistant to the Director General for Europe, give their holders both the particular advantage of the global view of a large and complex firm that managerial tasks require and a chance to increase visibility by influencing the organisation of the company:

I was taken on by E. [a large British multinational] in July 1975 through INSEAD. I was then assistant to the Director General for Europe. My task was to perfect a system of budgetary control for the headquarters of all the subsidiaries in Europe (sixty companies in fourteen countries, 5,000 employees). *It was a financial task but at the same time it was more than that, it was really the whole reorganisation of the company headquarters and its operations* . . . In July 1976, I became Director of Marketing, based in Switzerland.

Recognising that his task was made much easier by good personal relationships ('Let's say that having very good relations with the Director for Europe helped me a lot'), the respondent emphasised that the nature of the task, headquarters reorganisation, had been very important.

It was a trampoline for me. My function was primarily to put some order into the coordination of central offices which had been poor. I thus still had a foot in finance. But there were a few problems. The French subsidiary wanted to buy a rather dicey company . . . We gave a contrary opinion but the French manoeuvred round our backs. It was then that I was sent to France, again by the Director for Europe, *to try and get the situation back in order. I stayed there a year and managed as well as I could. In the end it worked quite well.* It was by doing this that later on I got to be Director General of a subsidiary.

This, then, was a promising situation but it could have gone wrong because 'in the meantime the Director General for Europe retired and the British decided to close the offices in Switzerland.' At that point, he could have gone to London but decided instead to stay in France because:

I felt the wind change and I preferred to take over control of the French subsidiary. [But there have been problems.] Indeed . . . one part of the company got taken over last Christmas by another firm: there have been several problems of that kind and many people didn't survive . . . Now, looking back, I think my position here is more interesting than if I had gone to London. But at the time, that wasn't clear.

In this case, several risks were taken in fairly quick succession, involving company reorganisation, change of function (finance, marketing and then top management) and moves between countries, all within the short period of four to five years. Accepting such risks paid off handsomely – for both manager and the company he was given charge of. 'Oh well, I had tried to put the subsidiary company back on its feet, and it didn't go bankrupt. *The future looks really quite good now.*' Unfortunately, problems arose elsewhere and the company as a whole is not doing well so that 'there *are* possibilities for promotion but not in the short term and here [in his subsidiary] they don't need me any more'. So, yet another new departure has been chosen. The respondent, when interviewed, was about to leave for a new job in Switzerland, in a large company, in a totally different and socially very prestigious field, wine.

I got the job through a headhunter who organised the meetings. I will be Secretary General of the firm and then will become Chief Executive Officer (*administrateur délégué*). It's a promotion, of course, because it's a multinational whose turnover is twenty times greater than the company where I am now.

This kind of movement, taking profit responsibility in a series of difficult situations, represents a major form of risk-taking and an important constituent of successful careers. It typically involves a manager both in developing a global view of enterprise activities, covering perhaps more than one company, and in taking over a profit centre (such as a subsidiary) which is in trouble, making a financial success of it and then moving on either up to a larger and more important subsidiary or, and this may be more likely, moving out of the group altogether to run a business elsewhere.

The following is a second example of a manager successfully pursuing a similar career, taking risks, changing direction and ultimately making profits for a firm. The respondent is a Dutchman, who, after INSEAD, worked first for a French multinational, ultimately taking over the running of a German subsidiary before returning to the headquarters in Paris, and then taking on another subsidiary in difficulty. On leaving INSEAD he had several offers and had finally chosen a French company, which offered what many INSEADs seek, 'adventure':

I met the new Director General who had just arrived from the USA and who wanted to create a team that he thought would be young, full of initiative, keen to take risks. In short, it sounded a fascinating adventure for three years.

During that period he rose through the sales side to be *chef de groupe* in control of a group of existing products, and at the same time to be New Business Manager, in charge of creating and developing new products and deciding on product orientation for the future. After a while, however, internal problems arose in the enterprise and the team broke up. R. decided to move on and chose another French firm

which offered me a huge increase in salary and a new function . . . I stayed there for four years. During those few years I created the post of Marketing Manager. My team was responsible from A to Z for the profitability of our product lines. *Sales increased enormously.* In spite of this, because we were only a subsidiary we suffered a lot from the silly decisions taken by the mother-company. We had four years of constant struggle.

Already working outside his home country, the respondent decided to go on playing on the international stage but to change the products with which he worked and move out of mass-market goods. With this aim he joined another French company in the International Affairs Division (*Direction des Affaires Internationales*). Then disaster struck, but a disaster soon turned to good effect. A motoring accident forced him to take a new direction. He was asked by his firm to make a study of a German subsidiary of the company which was in bad financial shape. The study took a year and following it, recovered from the accident, the company asked him to run the subsidiary in Germany. 'It was suggested that I took the subsidiary over. *Profits were quickly made.*' Soon after this, another part of the Group was found to face financial troubles and on the basis of his track record, the respondent was asked to move once again, back to Paris, to take over the firm in difficulty

So then another sector began to fail. This was the export section of the 'brown products' of the Group . . . I took it over. I'm still there. *Next year for the first time we shall make profits.* You have to persevere.

By dint of a series of zigzag career decisions, moving sideways when necessary, always into positions where his worth to the company could be clearly demonstrated, this young forty-year-old faced the future with optimism and a clear sense of where to go next.

My career plan? One day I hope to be running a large company. To get there there's only one path. First you have to become Director General of a subsidiary in the Group, then take over bigger and bigger subsidiaries. These might be subsidiaries that are outside the Group, for instance, companies that have been bought up. In any case, I shall stay in the export business.

A slightly different pattern of advancement but one which also involves the same kind of visible financial success is seen in the career of another respondent. German by nationality, he already had well-placed international connections before INSEAD and had worked in a French merchant bank in Paris. After INSEAD he joined an American multinational manufacturing company and worked in both Brussels and Zurich, becoming marketing director. Then he left and took the highest post in a totally different kind of company, in a different country again. Why and how he got the job and how he succeeded in it he describes as a mixture of luck (friends) and financial risk-taking.

If I left in 1978 it's not because I wasn't happy in Zurich but because I had received a more interesting offer. That was the position that corresponds to the one I hold now. The proposition was the following: I had to try to get a French company . . . that was bankrupt . . . back on to its feet. I had to redress its financial affairs. To do that I was given all possible powers. I got this proposition through chance contacts, *through friends if you prefer.* For the last three years I have been trying to get the company going again. I am Chairman of the Board (*Président du Directoire*) . . . in charge of new initiatives, that's where my work is most interesting, nothing is very precise, I have to develop everything to the maximum possible. Over three years *turnover has increased 60%. Instead of having huge losses we now are making small profits although not yet enough!*

Not only had the respondent managed to turn around the situation of the company but he had been able to do so principally by changing methods of working, managing to avoid the difficulties associated with the shedding of many of the 800 employees while at the same time making considerable new investments in machinery which almost doubled the company's productivity. The firm still faced problems because of late payments by clients (mostly public bodies) and difficulties with suppliers but the situation had greatly improved, with the firm returning to profitability. As the firm's financial viability had not yet been maximised the respondent felt that, while he had already been successful, he had not yet done all he could for the company and would therefore stay where he was, at least for the time being.

When I accepted the offer, I gave myself two and a half years to get the company going again. At present, the company could still do better so I'm waiting a bit longer before leaving . . . I'm waiting for 1981, the end of the planning and budgeting period, so I can see the fruits of what I sowed. I don't particularly want to go elsewhere at the moment . . . If after 1981 someone makes me a more interesting offer, which would give me more satisfaction, I'll change. But in fact I don't expect to change until I've been here five to eight years because it's after six or seven years in a firm that the job gets routinised . . . So I've still got two or three years of non-routine here.

Success in a task of clear financial benefit to the company is thus the secret of many fast promotions. A final example can be seen in the experience of a Belgian high-flyer who, having internationalised himself by working for a Swiss company in North Africa, returned home to Belgium with a mission to take over and 'mend' an ailing company.

Then I joined this company [a manufacturing firm] . . . which was bankrupt when I arrived. *I came to get it back on its feet.* I was taken on as a consultant to organise a new structure and then I was appointed Chief Executive Officer (*Président Directeur Général*). *By 1976, the firm had been reorganised and had become financially sound* . . . I am now a member of the Board of Directors (*Conseil d'Administration*). There are two groups, ten companies in all . . . I am in charge of everything . . . I prefer to work in a small firm (here there are 600 people) and be totally in charge . . . *Our turnover doubled in two years and tripled in five years* . . . My plans for the future? *To create new businesses. In another two years I'll leave – there's nothing more interesting than taking over a business.*

(Belgian, 1969; Belgian firm, Brussels)

Thus, a decade only after receiving his MBA from INSEAD, this respondent was chief executive officer and a member of the board of directors of a medium-sized manufacturing company, itself a member of a larger group, with profit control of ten companies. Leaving a successful international career to take a financial risk at home he had acquired a top job at a very young age. The doubling and tripling of turnover was the basis of a financial success visible to all.

The biggest career rewards then seem to be closely linked to financial achievements: rapid and visible financial success. Even though in some cases, including one of those cited, the functions held were apparently in other fields, such as marketing, the creation of profits for the firm was crucial. Success in this, seen as indicating 'general management' ability, led upwards fast and gave rapid access to positions with a fully recognised general management content and power.

To be chosen from many, or to force recognition of one's talents, in this way involves locating oneself in a public field of operation. Access to such a field of operation may be obtained early by moving to hold a position close to the centre of corporate power, even if at first only in a personal assistant capacity. As one said, 'you have to go straight away to the seat of top management, that's certain, or at least get as close to it as possible.' Others agreed.

The particular mechanisms for demonstrating general management ability vary in different business environments. In banking, achievement is visible principally in the number and importance of clients introduced to the bank and hence in the contribution made to the bank's financial growth. A profile of a young banking high-flyer, French but working in London, indicates this clearly. The banker concerned is not an INSEAD graduate but could easily be guessed to be so from the description. 'Philippe Bieler is a young-looking thirty-six with enormous energy. He was introduced to a new company by Clark. He first met Jacob Rothschild in July and created an instant impression by turning up with a client for the bank the very next day (*The Times*, 2 January 1970, p. 19). The INSEAD MBA, allied to high social origins and prestigious education, makes such exploits easier. In manufacturing, profit-making skills may be demonstrated early through controlling activities such as budgeting, corporate planning and investment. Marketing may also offer the same possibilities but only if the marketing manager is the effective decision-maker about the directions chosen, for the financial returns must be clearly attributable to an individual's activity. Only in that way, especially in large companies, is it possible to distinguish oneself sufficiently from peers so as to rise rapidly to positions of power.

Paradoxically, then, the study suggests that, while our most successful respondents are publicly defined as managers, in practice they are essentially risk-taking entrepreneurs. In developing their careers they concentrate, through their choice of sector, function, type of company and place of work, on acquiring the skills and experience which allow them to bid effectively for the risky tasks that challenge the manager to prove his worth at what still lies at the heart of any enterprise's activity – the making of profits. If he cannot prove himself in that, be he a genius at marketing or production, new ventures or long-term planning, he will probably never be trusted with the highest office, let alone be so trusted at the early age an MBA feels appropriate. The way to the top thus does not lie in marketing or organisation redesign as such; it lies in the use of these areas to make money in a visible manner. The constant need to prove oneself, to acquire the range of skills necessary to the global view of the enterprise, means sideways moves, see-saw careers, zigzag routes in all but the most staid and least expansionist enterprises. It is precisely because the MBA gives skills and confidence to many who were previously less-well-trained entrepreneurs that their opportunities on the European stage are so rewarding: in innovative businesses, making new products and operating in expanding product markets, they refine their entrepreneurial and managerial experience, which then enhances their image as the panacea to the problems of the more traditional enterprise at home or abroad. In this way their career opportunities are doubled: they may choose either to pursue senior positions in major European enterprises, reaching the highest posts later, or to move sooner into top positions in small, more national enterprises.

7. Invisible resources: families of origin and marriage

Managers moving on and flying high as organisational entrepreneurs do not make their careers alone. While individuals occupy positions, in business families do much to make many careers. Families of origin structure choices, develop ambitions and expectations, and determine effective education opportunities. Families of marriage later provide assistance with venture capital, nurture networks of contacts and channels of information and take up the task of assistance with managing the public image or persona of the occupant of a particular post. Being a manager in European business is at minimum a 'two-person' career (Papanek, 1973) and more usually a multi-person enterprise. Wives and uncles, grandfathers, mothers and cousins all contribute to an individual's portfolio of assets whose yield with good management increases over time. Paid largely in kind, the income from this investment is untaxable, while the capital is continually renewed.

In short, families of origin and families of marriage in the Europe of the latter decades of the twentieth century continue to play a considerable part in the life chances of individuals seeking high office in European business enterprise. Families, nuclear, extended, and affinal, remain close to the centre of career decisions and trajectories. In principle indefinite, the size of an extended family is only a function of the number of relatives recognised as such for the purposes of duties, claims or services and the spread of any group of relatives may vary over periods of time and over geographical space, giving a different 'shape' to the family as prominence is given to particular individuals or groups of relatives by the needs and circumstances of the moment. However defined, a large family is an asset beyond price for the sons of the upper classes to use in the competition for scarce rewards in the European business world.

Potentially at least, this pool of relatives provides many services, from information on the job market to suitable places to spend holidays, at home or abroad. The kind of pool which an individual can call on at any given moment is the result of a series of marriages, occupational choices and wealth holdings, developing over time and over space. The higher the status of the family members concerned the more resources they control and the greater the space, both social and geographical, which they cover, either directly as a primary group or indirectly through each member's own extended network.

These resources take various forms and are used in different ways. They include economic assets, both capital and income, cultural resources, education and knowledge of the world of high culture, and social capital, a network of social contacts and mutual rights and obligations. These together form the sometimes public but officially invisible strengths of a person applying for a position, being considered for promotion, deciding on a career change, making the deals which mark a man out from competitors. Above all perhaps, they provide, on the one hand, the safety net for the risks taken by high-flyers in the international managerial labour market and, on the other, the attributes which make up the social persona in whom others will have confidence so that they will also take risks in hiring. In short, families provide a pool of persons on whom an individual can make claims for assistance and who form a group in most cases more tightly knit than any network based simply on ties of friendship or common professional or recreational interests and in this do much to make a man what he is socially perceived to be. Kin relationships in high-status milieux both create their own links and underpin other links based on more fragile ties. To the degree that he has a large and successful family a manager is richer and more powerful in every sphere.

Families of origin: a wealth of connections

The quantities of social and economic capital available to an individual from the European upper class are considerable even if he does not control them directly. There is value first in the number of relatives available and their position in the economies and societies of Europe. Families of origin in this milieu provide business connections of many kinds, for they have overwhelmingly invested their members in the business world. Professional 'inheritance', entry by sons to occupations identical or similar to those followed by their fathers, continues to mark the social structure of modern Western societies, as many studies have shown (Girard, 1961; Higley, Lowell-Field and Crholt, 1976; Bertaux, 1977; Heath, Ridge and Halsey, 1980). The alumni of INSEAD were no exception to this picture. Most alumni came from families long established in the upper classes of European society, and indeed principally established within the business fractions of those classes, either as entrepreneur–owners or managers of enterprises.[1] As we saw earlier, half their fathers owned their own businesses (although these may have included some doctors and lawyers who of course own their practices, which may legally be businesses). Of this half, the largest proportions owned companies engaged in manufacturing. Such ownership was not new. In good part, these independent business fathers had succeeded their own fathers, for among the grandfathers

Table 7.1 *Occupations of respondents' fathers and grandfathers.*[a] Percent.

Occupation	Fathers	PGF	MGF	French[b] PGF	French[b] MGF
Own business (patron)	33	28.5	26	25	17
Top management	13 }24	6 }14	4 }8	7.5	13
Senior management	11	8	4		
TOTAL SENIOR BUSINESS	57	42.5	34	36.5	30
Senior civil service	8	5	4	7.5	12.5
Military and naval	3	4	10	1	1
Law	3 }13	4 }10	4 }9.5	7.5	14
Medicine and similar	10	6	5.5	7.5	14
Other professional	3	4	3	—	—
Writers and other cultural	0.5	1	1.5	5	1
University teachers/research	3	1	3	0.5	1
Other teachers	2	3	3	1	2
Routine non-manual/lower mgt./technical/white collar	1	5	6	6	8
Shopkeepers/artisans	4	7	7	14	12.5
Manual workers	1	6	4	7	5
Farmers and landowners	1	10	11	13	6
Misc. (clergy, organist, etc.)	1	2	2	5	6
N =	292	276	273	173	152

[a] As in chapter 5, unless it is specifically stated otherwise, the French are *excluded* from the figures in these tables
PGF = paternal grandfathers
MGF = maternal grandfathers
[b] Data from first French study only

between a quarter and a third also owned their own companies. In many of the families, indeed, both paternal and maternal grandfathers were business owners. Adding to these entrepreneur ancestors, the fathers and grandfathers who controlled companies through jobs in top or senior management raise the proportions of direct male ancestors in the senior echelons of business even further to 57 % among the fathers and a very high 42.5 % and 34 % respectively among paternal and maternal grandfathers.

For at least three generations, then – the students, their fathers and grandfathers – alumni families had in large proportion earned their living from business. For three generations business origins had almost always led to a career in business: 80 % of the students whose grandfathers (on one or both sides) owned and ran their own companies had fathers who also owned their own businesses. Moreover, the predominance of business origins becomes even more striking when it is seen that professional inheritance sometimes skips a generation. By definition all the present 'sons' are in business, although not necessarily as owners; not only did many of the fathers and grandfathers own and/or run companies but 78 % of those with fathers who were doctors or lawyers also had grandfathers who were business owners. This concentration in the business world was also apparent in the origins of fathers in cultural, military and public-service occupations, for 59% of their fathers were entrepreneurs. The importance of business as the source of the wealth and resources which in the fathers' generation led to high-status non-business careers is clear. The close relationship of respondents to the business world can thus be seen through looking at the grandfathers' generation, even though the fathers had moved away. In such cases, our MBAs were returning to an older family tradition, not straying away from an established family line. Perhaps, like the textile families of the north-east of France, these families had bought prestige by investing business profits in their sons' (respondents' fathers) entry to the liberal professions and the public service. With passage through prestigious educational establishments and the rise to prominence of the 'professional' manager, such migrations may be less necessary and equal prestige may be found within the confines of the business world.

Moreover, students with fathers in top management in non-family businesses and the independent business professions such as chartered accountants, who stand out as a 'new group', frequently had business origins; 40 % of their grandfathers owned their own businesses, a proportion which by the national standards of any European country is remarkably high. Here, too, business had undoubtedly led to business. In comparison with the businessmen of each generation, the public sector was much less well represented – only 11% among the fathers and 9–14% among the grandfathers – as were the 'old' professions of law and medicine and those involving cultural activities.

Marriage in the grandfathers' generation created some links between business and non-business backgrounds, but only to a limited extent. There were close links between owning a business in the students' fathers' and *paternal* grandfathers' generation and the occupations of *maternal* grandfathers. An outstanding proportion, more than two-thirds, of the students who came from families headed by independent businessmen had 'both sides' of their family in earlier generations owning their own businesses. In other words, a high proportion of students came from families where both fathers and mothers themselves had parents who owned their own companies.

From the grandfathers' point of view, they saw their sons (respondents' fathers and fathers' brothers) largely staying within the business world. Almost half (46%) of all paternal grandfathers who were independent businessmen had some sons at least who in turn became business owners, while a further 16% of sons remained in the business world in a different capacity, as top or senior managers. In contrast, only 12% of sons migrated into the public sector and cultural occupations while 20% entered law or medicine. About two-thirds thus entered the business world, the others choosing high-prestige professions. There was very little downward mobility at all.

There had, however, over the generations been some social mobility. In the grandfathers' generation there were more extremes; at the top, more landed aristocrats who lived from their *rentes* and had no 'occupation' and at the bottom more manual and white-collar workers, more shopkeepers and artisans. The latter, of course, can be described in some senses as owning their own businesses and in the next generation their sons may well have become company owners in the more generally accepted sense. In these cases, again, business had come very largely from business.

Returning again to the grandfathers' vantage point, the group of maternal grandfathers owning businesses had also been fairly successful in maintaining their families in the business world in the next generation by marrying their daughters to men who were also independent businessmen, as a third had done. A further quarter had married their daughters to men in other positions in the business world, top or senior management, and just over a fifth to doctors and lawyers. In contrast, they had only married 9% of their daughters to people in the public and cultural professions and a final 9% to men in less prestigious occupations. The range of effective marital choices was thus extremely narrow and there was a much greater chance of a daughter of an independent businessman marrying a man with the same profession as her father than of marrying one in any other single major professional group. The proportion remaining in business as a whole is even higher.

An educated élite

In addition to their investment in business ownership and control these families had already, before the INSEAD generation, invested heavily in the symbolic capital of education. While the 'new' bourgeoisie of Europe may be characterised as making particular use of formal credentials both to consolidate its skills and demonstrate and legitimate its social prestige, that strategy is by no means new. Families of respondents here have been investing in their sons' futures through extensive use of the education system for a long time, and the socially prestigious and exclusive family pedigree of the MBAs has long been sanctioned by degrees and diplomas. When the grandfathers were young, only a very small proportion of the total population even entered secondary school, let alone completed it and obtained a secondary school diploma. In the fathers' generation, and especially in the grandfathers' generation, very few people indeed in any European country obtained

Table 7.2 Men, wives and grandfathers: social homogamy over the generations among the French (percentages of respondents)

Socio-professional origins	Respondents			Wives		
	Fathers	Paternal GF	Maternal GF	Fathers	Paternal GF	Maternal GF
Rentiers/landowners	0.5	4	5	—	6	4
Patrons[a]	28	25	17	23.5	24	13.5
Cadres supérieurs[b]	19.5	7.5	13	21	9	16
Liberal professions[c]	11	7.5	14	16	7.5	12
Senior civil servants	2	1	1	3.5	1	1
Military/naval personnel	7	7.5	12.5	2	9	12
High-tech./research staff	2	0.5	1	5	2.5	1
Total upper class	70	53	63.5	71	59	59.5
Primary teachers	2	1	2	—	2.5	—
Lower executives/technical/white-collar workers	8	6	8	13	6	8
Artisans/shopkeepers	9	14	12.5	7	16	16
Manual workers	0.5	7	5	—	4	5
Farmers	4	13	6	6	6	4
Miscellaneous: cultural	5	5	1	2	2.5	4
Miscellaneous: other	1	1	1	—	2.5	1
Total other occupations	29.5	47	35.5	28	37	38

[a] Mainly industrialists
[b] Including *ingénieurs*
[c] Mainly law in grandfathers' and medicine in fathers' generations
Data from 1974 study of the French. Includes all the French and the wives of the married French

university degrees. In contrast, among the families of the MBAs studied here, very considerable proportions had both secondary and higher education credentials.

Their *fathers* had degrees and diplomas of many kinds. The overwhelming majority in each country had successfully completed secondary education, usually in the more prestigious 'general' streams of the school system. Thus, for example, among the Swiss, more than half had been to *lycées* or *gymnasia* and only a few to the technical or commercial schools which were nevertheless already well established in that country. The same was true of Germany – more than 99 % of the fathers had attended *gymnasia* and almost half had the leaving certificate, the *Abitur*. In Scandinavia, two thirds had been to *gymnasia* and almost half of those had passed the *Studentsexamen* graduating examination. Among the British, just under half had completed their secondary education in 'public schools', including the major major ones to which they later sent their own sons.

Remarkable numbers of grandfathers and fathers had also made use of the tertiary education system available in their countries. The proportion of *grandfathers* holding tertiary-level educational qualifications is striking indeed. Of the *paternal* grandfathers for whom we have information (about 90 % of the sample), two fifths (39 %) held university level diplomas, as did an even higher proportion (44 %) of *maternal* ones. The *fathers* had followed in their footsteps. In Switzerland, more than half had a university degree, and half of those had not just a first but also a higher degree. Among the Dutch, seventeen out of twenty-one had a university degree, and half of them had higher degrees. In Germany, nearly two-thirds held university qualifications, a majority holding higher degrees, a remarkable proportion even though it is, of course, difficult to separate out where a first degree is placed in the long period of university study in these countries. The percentages of fathers with university education must be at least ten times greater than the average for their generation. In Britain, the prestige of the universities attended was also outstanding. Not only had almost 75 % received a university education, including in that a small proportion who had received military-officer training at Sandhurst, but of these a fifth had been to Oxford and 31 % to Cambridge. Thus, half had been to Britain's two most prestigious universities, a proportion almost exactly identical to that of their sons.

The influences of family on sons' choices can be seen in fathers' choice of subjects. Engineering is even more predominant than among the sons, as is law, reflecting the prestigious symbolism of these disciplines in Europe at the time as well as their value on the élite labour market, but many sons and fathers had studied the same disciplines.

The wider pool of relatives

Fathers and grandfathers, of course are only a small part of the pool of relatives available to any individual. The pool also includes lateral and affinal kin – uncles, aunts, cousins and siblings – and all the family linked to each of these. The number of relatives on whom claims can be made is considerable in these large families and their 'value' can be seen in the professions pursued and diplomas held by uncles, cousins and brothers. The remarkable social homogamy, marriage within the same social group, evident among fathers and grandfathers, can also be seen in the concentration of extended family members in business activities of many kinds, interspersed with participation in a select few of the liberal and public-sector professions.

Respondents to the 1979 survey had between them 6,709 known relatives, ranging from grandfathers to cousins. They thus had a pool of at least 25–30 relatives each (allowing for non-responses) in their extended families of origin. This number only includes relative up to first cousins: some respondents undoubtedly had greater pools, knowing well many more distant cousins as well as more distant family members such as great-uncles and great-aunts.

Of this pool of almost seven thousand known relatives, the occupations of 3,164 (excluding housewives) were declared. Table 7.3 shows that a third of these declared were concentrated in the senior levels of the business world, including 11.5% who owned their own companies, 6% in top management and 15% in other managerial positions. The true network of family contacts within the business world is of course much larger than these figures suggest, as each person will extend the network further, but the figures give some idea of the mesh of the 'safety net' available to risk-takers in their careers at the same time as they indicate the 'degree of penetration' of a labour market which many candidates have. As with fathers and grandfathers, claims for assistance can be made on other relatives well established in the liberal professions, notably law and medicine, and in the senior echelons of the public sector and the cultural world. Here, again, however, one can see the considerable separation between the world of business and other sectors of the society and economy. The concentration of extended families in business professions is remarkable.

The families of respondents also included at least 1,479 housewives and 500 students and schoolchildren. The social capital represented by the housewives will be explored below. The students and schoolchildren in their turn will contribute to the continuity of the traditions of the family as they get older, for many will follow business and other high-prestige careers. The tertiary education which almost 300 were receiving at the time of the study will in its turn contribute to ensuring access to suitable positions for family members over time while protecting against the danger of downward mobility,

Table 7.3 *Occupations of respondents' extended family relatives*

Occupation	%	N
Independent business	11.5	364
(including independent business professionals)		(69)
Top managers	6	204
General managers/other managers/engineers	15	479
Total senior business	32.5	1047
Doctors/vets/pharmacists	7	233
Lawyers	4	142
Other professions	0.5	29
University teachers	3	84
Research/cultural administration	0.5	25
Architects/interior designers	2	65
Artists/writers/museum staff	3	99
Senior public servants	1.5	47
Military personnel	5	106
Total 'upper class'	59	1877
Other public servants	1.5	42
Lower managers/technicians	3	90
Teachers	10	315
Paramedics/nurses	5	168
White-collar workers	3	91
Secretaries	5	161
Shopkeepers/artisans	4	132
Manual workers	3	101
Farmers/farm workers	3	98
Landowners	0.5	19
Other	2	70
Total other occupations	40	1287
Overall total	100	3164

suggesting little social change even in the next generation of business managers.

The pool of relatives included 3,400 male relatives. It is, of course, mostly they who largely occupy the high-level business professional roles described in Table 7.3, although this is beginning to change as more women follow careers. Concentrating for a moment on the male relatives shows that the respondents' 250 fathers had between them 319 brothers, for 275 of whom occupations were given. As with fathers and grandfathers, the majority were in business. Of respondents' own brothers, two-fifths were in the senior managerial echelons of business (41.5%) with a further 8% in professional business positions such as those of engineers, bringing the total in senior business positions up to half. The public sector found little favour, with only 3 % in the senior levels of public administration and 5 % in careers as military officers. The liberal professions, too, were extremely poorly represented, with only 4 % of brothers practising law and 8 % medicine. A more 10 % were in other professions or were teaching, at university or secondary level. Almost none were lower down the social scale. White-collar, manual and farming jobs together accounted for only 2 % while a further 5 % were shopkeepers and artisans. These figures show remarkably little downward or outward social and professional mobility among members of a very large group of extended family members over two generations.

In the fathers' generation, families were particularly large and the fathers in the study had between them not only 319 brothers but also 289 sisters, of whom 235 were married at the time of the study. Mothers, too, of course have siblings, most of whom, in turn have spouses and children. In the respondents' generation, too, families continued to be large, especially among certain nationalities. Thus, for instance, more than half the Belgians had three or more siblings (families of four or more), as did one-third of the Italians, nearly a quarter of the Spanish and Scandinavians and nearly a fifth of the British and the Swiss. Some of the families were strikingly large by any modern standards: 5.5 % of the Italian families contained ten or more children as did 4 % of the Dutch, while 3 % of the Belgians had nine or more. Rather more modest but none the less large, 19 % of Belgian, 16 % Dutch and 14 % French families had six or more children. As most of these will marry, it can be seen how families in this milieu rapidly spread over a very wide social surface even in the present generation.

To the pool of 6,709 relatives recorded in the 1979 study must be added those of the French studied earlier. The 171 French respondents had between them 229 brothers and 171 sisters, most of whom will both exercise professions and marry. In addition, in the previous, fathers', generation, relatives formed a network for respondents composed of 481 uncles and aunts on their fathers' side and 395 in their mothers' families, not including the spouses. To these must be added their children, the cousins of the respondent at the centre of the network, who together number at least 1,200–1,500. Adding these and the spouses of uncles and aunts means that on average each French INSEAD had a network of around 25–30 people, exactly like that of the other nationalities in the study. Family sizes and patterns in the upper classes of Europe over the last half century have been remarkably similar across each country.

Among the French networks, too, male relatives were much concentrated in business and beyond that within a few select niches in the upper echelons of the society, as can be found in Table 7.4. Between 8 % and 18 % of close male relatives and affines (sisters' husbands) were *patrons*, while almost a further

Table 7.4 *Professions of members of French respondents' extended families*

Professions	Own brothers		Sisters' husbands		All uncles		Male cousins[a]	
	N	%	N	%	N	%	N	%
Rentiers/landowners	—	—	—	—	11	3	1	—
Patrons	16	8	15	13	75	18	46	9
Cadres supérieurs	60	29.5	50	42	91	22	128	26
Total senior business	76	37.5	65	55	177	43	175	35
Doctors	24	12	19	16	26	6	54	11
Lawyers	6	3	9	7.5	13	3	11	2
Senior civil servants	—	—	1	1	8	2	1	—
Military/naval personnel	1	0.5	—	—	32	8	10	2
Teachers	7	3	3	2.5	8	2	36	7
Low executives/technicians/ white-collar workers	43	21	10	8	43	10	78	16
Artisans/shopkeepers	12	6	2	2	45	11	29	6
Manual workers	1	0.5	—	—	8	2	18	4
Farmers	13	6	4	3	32	8	48	10
Other	20	10	6	5	28	7	40	8
Total other occupations	127	62	54	45	243	57	325	66
Overall total	203	100	119	100	420	100	500	100

[a]Information much less complete for cousins
Data from 1974 Survey of French alumni of INSEAD

quarter occupied posts as *cadres supérieurs* in French business. To those should be added the more junior managers, as many were still young and could be expected to rise to more senior or even top positions in their companies' hierarchies. As in earlier generations, there were also some in the liberal professions, but far fewer than among fathers and grandfathers in commerce and artisan businesses. Perhaps the small-scale industrial stage has been passed by relatives in the respondents' own generation.

As were fathers and grandfathers, these relatives, French and of other nationalities, were also highly educated. The biggest proportion had made outstanding use of the formal education system, for a third had not only one but more than one degree. In keeping with their business origins and connections, the biggest single proportion had engineering credentials (15 %), followed, at some distance, by law (7.5 %) and commerce (6 %). Languages accounted for a mere 2 %, the newer areas of social and political science for only 3 % and economics for 2.5 %. A very large proportion had studied 'other' subjects or had non-university tertiary qualifications. University education was perhaps felt less necessary by those who had entered family businesses in earlier years.

Families of orientation: marriage up and across

Capital, whether social, economic or cultural, is transferred between family group members in any one lifetime and over the generations in diverse ways. Access to resources is available to family members over a long period of time, even though ownership is not directly transferred until later. Some capital is transferred in lump sums at times of rites of passage – christening, barmitzvah, graduation, marriage, childbirth. Some is invested rather than transferred, put into education or another form of career apprenticeship with a long-term yield. Some assets are in cash, some in kind, some in exchange; some are transferred as loans, some as gifts, some as assistance, some as information, cultural, social and professional. In many families, some economic capital is handed on from parents to their children while they are young, in the form of educational and cultural activities, assisting the learning of skills of many kinds; much more is transferred on marriage and invested in the creation and maintenance of new links with other families.

Marriage in this milieu provides not only emotional but also the economic, cultural and social support which works to transform many potential career choices and possibilities into effectively open opportunities. Families of origin first shape values, ambitions and attitudes, but wives reinvigorate and reinforce them, helping to create and maintain the lifestyle and orientations which guarantee or underwrite the opinion formed of their husbands by others and which symbolise his appropriateness for high office. Wives' families increase the size and richness of the pool of relatives with the duty of and interest in assisting with information and advice. The social homogamy of marriage in this milieu means that affinal relatives, too, are well-placed in the professional world, notably again in business. International marriages, of course, greatly increase the spread of relatives in space and these contacts may be especially valuable in a career in the international arena.

Nuclear families created through marriage also ally two sets of kinship groupings which together create further pools of relatives. These groups may already have been linked by existing marriages between members but it is more likely that marriages will create new ties. In the first case, the new marriage confirms and reinforces existing relationships, binding together more closely by multiplying ties. In the latter case, new affinal relationships generating new rights and claims come into existence. These links will usually be cemented through the birth of children, joined by ties of blood to both groups.

There were 210 INSEAD respondents who were married at the time of the study and a further eighteen who had been married. Marriages among this group had mostly cemented the position of respondents in the upper classes of Europe and again in the business fractions of those classes, conforming to the pattern established by earlier generations of relatives and contributed in their own by their cousins and siblings.

If the young managers of European enterprises made socially and educationally homogeneous marriages similar to those of elder relatives, they were much more adventurous in contracting international alliances. Marriage for many meant the creation of kinship links transcending national frontiers and of ties criss-crossing Europe. Some nationalities were especially likely to have foreign wives, creating family ties linking country to country. Almost half of the British and Germans had chosen to marry foreign women as had a quarter of the Scandinavians and French. In contrast, the Belgians were parochial, very unlikely to marry non-Belgians, perhaps surprisingly unlikely, given their high proportion of foreign mothers. That proportion, however, may have largely come from an accident of frontier, for the textile kingdom from which many came crossed the Franco–Belgian border in the region near Lille-Tourcoing.

International connections made through marriage seemed particularly likely to link certain countries. Many seemed to prefer French wives – notably the British, the Germans and the Swiss, a choice made perhaps because many had worked in France in the years immediately before going to INSEAD.

Marriage reinforced the links between business and business which had already been established by marriages in families of origin. Like their husbands, the wives came from families well established in the upper classes of their society and more particularly they came from business. Almost half the MBAs responding had married women whose fathers owned their own businesses, while few had fathers in the liberal professions or the public sector.

Indeed, almost half the respondents who were the sons of business owners had married the daughters of independent businessmen, a proportion particularly striking if one bears in mind the whole range of possible marriage partners, both nationally and internationally. Business, moreover, seemed to attract others: doctors' and lawyers' sons in the study were more likely to marry the daughters of business owners than they were to marry anyone else, again perhaps renewing the earlier traditions of their families for, as we saw above, many were the grandsons of independent businessmen even though their fathers had exercised other professions. Respondents both from managerial occupations and the public sector were also likely to marry into business.

Among the French, for whom more detailed data were gathered, the *patron* and top-executive groups accounted not only for nearly half of wives' parents but, even more striking perhaps, for nearly a third of wives' grandparents, both paternal and maternal. French marriage patterns indeed showed even greater social homogamy than the broad categories would suggest. Of the French wives, married to Frenchmen, one quarter were from exactly the same occupational backgrounds as their husbands – *patrons* married to *patrons*, lawyers to lawyers, doctors to doctors.

In their husbands' families, relatively few links had been forged between business and the public sector or the intellectual professions in earlier generations of the wives' nuclear families. Little social mobility had occurred, although quite high proportions of grandfathers were found in artisan and shopkeeper families, suggesting that the fathers of the wives, too, may have taken over and expanded the small businesses founded by their own parents. Where close relatives had strayed from the ranks of businesses among the wives' families, too, they had mostly joined the prestigious liberal professions, particularly among fathers and maternal grandfathers.

Marriage for the respondents not only took place in a socially homogeneous circle but also in an immediate family circle which was highly educated, such high education in Europe again indicating the exclusive nature of this élite marriage market. More than half the wives had fathers with university degrees, in subjects similar to those studied by the fathers and grandfathers of the INSEAD respondents themselves. Overall, law holds pride of place, followed by engineering and, some distance behind, economics. The similarity is indeed striking between the wives' and respondents' families and suggests a Europe-wide educational pattern. For example, the proportions of wives' and respondents' fathers trained in law are identical and those of engineering and many others very close.

Appropriate marriage strategies allowed the men in this study to make potentially very valuable affinal alliances, whether or not they were consciously planned. The capital of connections provided by the family of origin was not just doubled but multiplied on marriage as the value of each link is, in Bourdieu's phrase, multiplied by the value of the whole. As seen in the 1979

Table 7.5 *Occupations of wives' extended family relatives*

Occupation	%	N
Independent	16	356
(including independent business professionals)		(53)
Top managers	3.5	77
General managers/other managers/engineers	15.5	347
Total senior business	**35**	**780**
Doctors/vets/pharmacists	6.5	146
Lawyers	4	99
Other professions	2	53
University teachers ⎫ Research/cultural administration ⎭	3	67
Architects/interior designers	2	47
Artists/writers/museum staff	3	74
Senior public servants	2	44
Military personnel	2	45
Total 'UPPER CLASS'	**59.5**	**1355**
Other public servants	0.5	16
Lower managers/technicians	2	50
Teachers	7	160
Paramedics/nurses	6	150
White-collar workers	2	47
Secretaries	7	163
Shopkeepers/artisans	4	104
Manual workers	3	65
Farmers/farm workers	2	48
Landowners	1	27
Others	2	49
TOTAL OTHER OCCUPATIONS	**36.5**	**879**
OVERALL TOTAL	**100**	**2234**

study, the social capital in the form of relatives brought by the wives was
considerable. The wives between them had a pool of relatives of more than
4,500. Like their husbands, the wives thus each had kinship pools of at least
twenty-one to twenty-five people. Not including grandfathers, 2,234 of the
total pool had paid occupations, while a further 678 were housewives and
almost 200 were students or schoolchildren.

Like their husbands and their fathers, the extended families of the wives
were also concentrated in the business world as Table 7.5 shows. Over a third
(35%) ran their own companies or held top or senior positions in other
business enterprises. Those who were in other occupations were again like the

relatives on the other side of the families, most often in the upper echelons of the society. Thus 12.5% practised one or other of the prestigious liberal professions while 4% occupied senior rungs in the public service and 8% similar positions in the intellectual and cultural sphere. In contrast, only 3% were from manual-worker homes and 4% from shopkeeper or artisan homes.

More detail still can be seen from the 1974 study of the wives of the French. The 134 wives responding had between them 153 siblings (89 brothers and 64 sisters) and, in their parents' generation, 215 paternal and 177 maternal aunts and uncles (not counting their spouses). These uncles and aunts have 219 male children, 83 female children and a further 97 whose sex is not reported, as well as a considerable number who were 'too many' to write down. This gives an average pool of relatives reported of 18–20. The French wives' extended families were even more socially exclusive than those of their husbands: between two-thirds and three-quarters of their male relatives, excluding grandfathers, held senior positions in economy and society (see Table 7.6).

Marriage in this milieu, then, mostly at least doubles the pool of useful relatives potentially available to a manager, both early on and later in his career. Through their families, respondents and their wives together each share privileged access to forty-five to fifty people on whom claims can be made and who will give extended and generous 'credit'.

The social homogamy so clear in most respondents' marriage choices – and those of their own families before them – is not a matter of chance. It arises from the structuring of opportunities for meeting appropriate spouses. Marriages in this milieu are no longer arranged but neither are they left to 'luck': rather, they arise from meetings in situations so structured by social and family circumstances that the field of competition for partners is severely limited. Among factors determining chances of meeting, the importance of family and friends is outstanding. The great majority of wives first met their husbands at friends' houses or through activities arranged by friends or family such as the *rallyes* of the French upper class, or dinner parties and other private receptions. Others had met their spouses through the clubs, associations or sporting activities engaged in by people from a privileged social milieu. Only a fifth had met their husbands in circumstances which might be considered more 'open', such as through studies, work or travelling. Even here, the possibilities are socially limited, given the selective milieu from which students, the major source of friends, are recruited in most of Europe, a selection which contributes to making international marriages as socially exclusive as more local ones. There were thus very few occasions where the influence of a family and its immediate friends was not felt, directly or indirectly, either because of the networks developed through childhood and locality-based activity or through contacts essentially made through education in exclusive institutions. For most of the wives, the likelihood of marrying someone from a very different social milieu was very small indeed,

much smaller than that of marrying someone from a different nationality. Affinal links spread outwards, seldom downwards.

Social capital

In this milieu as we have seen, social capital in the form of a pool of relatives, well connected and frequently affluent, is a peculiarly significant resource. Not only are contacts important, but the claims and obligations of kinship work to multiply the economic resources to which couples in this milieu have access and on which they can call.

Social capital has been defined as follows:

Social capital is the ensemble of actual or potential resources which are linked to possession of an enduring set of more or less institutionalised relationships of acquaintanceship and mutual recognition. It can also be expressed as belonging to a group, seen as an ensemble of agents who not only possess common properties (which can be seen by an observer, by other people or by group members themselves) but who are also united by permanent and useful links. These links are not reducible to objective relationships of proximity in a physical (geographical) space because they are built on exchanges, inseparably both material and symbolic, whose creation and perpetuation presuppose the re-creation and permanent recognition [*re-connaissance*] of that proximity. The volume of social capital possessed by any particular group member thus depends on the breadth of the network of links that he can effectively mobilise and on the volume of capital (economic, cultural and symbolic) possessed by each individual in the group to whom he is linked. This means that although social capital is relatively irreducible to the economic and cultural capital owned by any particular member or even by the group as a whole (as can be seen in the case of the *parvenu*), it is never completely independent of the fact that the exchanges which form the basis of mutual recognition of group members presuppose the recognition of a minimum of objective homogeneity and that *social capital exercises a multiplier effect on the capital possessed by the group*.

(Bourdieu, 1980: 3, emphasis added)

Contrary to much popular opinion, social capital provided through kinship does not lose its importance as the relationships between education, family and enterprise become more complex. On the contrary, as Bourdieu explains, family networks provide mechanisms for multiplying the value of the capital held by any family member and increasing individual earnings from the formally economic productive system:

It is as though the new mode of capital appropriation [by a salaried bourgeoisie] made possible (and even desirable) the creation of a truly organic solidarity between members of a family. In contrast to the position of the holders of an economic patrimony who are divided as much as they are united by their common claim to appropriation of the patrimony, which is, moreover, always threatened with division and dispersal through the chance happenings of inheritance and marriage, *the owners of a diversified patrimony, with a considerable capital component, have everything to gain by maintaining the family links that allow them to add together the capital resources possessed by each of the family members.* In that way, the network of family relations can form the framework for an informal or even clandestine circulation of capital which has the specific function of increasing the efficiency of the channels of official circulation and of counteracting any effects of that circulation that may be against the interests of the family. The dialectical relationship established between the formal and the informal, between the family network and the formal economic channels for the circulation of capital permits, here as elsewhere, the maximisation of profits procured through systems involving apparently incompatible demands. *It allows one, for instance, to add together profits obtained from prestigious educational qualifications and those obtained from systems of production that allow them to yield full value* and even to add to the advantages gained by links between firms, the secondary benefit ensured by matrimonial exchanges among company controllers [*dirigeants*]. In this way, the 'integrated family' owes its cohesion to the operation of a specific principle, sense of family' [*esprit de famille*], and affection as transfigured forms of the interest attached to belonging to a family group, or, more specifically, to participation in the patrimony whose integrity is assured by the integration of the family. Thus by the sleight of hand which is the mainspring of the alchemy of the collective, belonging to an integrated family ensures that each individual member receives not only the profits due to his or her individual contribution to the whole or even those that could be gained from adding together the contributions of others. *Rather, an individual member receives the profits that are the product of the multiplication of the contribution of each by the contribution of everyone . . . In short, if social capital is irreducible to the other kinds of capital, especially to economic and cultural capital (whose yield social capital can multiply) while none the less remaining dependent on these to some extent, it is because the volume of social capital that any individual family member (and thus the group to which he belongs) owns depends on the volume of capital held by each of the group's members multiplied by the degree of integration of the group.*

(Bourdieu, Boltanski and de Saint Martin, 1973: 85–6, emphasis added)

The families of origin of INSEAD clearly provide potentially important contact with different parts of business and its associated worlds. Kinship systems, in contrast to friendship or acquaintancy links, are lifelong. To be useful, however, there is a condition: they have to be activated. The price of activating them successfully is an investment in participation in occasions of importance to the group and in cultivating the relationships concerned, either on a regular or an occasional basis. It is here that the women of the families are crucial. The realisation of the *esprit de famille* and its transformation into well-nurtured channels of contact, communication and mutual aid are largely the work of women, mothers, sisters and wives. Many of the wives of respondents in this study do not follow professional lives and many others only do so part-time. They, therefore, are both perceived by husbands as having the time and perceive themselves as having the obligation to organise such participation, to render mutual services and to undertake other forms of necessary reciprocity, such as outings and dinner parties.

For the wife to be able to play her role, however, the new couple needs to be established as a member in its own right of both kinship groups and as one fully accepted by each. Ceremonies provide occasions for the public presentation and recognition of the new unit. The first of these ceremonies, both in time and frequently in importance, are the receptions held after the wedding.

Making the match

Reflecting their social importance and indicating their social role, weddings in this milieu tend to be large affairs. They together mix both sets of kin and include, in a quasi-familial position, personal friends and professional acquaintances: at a quarter of all respondents' weddings the wider social significance of the marriage was emphasised by the presence at the reception of professional associates of the fathers and sometimes of the husbands, often making up large proportions of the guests. Wedding receptions thus brought together many people salient to establishing the position of the new couple. Among some nationalities, weddings were large indeed. Almost half (44 %) of the French had more than 500 guests at their weddings, and 13 % had more than a thousand. A fifth of all non-French INSEAD marriages had been celebrated by more than 200 guests; of those, many receptions included numbers of guests nearer 500 than 200. The reason for the much smaller wedding-guest lists amongst the non-French may be the higher number of 'mixed' marriages, for where spouses come from different countries it is harder to bring together large numbers of family members and friends or professional associates.

Some sense of the physical and economic capital available to the young-marrieds can be gauged from the place of wedding receptions. In spite of the large numbers of guests, wedding receptions were very largely held in private houses (or gardens), principally in properties belonging to the family of the bride, but also, where appropriate, in properties belonging to the bridegroom's side of the family or in other private premises loaned by friends or other relatives. The place of reception suggests both the size of the houses concerned and the cost of the gathering. Between a fifth and half of receptions took place in restaurants or hotels, which also indicates considerable expense.

From the number of guests at a wedding it is possible to estimate roughly the amount of economic capital invested in the social establishment of the new couple. Even allowing for the lower prices prevalent in and before the 1970s, it seems likely that a reasonable average cost per head over the period 1960 to 1970 would be 200–300 1981 French francs. A reception of one thousand guests would thus cost 200–300,000 francs (approximately $50,000 at the time). A reception for 200 guests, which would probably have been average for members of all national groups in the study (although rather small for the

French) would have cost at least 40,000 to 60,000 francs (approximately $10,000). These figures, of course do not take account of other costs, such as clothes, transport and the provision of accommodation for guests travelling long distances to attend, possibly on average $5,000 more.

Most of the wives had sisters and frequently more than one. This means that the total cost of family investment in wedding receptions alone was truly considerable. Weddings thus appear as moments where the standing of the two families being allied is confirmed and where considerable investment of economic capital is made to ensure that the young couple are recognised as full members of the extended but integrated families on each side and that they share fully in all rights and duties associated with such membership. In particular, this initial investment establishes them as suitable people to share in the accumulated social capital of the families concerned. Gifts given by guests to the new couple symbolise its acceptance by members of the group as well as being a considerable transfer of assets, estimated by one respondent as equal to the cost of the wedding.

The same economic investment ensures that the male partner in the couple is recognised by potentially important professional colleagues in the widest sense as 'trustworthy' and, even more important, himself a member of the group who in return for assistance or support invested early in his career will be able to return a yield on that investment at a later stage. While such yields cannot be certain, the proper establishment of the 'son' makes it more likely that he will be able to return the debt and suggests his suitability as a creditor. In this sense, a professional group is constituted as a surrogate or complementary family, underwritten by the true families concerned. In this surrogate family, too, the profits yielded will not only accrue to the contribution of the individual 'son' but also grow as a function of the 'share capital' held by all members and be multiplied by the degree of integration of the group, as Bourdieu has suggested.

Establishing the couple in the joint social arena, however, is not sufficient to guarantee that full yield will be returned by the investment. Once established, the couple must maintain the linkages, both in the 'real' kinship networks and in the surrogate, professional, ones. International careers, of course, make the task of maintaining both kinship and professional links more complex and new strategies need to be developed to deal with this; geographical distance, however, is not necessarily a bar to the maintenance of strong kinship links, as Bell showed two decades ago. The telephone, the airline ticket and the bank draft transfer are the modern international equivalents of 'popping in', the exchange of cash, and the direct gift of household items. Even among members of families dispersed across Europe regular links are maintained and it seems likely that as managers move back to their countries of origin at later stages in their careers, regular visiting of kin and other members of the circle will be taken up again, for such links are easy to reactivate by direct contacts provided always that a minimum of indirect contact (telephone, letters) has been maintained over the years. Moreover, the wives and children of many international European families journey across Europe each year to the country of origin for family visiting. Sentiment guides such visits but their social and economic rewards are not inconsiderable.

The more detailed study made of the French INSEADs indicated the frequency of visits made to relatives. A third of the French wives visited their own parents once a week and a further quarter at least once a month. Just over a fifth visited their husbands' parents once a week while almost a third did so at least once a month. Thus, more than half the wives visited their own and their parents-in-law at least once a month. Moreover, almost half saw their own and their husbands' siblings with the same frequency, 15% once a week and about a third at least once a month. Similar proportions visited their own and their husbands' grandparents at least once a month while between a quarter and a third visited both grandparents and other relatives on each side of the family three or four times a year and a further 10% also visited them while on holiday.

Visiting of kin takes place not only in the evening or at weekends but also during family holidays. Indeed, among all the nationalities the single most frequent place (half) to spend holidays was property belonging to the families of either wife or husband. Among the French (including the French married to foreign wives), almost two-thirds went at least sometimes on holiday in the wife's family property and more than half to the husband's family 'estate'. About two-fifths did so much more frequently, saying that they used such property often or very often.

Use of family property plays a central role in the upkeep of kinship links. Some hold property in the mountains, some by the sea, some in the country. Visits made there are usually the occasion, at least in France, for reunions with other family members – siblings and cousins as well as uncles, aunts and grandparents, often in very large family parties. In this way, contacts are maintained and ties reinforced. The group of immediate family members present at a holiday house is usually supplemented by the presence of friends or of persons linked to cousins by affinal relationships quite distant to any given person. Given the homogamous nature of marriage in this milieu and the socially very limited origins of students attending the best educational institutions in most European countries, it is very likely that these extra 'cousins' extend the field of 'appropriate' and useful contacts. Many will themselves occupy central positions in similar family networks and be from similar schools, their presence perhaps creating links with students from different years from the same school or between schools. Such gatherings also are frequently the occasion for family networks to be reinforced by the creation of new links, for the cousins of one group frequently meet future marriage partners there, thus making them closer cousins and doubling up existing links by creating new ties between given individuals. Thus, in one French example, an affinal cousin present as a guest at such a house met and married a cousin of the other family, thus bringing whole groups of people already linked distantly into much closer relationships, with all their attendant rights and duties.

Family possession of properties is also important for another reason. Access to places appropriately located allows a relatively young couple, on a relatively low income, to maintain a life style which both confirms them as members of their class of origin and indicates their suitability for occupancy of higher posts. To be seen at the right places, the right ski resorts in winter and the right watering places in summer, is important both for the symbolic capital involved and for the social and quasi-professional contacts that can be made or confirmed by simultaneous presence. To gain these benefits it is not necessary for any given respondent to *own* the properties involved but only to have *access* to them. The high rents charged on the market for such places mean that access early in careers is impossible for those without the appropriate family backgrounds.

In such ways, the social capital provided by kinship substitutes for the direct ownership of economic capital by any individual and makes clear the sense in which the yield on capital may be received even though the contribution of any individual to the group may be delayed until that person in turn is able to supply the necessary property. Kinship links suffice, at least until inheritance occurs, and provide an 'anticipated' inheritance.

Economic capital

Access to economic wealth is, as Townsend says, not a passive factor in life chances. 'It provides advantages in securing admission to top private schools, supplementing education, offering the surroundings and leisure to meet well-endowed individuals of the opposite sex, secure credit and launch new businesses [and] offset risks' (1979, quoted Scott, 1982: 119). Considerable amounts of economic capital are available in this milieu as the earlier discussion of the business positions of fathers, grandfathers and other relatives has suggested. Moreover, as Lord Lytton remarked in 1893, 'the very possession of money at certain stages of life gives assurance to the manner and ... attraction to the address' (quoted Lewis and Stewart, 1961: 86).

Social and economic capital combine, recombine and reinforce each other, conferring cumulative advantages. Both kinds of capital are transferred and linked through marriage and similarly combine and accumulate. Economic capital can be transferred by families and wives at marriage or brought to the marriage over a longer period. It may be given as directly utilisable capital assets or money income, or it may take the form of the contribution to effective income that the 'non-working' wife makes by providing services that would otherwise have to be paid for, such as elaborate cooking and the organisation of entertainment as well as every day childcare and the design and maintenance of the home as an appropriate symbol of status and attitudes. The capital transferred at the marriage of respondents in this study was both in the form of wedding presents, brought by guests from both sides of the family and friends and in itself not inconsiderable, and in the form of a 'dowry', assets provided by the bride's father (or other relatives) to the bride on marriage.

The wedding presents given jointly to both partners were important assets for the couple. Half of the INSEAD wives had received cash as presents. Between 9 and 10 % of the non-French and 28.5 % of the French had received shares. Between 35 % and 39 % had received furniture and between 55 % and 65 % other major presents. Some of these 'other' presents were of considerable value. 9 % had received real property (flats and houses) while 8 % had received cars. The value of the presents thus contributes considerably to the young couples' ability to establish themselves at once in domestic environments appropriate to their status, measured both in terms of their families of origin and in terms of their expected future position.

Almost one-third of INSEAD wives declared that they had received a dowry. These proportions are enormous in relation to the total population and only somewhat lower than those which Girard (1964) found in France among families of roughly equivalent status but an older generation. The importance of the assets concerned is indicated by the high proportion of respondents (40 %) that had 'separate assets' (*séparation de biens*) marriage contracts protecting control by each family of origin of property transferred at or during marriage.

Where wives did not bring real estate as a 'dowry', families of origin also sometimes helped the young couple with the purchase of that most expensive item, a house or a flat, usually through money gifts and loans. A quarter lived in their own or family property after marriage; a quarter received family financial help with the purchase of their own house or flat, while other families contributed to the young couple's housing budget in kind, by allowing them to live in a house or flat owned by parents or relatives. One respondent reported that she had lived for some years in a family house in the fashionable 6th *arrondissement* of Paris. The house had five floors and each floor contained a household of cousins. As their financial situation improved, some moved out, to be instantly replaced by younger cohorts of relatives. Young members of the family were thus able to live in comfortable and elegant surroundings in an area of Paris which they would not otherwise have been able to afford. Many such houses in European cities have been bought as investments over the generations and now serve effectively as income in kind for family members, the owners relying on capital gain as a return on investment rather than on recurrent yield.

The wives also contributed money income to the marriage. Three-quarters of them had worked full-time before marriage and a further 8 % part-time. This proportion dropped considerably on marriage but, nevertheless, among the couples already married when the husband prepared his MBA, two-fifths of the wives worked full-time during that period and a further fifth part-time. Their incomes must have been important in maintaining the family while the husband was a student. At the time of the study, while the proportions working full and part-time were very different, more than half the wives had jobs outside the home, 28 % full-time and 28 % part-time. For some periods at least, therefore, the wives contribute economic capital directly to the household in the form of earned income. Just under half put their incomes into joint household expenditure, while the rest was divided between their own and their children's needs, or used as savings.

There were variations between nationalities in the proportions of wives working. The most likely to have worked or to be working at least part-time were the British (84 %), followed by the Germans and the Scandinavians (each 73 %), the Swiss (78 %) and the French (70.5 %). The least likely to be or to have been working were the Belgians (55 %) and the Dutch (57 %). The jobs they did varied little from those of their mothers. Much like their mothers and their husbands' mothers, they mostly remained in 'feminine' fields, although there was some movement towards the 'harder' professions. Of those who were working at the time of the study or who had ever worked, either full or part-time, the Belgians were the most likely to be teachers or secretaries (64 %), followed by the Swiss (50 %), the Scandinavians (44 %), the British and the French (each 33 %) and the Germans (32 %). While such jobs are not extremely well paid, they have the advantage of ensuring the free time necessary for the maintenance of the appropriate lifestyle and for activating family connections. They are also translatable across national frontiers.

Those wives who did not have professional lives also clearly contributed to the economy of the household. Even though many families employed domestic help, most wives were the domestic managers, organising child-rearing and education, managing the daily budget, enduring the production of the many social and professional or semi-professional dinners both frequent and elaborate in this milieu, performing many domestic tasks and, of course, arranging the family holidays and visits which ensure continuity of contact. Most important, perhaps, it was the wives who managed the families' frequent international moves. Many also had private incomes that contributed to savings, to household expenses and to private education for the children.

Cultural capital

The wives' activities at home, however, must be seen as having more than simply an economic or even social capital value. To use Andrée Michel's term,

Table 7.7 *Occupations of wives (percentages of respondents)*

	INSEAD	INSEAD[a] French 1974
Secretarial and other office workers	23	23
Teachers/research staff	20.5[b]	27.5
Business managers[c]	11	6
Lawyers	4	—
Doctors/pharmacists/psychologists	5	12
Journalists/public relations personnel/writers	9	8
Translators/interpreters	5	5
Interior decoraters/designers	2	2
Paramedics	2	5
Others[d]	14	14.5
N=	120	128

[a] These figures are averaged over past and present jobs. There were some notable changes over time, especially in the number ceasing to teach
[b] Including 2.52% who were university teachers
[c] Including own and family business
[d] For example, air hostesses

they contribute considerably to the non-material goods, the *biens non-marchands*, that the household has at its disposition. In this milieu, it is the wives who are principally responsible for the style and quality of the decoration of the domestic interior which provides the setting to which their husbands can invite guests and colleagues and which 'places' him in relation to others. Bourdieu, Delsaut and their colleagues have pointed on numerous occasions (e.g. 1975, 1976, 1979) to the combination of the elements of an interior into a particular style that 'distinguishes' a person from others, while at the same time it suggests a set of attitudes and beliefs that is associated with the style. Comparisons between the interior decor, eating habits, vestimentary choices and cultural activities of some social groups in comparison with others indicate ways in which, for instance, members of the 'new' bourgeoisie distinguish themselves from their 'old' counterparts, while the cost, quality and exclusivity of the elements of their lifestyle still mark them off as belonging clearly to the upper classes.

Wives are, of course, also responsible to a very large extent for the raising of the couple's children, because of both the long hours worked and the frequent trips away made by their husbands. The wives' values and the attitudes and aspirations which they instil are particularly important. So, to the busy husband, are the cultural activities in which the wives participate or which they organise for them both, for, especially in cities such as Paris, one of the important ways in which a man is 'judged' is through his knowledge of trends on the cultural scene. The extent to and way in which wives do this is, of course, itself in part a function of the *éducation* which they themselves received as children, for cultural capital is composed of two elements, the configuration of attitudes known as 'taste' and the cultural knowledge inculcated through formal education and symbolised in the possession of specific educational credentials.

The wives were indeed highly educated in the formal system and hence well able to advise on and supervise their children's educational choices and careers. Nine-tenths had successfully completed secondary education, including about 5 % who had done so abroad. Just under half – a very high proportion in relation to their age cohorts in the total population, but common for their class – had attended a university. Of these almost 46 % had obtained a first degree, 15 % a master's degree and 12 % a doctorate, while 10 % or so had done 'professional' degrees with a different structure, such as medicine or architecture.

The subjects they studied were still very largely the 'feminine' ones, although there were some movement away. Particularly useful in this milieu, one-third had studied languages and literature, of which by far the greatest proportion were those of cultures foreign to them. Another fifth were distributed across a wide range of disciplines, including arts, classics, history and geography, all culturally valuable to the lives they lead.

Wives also organised both the cultural and the sporting activities in which their families participated and which were those both typical and socially expected of members of their group across Europe. The overwhelming majority of both respondents and wives practised at least one sport regularly. The favourite was tennis followed by skiing, swimming and horse-riding. These sports all have one characteristic important to this milieu: they are transnational, easily exportable and the key to new and appropriate social contacts when the family has to relocate. Bridge, played by many, provides a similar key, as several respondents pointed out.

The wives, thus, both participate in many activities and manage the social, sporting and cultural calendar of the household. Active in a wide range of cultural events, visiting regularly theatre, cinema, exhibition halls and art galleries, reading specialist journals, magazines, books and newspapers in a variety of languages, the women keep the household abreast of the current scene, political, social and cultural. And they can do this in most countries of Europe for the number of languages they spoke outstripped even that of their husbands: two-thirds spoke three or four languages, 10 % five and 4 % six languages or more, while only 2 % spoke their mother tongue alone. In all, more than three-quarters of the wives spoke between three and eight languages, skills particularly useful to women called upon to manage a husband's international career where the family is highly mobile and settling into the new country is in practice very largely left to the wife. The pattern was summarised by one wife who remarked that even her children were quadrilingual – English herself, married to an Austrian working for an American bank, over the preceding five years she had set up house in France, Belgium, England and Sweden, where she was at the time of the study. To the two languages at home had been added French, some Flemish and Swedish. Another, an Italian married to a Dutchman living in Brussels, explained that her two children, both under five, spoke Dutch with their father, Italian with her, English, the only common language of the household, with both parents together, and French at their nursery school. The women are managing not only their own and their husbands' international lives but also the special environments of their children, while not losing contact with wider families and attempting to maintain some emotional stability in the household.

This task is especially demanding because international careers not only demand the frequent relocation of the family but also require that many husbands travel incessantly from any given base. Many of the men spend at least 40 % of their time travelling and a considerable number up to 60 or 70 % of their working life outside their own offices. Even when 'at home', many work very long days, between fifty and seventy-five hours a week, so that 'home' is the office rather than the house. The wives' managerial skills thus become essential for the maintenance of domestic order in a range of activities from the provision of an endless succession of clean clothes to the proper *éducation* of the children. The wives' own education and the attitudes, values and skills they received from their own mothers, are thus brought to the husband and their companies as both back-up and back-drop to international business careers.

Moreover, while contributing their labour, and their income if working outside the home, to the maintenance of the household, the wives seldom pursued careers that conflicted with those of their husbands. Recognising the importance of their role as domestic managers, many explicitly gave this as the reason for not taking an outside job, mentioning also the need for an impeccable house 'because of visitors', the need to organise receptions and social occasions and 'to entertain guests' (for 70 % entertained for business purposes at home) and the necessity in the absence of the husband 'for children to have one parent at least'. Many felt that the decision was also right on moral was well as practical grounds, for 'traditional family values are important' and wives should 'be free for both husband and children'. While some dissented and felt their own careers important, only a very few would be prepared to argue for equality and fewer still to consider following the example of one couple where each partner lived and worked in different countries and the family 'lived in both Paris and Milan'. More acceptable would be the model of the American wife managing in Germany the household of three young French- and English-speaking children while her German husband worked in Paris, returning only once a month for a period of

8. A family of beliefs and character

The world of management, like any other professional milieu, has its own symbols of excellence and has developed a language which, by concentrating on certain characteristics and qualities, 'explains' the success of its members. Many studies have shown that managers (in common with others) attribute their success to personal qualities rather than credentials or track record, while in the management world there continues to rage a nature–nurture debate about the extent to which managers are 'born' or 'made'.

It is clear from this study that managers are both born *and* made. As very many of those who attend INSEAD are from families whose male heads occupy positions in the most senior echelons of the business world, many MBAs have been born into the business world in a literal sense. The normal processes of child-rearing and family interaction inculcate in them a view of themselves, their qualities and their place in the world which makes them the direct heirs to a particular view both of the 'nature' of a manager and of the 'natural' place of business in the social and economic orders of Europe. The same period of their lives also allows them to develop a strong sense of their own worth and a considerable faith in their own abilities. Above all, it allows them direct access to socially dominant definitions of 'character' and the values which the definition implies, as well as with early opportunities to develop these themselves. They are constantly bathed in informal advice about the behaviours and reactions which are desirable in business. They are early able to seize the nuances of acceptable rhetoric and to absorb the subtle distinctions involved in debates about acceptance of the need to 'modernise' and 'move with the times' while maintaining the essentials of the socio-economic structure – and the organisation of private business – intact. Formal education and informal *éducation* combine to make them obviously eligible to become the quintessential 'young Turks' of many business modernisation strategies, while the companies which employ them can remain confident about the 'soundness' of their underlying values and judgements. Combining the skills gained from 'nurture' and the qualities with which they have been

153

endowed by 'nature', they are well equipped to guide the acceptance of change while also ensuring the desired continuity.

Candidates for routes to top positions who are not from families high in the business world of Europe's major countries are less able initially to present themselves as the possessors of the 'nature' appropriate to top management careers. Young men from the public sector or professional, and, *a fortiori* backgrounds on the 'other side' of industry, with values perceived as different if not antithetical to those of business, need to prove their loyalty and, above all, to learn the language which characterises élite managers. Passage through INSEAD is one mechanism which allows them to do both, for its values are clearly those of business, while the business language taught there not only is perceived by many employers as belonging to those at the forefront of management's professionalised world but also guarantees that those who use it will find colleagues across Europe who understand and justly appreciate the skills which possession of the MBA symbolises. The language learned is the 'universal' one of 'management', crossing national frontiers and allowing its user to participate sensibly in decision-making processes in a wide variety of countries, sectors, and companies. The values implicit in that language match well those suggested by Bourdieu and his colleagues as characterising the 'new' business bourgeoisie. Possession of it facilitates full acceptance in the managerial world of those whose origins are outside it, while also allowing them a sense of fellowship with colleagues elsewhere, thereby strengthening their sense of the 'rightness' of their managerial approaches.

In their 'Encyclopédie de la Technocratie', Bourdieu and his colleagues (1976) pointed to the 'modernising' language developed and adopted in France in the post-war decades up to the 1960s by politicians and businessmen alike and to the conserving nature of the discourse thus developed. Emphasising that the theory of social change presented through the discourse defines the desirable mechanism of change as 'evolution' rather than 'revolution' and the end-state as 'modernity' with little clear content except 'state-of-the-art' technology, the 'Encyclopédie' illustrates the manner in which a perceived need for alterations in the methods of business and the structure of the economy could be incorporated into an apparently neutral process of 'modernisation' presented as the 'progress' all were seeking. In particular, only one set of social and economic projects could be desirable because only one set could be characterised as 'modern'. In the early post-war period especially, the development of the discourse was part of the search for the 'third way' of social and economic change desired by many public people. Central to their image of the 'third way' was a belief in good 'management' as the deciding element in economic choices, as the essence of the appropriate economic role for government and as the means of reconciling the interests of the social partners. Internationally, 'progress' lay in 'Europeanism' and the Common Market, as an economic stimulant and as a political mechanism for unifying Western Europe, notably against possible threats from the Eastern areas, as well as overcoming the internal conflicts of the recent past. As the economy developed and Europe stabilised politically, 'third-way' rhetoric gave way to an emphasis on social 'progress' through economic growth in the common interest of all: 'management' has thus, in the European context at least, always carried a heavy-value load and implied a whole social and political view.

These 'consensus' views are present in the discourse of INSEADs, as seen in their statements made on application to the Institute and in interviews carried out in 1980 with alumni. The nature–nurture debate and beliefs about the most appropriate qualities of a manager, as seen in descriptions of self, slip easily into descriptions of socially desirable attributes and acceptable political attitudes, and ultimately into the internationalism consonant with the belief in the desirability of a united Europe and the 'management', social, political and economic, of Western Europe as a whole. Like Jacques Delors, INSEADs typically 'attach much importance to the strategy of change' and, like Prince Poniatowski, they believe that 'the will for progress and modernity must overcome the rule of ideologies which sacrifice the future to the past', (quoted Bourdieu and Boltanski, 1976).

Successful characters

Emphasis on personal qualities and particular skills in explaining a manager's success or failure is important as a legitimating device within a competitive individualistic system, because it diverts attention away from the structure of the enterprise, whether managerial or productive, and from the social structure of opportunity, and gives all the explanatory weight to individual factors. An individual who 'fails' thus takes all the blame and, while some of the structures surrounding the 'failure' may subsequently be modified, emphasis on individual performance as a basis for promotion remains intact, underlining the ideology of individual leadership, both in the enterprise and, by extension, the society.

INSEADs, like most managers, believe strongly in the importance of individual characteristics and have developed an explanation for their success which combines the 'modern' and the conservative. They believe particularly strongly in 'character'. Speaking of the character traits they divine in themselves, these young managers evidence both a belief in the qualities of 'dynamism' and 'creativity' and in the importance of the 'sense of human relations' identified by Bourdieu and others as the mark of the modern manager, which they blend with more traditional views of the qualities needed of the *patron*. They see themselves as possessing 'self-confidence and modesty', 'intellectual rigour without "cleverness"', combining openness of mind with firm convictions about correct behaviour, tenacity without rigidity, the ability to be both analytical and practical, to have 'character' and to know how to command but yet retain adaptability and sociability, to be ambitious without being one-sided. Even the apparently 'negative' traits they admit to, such as 'coldness of approach' or 'stubbornness', may be useful qualities in business. At the same time as they use these terms to describe themselves, they also use them to explain implicitly why it is that they will be successful: the mix of the traditional *patron* with the modern manager is the secret. Writing at application to the Institute, they declared:

At once very realistic and fond of action in all its forms, I like to be confronted with difficult problems . . . For a long time I was very shy but responsibilities I have taken on have little by little made me lose this trait . . . [I have] *the will to succeed.* Life for me is a service one renders rather than a personal characteristic.

I am *open-minded* . . . By nature *I am enthusiastic and active.* When a problem has aroused my interest, I *persevere* in studying it until I have completely overcome it. I am . . . *tenacious* in my projects. I have acquired the conviction that *perseverance is a prime factor in success* . . .

I have always lived in a milieu intimately involved in the problems of economic development . . . I have *good practical sense* and *an open mind.* I know that in some circumstances, I have a rather rigid mind and do not welcome contradiction. *I have the mind of my milieu, with its qualities and its defects.*

My frankness is my best trump card because *everyone has confidence in me* . . . I am not selfish but I am not entirely altruistic . . . I like to choose my friends, who I prefer to be small in number but to be for life. I have a strong character [*caractère entier*] and *I like to be right.* I am very sensitive . . . I don't like to do anything by halves and everything interests me on condition I don't go into it too deeply. I don't like reading but I like to discuss matters without showing off my knowledge too much . . . I do everything *conscientiously* . . . *I abhor laziness* and I feel sorry for those *who don't know how to occupy their leisure time intelligently.*

I am said to *have character*, to be *active, serious, reflective, polished, sociable* and to like the *happy medium.* People reproach me with *not being very conciliatory*, with often *preferring my interest to that of others*, with being sometimes *distant* and rather *jesuitical.* I have an *open mind* and cannot remain unmoved by a problem I know I could do something about. When I am prevented from acting, I sometimes make bitter comments about the obstacles I meet. *Above all else, I appreciate efficiency, and work well organised, properly carried out and finished off.*

Strongwilled, positive, I am at once *active* and *sensitive* but my nature is *phlegmatic*, well balanced. I have a mind that is *concrete* but *generalist* and I am quite *ambitious.* My qualities are *curiosity*, good facilities of *adaptation*, a *taste* for *human relations* and for *authority*, the *will to succeed.* On the other hand, I am ill-served by a nature that is not very outgoing and at first sight gives an impression of coldness.

By character I am rather *optimistic* but I remain *conscious of my responsibilities* and I keep a sense of *duty.* *Work does not frighten* me and I find *much satisfaction in accomplishing a task perfectly.* By character fairly *independent,* I am nonetheless sociable and I *participate well in a group.* I am a bit too sensitive in the sense of emotions, I remain *faithful* to certain *ideals* and *principles* while also being open-minded.

I have a taste for *new situations . . .* a faculty for *adaptation* to new problems, a *taste* for *travel* and for *change* in general. I think I also have a good *psychological* sense, good humour and I am calm. On the other hand, I have an *independent character* and can be *slightly selfish.*

Many such characteristics are, of course, a result of family *éducation* in the milieu common to so many in this study, an *éducation* recognised by the respondent who said that he had the spirit of his *milieu* with its qualities and faults. Another, too, specifically acknowledged the role which his parents had played both in shaping his character and in endowing him with a sharp sense of duty:

I am grateful to my parents for my happy childhood to which I owe a good *emotional stability* and an *acute sense of duty.* In increasing order of importance, I think my main qualities are gaiety, curiosity, *tenacity* and a certain *taste for teamwork.* I think, however, that all these characteristics are dominated by my *will*, a will which is based on reflection and discussion and which influences all my actions. It is this *will* which I consider to be the *major quality* of my character. But this same will engenders a certain apparent coldness which hides my sociability and which is often interpreted as shyness . . . That also comes from a certain *sangfroid* that I do not seek to overcome.

These lists of individual qualities and defects match extraordinarily well the stated views of employers on what a manager should 'be like'. In one survey (Harmon, 1977) where businessmen across Europe were asked what they thought of on hearing the word 'manager', more than half of the survey's respondents put personal traits and leadership quality first. Such factors as 'leadership, ability to communicate, social attitude, ability for teamwork, persuasiveness' went with 'sense of responsibilities, performance of duties, creative talent, superior technical knowledge and skills, decisiveness, personality, broad general knowledge, readiness to accept risks, vitality, ability to make things happen, intelligence'. The survey concluded that it is clear therefore that:

The director and manager must have a good general education, good breeding, ability to command, psychological talents

and that:

A man in a leading position has a distinctive personality, good professional knowledge, strength, energy, common sense, leadership qualities, knowledge of human nature, organisational talents and rational thinking.

He must therefore have:

Character, knowledge, corrected and improved by experience. The manager is determined by his character. Education and knowledge rank in second place . . . A manager must be vigorous, healthy, obliging and just.

(Harmon, 1977: 14)

Or, as a leading French businessman put it two decades ago:

I believe no-one can say 'I trained a *patron*!' You can give skills to a man but he will still lack certain elements given by nature, innate in the human being and in the *patron* who will become a good *patron: human contact, ability to command, sense of responsibility* . . . The *dicton* 'chase away what's natural, it will come back at a gallop' applies equally in business. If you don't like to command, if you don't like human contact or if you don't like responsibility or if nature did not give you these three qualities . . . you will never be a good *patron!*

(Michel Calmettes, *Président-Directeur-Général* of the Société des Produits du Maïs, quoted in an unsigned article in *Enterprise*, 26 May 1962: 53)

Again, as a spokesman for Renault pointed out in 1977,

We're not recruiting for a post but for a professional life and therefore qualities of character are very important.

(Quoted Fontaine, 1977: 68)

The majority seem to believe that the most that business education can achieve is the development or 'bringing out' of innate talents and abilities. As Xardel sums it up:

Let's be clear; in a [business] school one acquires information [*connaissances*], one can develop aptitudes already existing in an embryonic state, but one can hardly create them.

(1978: 25)

The manager who succeeds is said to need qualities of 'openness', 'intuition', or 'sensitivity' with regard to other people, which he must possess in quantities greater than those of the common herd. The French Foundation for Management Education itself even went so far as to state:

Management is an art. It can therefore not be taught, even if one can develop it. It cannot be described rationally in its entirety and in its substance, even if one apprehends certain of its aspects. *It is an affair of character and of personal qualities.*

(Quoted in Xardel, 1978: 61, emphasis added)

INSEADs explanations for their success are exactly in this mould, as became clear in the interviews in 1980.

From 1961 to 1971 [my career consisted of] an evolution within the confines of the company, very interesting and very rich. I have good memories of it. It gave me a good training as well as some responsibilities. In 1971 I joined the bank. *I was sure I would succeed. I had a strong internal conviction,* accompanied by *in-depth knowledge of the profession.* I am still concentrating on what I do – that's one of my principles. *I am a banker to the very marrow of my bones:* it's the only thing that interests me. I like this *métier, the independence and responsibility* it entails . . . I've always had responsibility even at the BNP. I had intelligent superiors who had confidence in me. I know I was lucky. *But you also have to know how to make the most of luck. I took a risk* when I joined the Y. bank and again when I took over the X. bank. In the first, there were 140 employees – in the second, 6,000.

(French, French bank, Paris, 1960)

While others emphasised a mixture of 'competence' and 'flair' when explaining their successful career, the explanation is still individual.

It was the sector in which I could feel *most competent.* Partly my success was thanks to my *past experience* (at INSEAD I was the student rep.), partly it was because I have a *feeling* for this kind of work and partly because it's a job that means you have *to get results* (as it is in advertising). I wouldn't go into consulting for anything in the world! *There you do nothing but diagnose* – most frustrating!

(French, 1974, American company, Paris, interviewed 1973 and 1980)

Indeed, their motivations for the work they were doing emphasised the rewards accruing to individual determination, not to the teamwork or 'human relations' said by some observers to characterise the modern manager. The rhetoric of employers may emphasise the team; the reality of business success relies on and rewards the individual.

My main motivation for this *métier?* The fact that one can *progress intellectually, one can't go to sleep* like those who remain in industry . . . In this *métier* you can *progress much more quickly* than in industry. Salaries are similar to those paid in industry but there's more *work* and above all *more risk* – *one failure and you're shown the door.* That's what I like.

(French, 1974, multinational consulting firm, Paris,
interviewed 1974 and 1980)

It is recognition by the company of both specific skills and personal qualities which makes further promotion possible:

After 7 or 8 years of business experience the diploma hardly matters. Its rather the *results obtained* that count, the *success* one's hand in the posts one has filled and especially one's success in human relations (*rapid adaptation to new situations, capacity for working in a group, knowing how to be flexible while at the same time keeping one's sights on a specific objective).* There is one exception to this rule: big multinational firms are more willing to hire people with high-level credentials than are small or medium companies. *For them it's a guarantee.*

(Swiss, 1975, British multinational, Paris)

As one summed it up, 'you have to work hard, really keep at it. I think I have succeeded'; another said, 'I must have an enterprising spirit.'

These analyses of the way in which individuals demonstrate talent and successfully manage companies can be seen to reflect the most typical bourgeois values of success through enterprise (whether managerial or independent) supported by work, ambition, and duty, with rewards accruing to the individual. It is the individual leader who is recognised in spite of the need to thank a 'team'. Moreover, only occasionally does the aristocratic notion that life should be fun and that work, if it has to be undertaken at all, should be a means of entertainment, leaven the mix. Even here, however, the fun lies not only in doing but also in the possibility of increasing individual rewards.

I think *I am not really a man of the big machine*, advertising *continues to amuse me*. Sometimes I wish I had a bigger organisation, that I didn't have to do everything myself because managing and controlling everything don't amuse me . . . *What amuses me is earning money* and advertising is a means of doing that without needing a lot of capital at the outset.

(Belgian, 1963, American company, Brussels)

The successful contrast strikingly with the other extreme, the failures, depressed by their situations but still explaining their lack of success by personal qualities:

I won't climb much higher because *I don't have the qualities necessary for climbing* . . . Personally, one can accept not climbing but *one is constantly pushed by one's family* and friends . . . You need a particular kind of philosophy not to climb . . . In a bank you need *a certain aggressivity to climb* because *nowadays there's very little promotion*.

(Belgian, 1976, Belgian bank, Brussels)

They explain that they are 'too prudent' to make the changes necessary for promotion:

Changing company? I don't know. Top managers or those in the hierarchy in positions just underneath them say they would agree to move, but in fact they don't go because they can't find anything elsewhere. Here salaries are very high. *Of course one can agree to a drop in salary if in exchange one expects to move up but now is no longer the moment, there is a malaise everywhere. There's no will to take risks* and to be *no longer protected by years of service*. Here there is little turnover in personnel . . . you see, the picture is black . . . I nevertheless keep an eye on what's happening outside but *by a certain age it's hard to change. I'm nearly 40 . . . One becomes perhaps too prudent* . . . [but] an enterprise won't take on anyone just average. The crisis has favoured people of a *higher level*.

(Belgian, 1976, Belgian bank, Brussels)

The world thus continues to be seen by the successful and the failures alike as one in which it is individual attributes, individual efforts and individual enterprise that count. The value of the individual both underwrites activity at work and is the justification for the hierarchical structure of the enterprise and beyond it for the stratification of the surrounding society.

Ideological internationalism and political concern

Part of the process of creation of an élite is the definition of its boundaries through a common belief system and adherence to values reinforced by activities in which only group members take part. The public activities in which they engage as part of or in addition to their professional responsibilities and the beliefs which they bring to them are an important element in the definition of a group seen both as the 'moderniser' of business and the beginning of a 'new' national or transnational business élite with the power for dissemination of ideas which that position implies.

The views about the organisation of the world and the place of business within it which alumni from INSEAD hold are important because they are people who occupy responsible positions in their professional lives. Many hold or will hold positions of influence inside the business world, in companies and business organisations, and their views extend beyond that world to the public domain, through activity in politics, local or national, in education and other public organisations. Many are or one day will be running companies, small or large, be advising others on how to reorganise their enterprises or, increasingly, be advising on the reorganisation of institutions in the public sector and, directly or indirectly, be advising government on a wide range of policies in interaction with public officials and politicians. To both private sector and public spheres they bring approaches and values which are given legitimacy and force by the positions they hold. Through the interviews, it became clear that there was an enormous diversity of opinion both about 'what' the INSEAD MBA person essentially was and whether that person had characteristics that distinguished him or her from others. Some respondents clearly went to INSEAD with a more or less strong value-commitment to the idea of a united Europe and of contributing themselves during their careers to the realisation of that ideal, while others simply saw Europe as a professional stage. There was also much disagreement about the extent to which it was either possible or desirable for people in business careers to be involved in politics or public institutions and activities of different kinds. Behind these divergences, however, there lay a considerable amount of common ground.

Some of this common ground appeared in their political orientations. Essentially, they felt themselves to occupy the centre of the political field. Two-thirds of the respondents to the questionnaire situated themselves politically in the middle of the spectrum, either in the Centre or the Centre-Right (together almost half) or the Centre-Left (16 %). It is sometimes said that one may associate a belief in a neutral 'efficiency', especially in the management of what is seen as the 'economy', with adherence to the 'technocratic' policies and discourse of parties such as that headed in the 1970s by Giscard d'Estaing in France and an avoidance of the extremes in both policy and discourse of the kind which became evident in the 1980s in the UK and the USA. This seems to be borne out here, for members of the group both believed that government was essentially about good management and supported centrist parties. The great majority were advocates of moderate positions on the current European political scene. Relatively few were prepared to admit that they were on the Right (14%) or far Right (0.3%), and even fewer on the Left (2%) or far Left (0.3%).

Part of that avoidance of political extremes may arise from their 'internationalism' and 'Europeanism', both of which generally involve the feeling that many of the problems of the twentieth century in Europe have been the result of extremism, of political nationalism in particular. There seems to be a sense in which 'Europeanism' is perceived as being 'anti-ideological', as a means of bringing together of people of 'good will' in different countries to solve problems in a mutually acceptable manner. To that extent, internationalism or Europeanism as a value implies a belief in a process of negotiation, of reaching common terms, of seeking solutions rather than imposing policies or politics, using national entities rather than class as the unit of analysis. It also encourages people to think beyond national boundaries and thus, in the present context, to concentrate on similarities between countries rather than on political differences internal to any given country's system.

Moreover, to the extent that 'Europe' has yet (pre-1992) to be made in any political sense, a belief in 'Europe' implies that those who share in it dissociate themselves from the political stances taken by extreme parties in any European country and brings them closer to parties which seem to believe most strongly in the same road, effectively in practice the 'centrist', or some social-democratic ones in their various guises.

To some extent, too, a belief in Europeanism may militate against active political involvement and encourage a 'supra-political' stance, a feeling that *la politique politicienne*, politicians' politics, necessarily involves deals which can only operate at a national level and which are therefore inappropriate. Moreover their professionalised management, ultimately technocratic, views of the world suggest that politicians' decisions are based on criteria which lead to outcomes that are not 'efficient' in their use of resources – and probably extremely 'inefficient' – and are therefore not worthy of considerable personal involvement. In this professed attachment to a Centrist political stance can often be seen an association in Europe with the 'technocratic' ideas about the management of the economy and with the political language, developed especially in France, by post-war political and business intellectuals, such as Lionel Stoléru or François Dalle. Their language expresses a search for 'consensus' and 'progress' which is often associated with the Centre or Centre-Right.

The economico-political beliefs expressed by INSEAD MBAs are developed, modified and disseminated by everyday contacts with the national and international political worlds of Europe. Through both their work and other activities they act as transmitters of ideas from the private to the public sector. Their internationalism and their geographical mobility do not prevent alumni making frequent contacts with politicians, notably in the course of their professional lives. Many work in politically sensitive fields and banking and consulting especially involve close and continuing contacts with governments, both with politicians and with public servants. A professional concern with political issues and decisions frequently spills over into social gatherings and stimulates political and policy interests at the same time as it provides opportunities for the expression of views and exchange of information with political representatives. Many respondents declared an increasingly lively interest in politics, as one said, 'by necessity and utility'. A number, notably in Britain, Germany and Switzerland, emphasised particularly the frequency of both professional and social mixing with representatives of the political world both in the countries in which they lived and worked at any one time and elsewhere.

I'm interested in politics and I have both professional and friendly contacts with members of governments and social links with many politicians.

(German, 1969, American bank, Frankfurt)

I have lots of friendly links with politicians. We belong to the same clubs. I'm interested in politics, both at *canton* and federal level. I have lots of contact with governments in several countries.

(Swiss, 1972, Swiss firm, Zurich)

I'm interested in both national and international politics and I'm active in the political arena. I have a lot of contacts with the government at Ministerial level and I know personally many politicians both in Switzerland and in Germany where I was brought up.

(German, 1968, Swiss consulting firm, Zurich)

I have many professional contacts with several governments and lots of social links with politicians.

(Swiss, 1972, international legal firm, Zurich)

I have social contacts with members of the government and with many other politicians.

(Swiss, 1965, Swiss firm, Geneva)

The close connections between business and politics in the banking world in particular were indicated by several respondents. One described his role as follows:

I take part in no political activity but I have frequent contacts with politicians, or rather very often with ex-politicians, taken on by the bank precisely because of their network of contacts. I also work for one government. And France is much interested in its ex-colonies . . . The Elysée wants to know what we're doing in Gabon, as does the

Ministry of Foreign Affairs in London. In London, political dinners are frequently held. We only go as bankers . . . A bank is an apolitical organisation but it necessarily has political impact because of its activities.

(British, 1973, British multinational bank, London)

Close contacts with politicians on the social and more informal levels may be much easier in countries with a federal political structure, such as Switzerland, Germany and Austria, because there many important political decisions are taken outside the federal capitals at State (*canton* or *Länder*) levels which frequently contain only one major city. But they also occur elsewhere, for even internationally-oriented businessmen work in the same city, live in the same *quartiers*, frequent the same clubs and restaurants, and play tennis on the same courts as politicians with considerable power. The frequency of 'chance' everyday contacts between private businessmen and public decision-makers in the normal course of living a fairly prosperous life is considerable everywhere; the dominance of the capital city in most European countries and the tendency of the majority of respondents to live in the fashionable areas of their cities facilitate interaction between senior public- and private-sector decision-makers. This geographical concentration is particularly high in cities such as Paris, as we saw in an earlier chapter, but also occurs in London as well as in smaller capitals such as Brussels and Stockholm. For respondents who work 'internationally' but who reside in their cities of origin the INSEAD network is added on to existing *grande école* or family connections, multiplying the effectiveness of each and multiplying the possibilities of formal and informal interaction with a variety of worlds. As international managers move back 'home', so their ideas find more powerful channels of dissemination and their ideas may become more influential.

In contrast to the frequency of their social and professional interaction with the public sector, respondents seldom engage directly in political or community activity. A fifth of those questioned, however, did belong to a political party and a few even envisaged a political career later on. One, a member of the British Liberal Party, recognised that he had very little hope of a political career but 'if things change I might go into politics'. Others, who felt strongly on issues such as the creation of a political 'Europe' were paradoxically excluded from a political career which could give power to their ideas by the very fact of their internationalism – as well as more material considerations.

I'm interested in politics but I am a multinational. Who would want me? And anyway you have to be rich to take part in politics in England: I have a brother-in-law who's a Minister – he hardly earns more than my secretary!

(German, 1965, American firm, London)

In spite of little opportunity for direct political activity, many implicitly saw their role in life as much wider than purely professional activity, feeling that they had both ideas and ideals and skills to contribute:

I should add that I believe in the future of free enterprise in France and Europe, and so I think that the role of a top business manager [*chef d'entreprise*] must develop much more along the lines of what it has become in the United States, that is, *the role of a man who is responsible not only for his enterprise but also for his city, his environment and his society in general.*

You have to have a certain presence in the local society, in local or neighbourhood activities. It's unimaginable that one doesn't use one's skills in the service of the community.

(Belgian, 1969, American firm, Brussels)

This, however, is largely for later. At the earlier stage of their careers, lacking both time and geographical stability, few contribute actively to business or other organisations, although some were treasurers or secretaries of local associations, very few (11 %) are active in local politics and even fewer (8 %) in local economic or employers' organisations. That involvement is likely to increase, however. Already a third belong to professional associations and between a quarter and a third to business clubs, while two-fifths expressed the intention to join 'when I am older'.

Personal and professional Europeanism

A sense of a common and separate identity as a group is reinforced by personal relationships and ways of living. These strengthen the political orientation towards internationalism and heighten consciousness of the distinctiveness of the international experience of the group: 'being international' is applied and confirmed in daily life. This is, of course, especially true of the group with foreign wives, working for foreign companies in foreign cities, but is also the case for many of the others who work in international environments. The sentiment of personal transnationality or internationalism as lived in daily relationships reinforces the belief that the way forward lies in a political and economic (Western) Europeanism, for it is 'internationals' who are perceived as the most open-minded and progressive. Less locked into national structures and prejudices and ways of thinking than their 'national' counterparts and as a minority group seldom truly 'at home', international managers feel that they are able to perceive problems in more rational terms because of their comparative perspective. Their transnationality is positive; perceiving themselves as the 'true' Europeans and as such as members of a rather special group, Europe as a whole is 'home', both professionally and personally.

I feel European. I consider Europe to be one geographical unit. I have spent 13 years outside my country of birth and *I feel at home everywhere I go*.

(Dutch, 1971, British multinational, Frankfurt)

Yes, I think of Europe as a privileged space for professional mobility; to me *it's all one country*. As a general rule, I feel international although there are still a few areas where I feel German.

(German, 1969, American bank, Frankfurt)

Others both recognised the potential of Europe as a professional field and knew that they would find going to any national 'home' impossible.

I feel cosmopolitan. I have spent 10 years outside my country and re-entry would be difficult. I wouldn't go back now, although my wife would like to live there.

(British, 1970, American bank, Frankfurt)

I feel more European than Dutch. I am an 'international' in the full sense of the term. I feel good like that. I don't have any preference for any country over any other. But yet I don't feel in any way rootless.

(Dutch, 1971, American firm, Paris)

I am thus an international in the full sense of the term. This life suits me well. I feel at home in every country . . . I live both in Paris and Milan as I work in Paris but my family is in Milan.

(Italian, 1969, American company, Paris)

Others made new 'homes' elsewhere.

I was born in one country, brought up in another and I have worked in seven others. I think I'll stay here for a while.

(British, 1972, American firm, Zurich)

A few felt some residual national feeling, but recognised that having lived abroad they also had outsiders' views.

I feel European but not international. You notice that outside Europe. But I also feel Dutch in France. I feel that because there's something I don't like in the mentality of the people.

(Dutch, 1961, American company, Brussels)

I feel more international than European with nonetheless a strong affinity for old Europe. From time to time I feel German, because of the past, especially in France on 8 May and 11 November. But when I go back to Germany, I feel more critical of it. *Because I've lived abroad, I have a different point of view.*

(German, 1969, French firm, Paris)

Many respondents feel less at ease with nationals of their own or their host country than with other transnationals like themselves. Most find purely 'national' social mixing less interesting then international occasions, for 'nationals' make different sets of assumptions and do not share the experience of the international.

Do I feel European? Yes and no. Certainly at a dinner party we prefer to have an Italian, an American, rather than just French people.

(Swiss, 1975, American firm, Paris)

There was, however, the occasional dissonant voice opposing the general consensus that the INSEAD 'family' is one both truly European and a model for others; one person expressed his total disillusion with the European ideal as experienced at INSEAD. He was, perhaps not surprisingly, as Englishman.

I became completely disenchanted about my European vocation at INSEAD. While I was there I became aware of the difference between the French, English and Germans. And I said to myself that the European community would be likely to take a very long time to create!

(English, 1972, English firm, London)

Professional careers reinforce personal 'Europeanism'. Most respondents believe very strongly in the virtues of Europe as an international professional arena and few consider working outside the boundaries of Europe for any length of time. 'I wouldn't go to the Middle East, for example, or to Asia for any length of time – a question of culture and customs.' For most, the USA is a place to spend the early days of a career, to train quickly, especially in areas such as finance which at least at certain times were 'well in advance of Europe', but not a place to stay. In part this is because in most American companies, career prospects are limited: 'The road is blocked. The key posts remain in the hands of Americans.' But choice of workplace is also a matter of values and preferred environment. Europe is their 'country', both professionally and personally. Their careers and their families focus on Europe. Typical of this group is a German, at the time of interview working for an American company in London, who, since gaining his MBA fourteen years before, had worked for a Swiss enterprise in Basle and an American one in Brussels, as well as creating companies in England and Ireland in conjunction with a French and an English partner. He was also on the board of several French firms in France, did a great deal of publicity in the Middle East and New Zealand as well as in Europe and had many contacts with international organisations. While INSEADs divide themselves into two groups – those who are truly international, as is the case for most of those quoted here, and those who go back to their countries of origin, perhaps retaining some international preferences and orientations – many are rarely in their country of origin, or only by chance; they work for foreign firms and feel the whole of Europe to be their special field of operations. They feel themselves as a group to be distinctly European with a few with an even wider world orientation. Such people, at least while building their careers, have no national 'home' and are clearly unlikely to espouse an exclusively national view either about which are the important policy problems faced by enterprises or governments or of possible solutions to them.

Both political or ideological internationalism and belief in a universal managerialism are also reinforced by career structures in multinational companies, which very often involve both frequent relocations and constant travel. As we saw above, many respondents spend at least 40 % of their time travelling and a considerable number so spend 60 %, 70 % or more of their working life. They are thereby in their daily professional lives also constantly reinforcing another important idea, that in every country business problems and decisions share basically the same parameters, are subject to the same opportunities and constraints and are open to solution and control by the same managerial techniques. The issues to be faced may vary temporarily with the state of an economy or with the political complexion of the government of the day but changes are not likely to be seen as fundamental. Working the very long hours which many do may also reinforce in their own minds the image of the MBA as a dynamic European at the very heart of important decisions. Many consider themselves as a group to constitute an international business stratum and for them 'supranationality' in views and in decisions is both a matter of pride and a characteristic they will seek in subordinates, thus reinforcing it down the managerial line. In these ways, their views take on public importance because of their effects on the crucial management decisions of major European companies, regardless of whether as individual citizens they engage in any overtly political activity.

As managers, however, they also know that they must be interested in politics. With this emphasis on the international perspective and their living of a European professional life, respondents stand in marked contrast to more nationally oriented managers. Their views of the role of business in Europe as a whole, which they see as a free enterprise but 'well-managed' economic zone owe much to their transnational outlook and practices. They see large corporations as the essential economic managers of the world stage, the force for the future, both because they see their power and because they see them at the forefront of economic progress. The outstanding economic success of many of the companies they help to direct itself continually suggests to them that such organisations represent the future shape of the European economy. But they also recognise clearly that they share their power with governments. Their fundamental belief in a Europe based on *libre entreprise* is tempered by 'managerialism' and explicit recognition of the importance of government and public authorities in creating the 'right' environment for business. That environment includes a recognition of the role and powers of the other social partners and a good sense of the contingent nature of particular structures and practices. The relativism implicit in an internationalist and essentially comparative perspective allied to the distancing of internationally operating managers from the more established business groups and organisations of their societies of origin seems to mean a belief in 'economism' which also appreciates the importance of public authorities. Just as they see the benefits of 'good management' in an enterprise, so it seems they are prepared to admit a role to government in the good management of the society. This belief fits well into the 'post-ideological' view of modern European politics and especially well into the post-war societies created in Europe, where the economic soon became central to the political, where government and public action form the essential backing to the economy and where most groups implicitly or explicitly espouse the view that the only way to greater social justice lies through increased economic productivity. While in the 1980s in much of Europe that view may seem a little dated, it was the progressive ideology *par excellence* of the 'productivist' group in Europe in the 1960s and 1970s and well fitted the image of the dynamic but socially sensitive corporate entrepreneur. That last image, although tarnished somewhat in the 1970s by corporate failures with employment, remains strong in the 1980s when many companies have become increasingly interested in many aspects of the 'public–private' interface in economic development strategies. Where necessary, these young managers in tougher times can supplement their world view by falling back on the older business values they absorbed in their families of origin.

As a result, the political views of these rising young corporate entrepreneurs are conservatively capitalist but socially aware and comparatively based, not narrowly nationalistic; they recognise the strengths and weaknesses of many systems and respect governments as crucial players in modern economies.

Creating a new family: the 'esprit INSEAD'

To the extent that they subscribe to a central group of political and managerial ideas, as we have seen that they do, INSEAD MBAs have the makings of an international élite which shares more than just background and training. The group and their ideas are developing over time a social presence, and hence political as well as economic power, as they find ways to express and reinforce those ideas and give concrete expression to their beliefs. The sentiment of group unity and mutual recognition is centred on the use of a common but exclusive language, but it is concretised and expressed through mechanisms creating the occasions for interaction, mutual aid and the encouragement of the translation of ideas into practice. INSEAD teaches people to think alike: constant mixing with those of like mind reinforces the sense of unity and difference from others. Joint group activities provide the framework for the exchange of information and ideas and that exchange further creates a sense of obligation for mutual assistance.

The international managerial group of MBAs is first created via the year at INSEAD. The socialising power of the experience at the Institute in forging attachment to the 'esprit INSEAD' must not be underestimated. A study of alumni of an equally intense executive in-service training programme at the Massachusetts Institute of Technology (MIT) found that one of the most powerful features of the Sloan programme was the peer-group ties formed during the tough year. These ties were subsequently one of the key supports to the maintenance of the values and attitudes learned in school. The power of this socialising force can be seen in the fact that alumni stated that whereas before the programme they had identified with their firms, afterwards, they referred rather to the other Sloan fellows (Schein, 1967: 6). At INSEAD, the teaching methods in particular, linking people into small groups for the whole year, have a powerful structuring, unifying and consciousness-creating effect. Linking together people as diverse as engineers, economists, lawyers and arts graduates, British, French, Italians and Germans in a common endeavour in which all must cooperate to succeed in the valued task, the syndicate experience shows how to overcome differences of approach, experience and language and mould a functioning group out of unpromising bedfellows. Such cooperation, tolerance and flexibility, while they occasionally fail, become accepted as the normal way to work and from endless discussions, arguments and analyses, a common approach and a common language emerge.

Once that year is over, the approach and language remain. In all the cities where interviews took place, many MBAs felt that there was indeed an 'esprit INSEAD' and that the INSEAD outlook or approach was expressed through a common language. That language they saw as composed both of technical terms and of nuances, expectations and *sous-entendus*. Bringing together expression of both attitudes and skills, this language was felt by some to be *the* tongue of modern management. They suggested that it had already been or would soon be adopted by top management, particularly in banking, whether Swiss or American. The utility of the language appears in daily life, thus increasing its value as a unifying agent. While French, British and Belgian banks seem to be further behind in acceptance of both rhetoric and skills, at least one senior person expressed the view that, without being fluent in the jargon, without the terminology he had learned at INSEAD, working his way upwards would have been much harder. Its value to him reinforces its value to others.

Using less formal images of career and hierarchy, some expressed their sense of group feeling by stating their liking for mixing and working with other INSEADs for whom they felt fellow-feeling, whether in banking or in engineering. They perceived their group as special because of common understandings, attitudes, values and centres of interest which transcended sectors of work and national frontiers.

I feel different from the other nationalities at INSEAD but similar too. *I really like being able to have discussions with people who share similar beliefs and the same spheres of interest as me . . . Alumni of INSEAD are beginning to form, in a good sense, a kind of mafia*, like the alumni of Harvard [Business School]. *It's automatic*, it's obligatory, that a certain *genre* exists because *we understand each other better at once.*

For some, the passage through INSEAD was felt to be the final factor which had brought together people who would otherwise in any case have had many things in common, and who selected themselves as a group. Common INSEAD experience, however, bound them into an identifiable unit.

The *esprit INSEAD* can first be seen in the choice made of going to INSEAD. *There is an ambition there right from the start. That shapes a kind of mind, reinforced by the international education we receive. We have the same 'optique' for looking at things . . .*

(Dutch, 1971, American firm, Paris)

Many reinforce that *optique* in the practice of their daily business lives.

I think that what INSEADs have in common is the same way of analysing a problem. I'm going to pass that on to the company where I am now.

I think there is an INSEAD language. Yes, I'm sure of it. Whether there's an *esprit de corps* I'm less certain. I am an individualist and therefore a bad judge. Yes, there surely is something. I would say yes. Perhaps there's more group cohesion than elsewhere, although that depends a bit on the quality of the person . . . Among the young, an *esprit-INSEAD* certainly exists: we are the best! . . . When I was there I felt that there were a good few pretentious people. But that's explained in fact by the nature of INSEAD. It is after all a school for businessmen and in business one mustn't be afraid to push oneself forward. I think that's a necessity.

(French, 1969, French multinational bank, Paris)

Some indeed went further, remarking that 'INSEAD was a very slick course of indoctrination', while a few were less than complimentary about this, saying 'Yes, there is an *esprit INSEAD*. There they create people with very high opinions of themselves!'

In defining and reinforcing the sense of group, contacts with other *anciens* are important. Although some people do not recognise these contacts as being on any but a friendship basis, others consciously cultivate other INSEADs, seeing their importance for business contacts, useful at present or in the future, for 'testing' the job market by comparisons with others and, more directly, using them to solve problems that arise overseas, such as those needing legal advice. Here the 'family' nature of the alumni network becomes important because mutual membership of that 'family' guarantees trustworthiness, overcomes barriers of language and provides an entrée to a national culture where the non-national could otherwise encounter difficulties in conducting business operations successfully. Even for those not of the same *promotion* (year), a phone call to another *ancien* located through the Address Book is sufficient to establish the rights and obligations of the surrogate kinsman. An Englishman working for an American company in Paris recounted that he had recently been on a business trip to Geneva and as the environment of his particular business there was unfamiliar to him he had picked up the Address Book, looked up Geneva and within half an hour had arranged a dinner for a dozen people, most of whom he had never previously met. Many clearly feel that 'such contacts can be useful and I multiply them deliberately'. As another emphasised,

I have a lot of contacts among the alumni. My friends are very mixed – French, German, Swiss and a lot of English. If we have a [business] problem in a country we telephone to a friend. It's a good mix – we are good friends *and* we help each other.

(British, 1968, Swiss multinational, London)

Contacts may also be key elements in the non-formal labour market for important managerial positions. For a group of people with high ambitions and usually much enthusiasm for seizing new opportunities, the job market is a constant source of interest. It provides the focus of conversation and exchange in INSEAD group dinners and reunions, formal and informal, as people compare promotion, remuneration and other conditions of employment, placing themselves in comparison with others and evaluating offers and opportunities. These contacts and discussions sometimes lead directly to new jobs; in other cases, they are useful later, for knowing what is happening in the world of job exchanges even if they do not immediately lead to a new post.

The club can help you to position yourself [in relation to others on a similar career tree] and can teach you how to go about looking for another job. You can even use your contacts with friends to get advice on how best to sell yourself [to a particular buyer] even if the friends don't give you a direct introduction to any specific bank.

(Belgian, 1975, American bank, Brussels)

Friends help to fill in the details behind the public descriptions of job vacancies, can indicate the internal politics surrounding the posts, outline the attributes, positive and negative, of other potential contenders, suggest what the company is 'really' looking for and in that way considerably enhance the chances of an INSEAD candidate, while at the same time they can suggest to the company where one might look for a suitable incumbent. Friends can also, in response to an inquiry, indicate what a given job is 'really' like, so that a potential candidate can decide whether or not he wishes to take the rather public step of applying.

Whatever the direct job outcomes, contacts made among group members reinforce feelings of similarity and of the success 'due' to the possessors of the many qualities of an international MBA.[1] In many cities, there are regular lunches and dinners at times and places announced in the Address Book so all who are in town can take part. In the major cities, too, there are fund-raising dinners, bringing the *anciens* of the area into contact with public figures, politicians, business leaders, even academics, and providing useful informal mechanisms for exchange of views and information, for doing deals and for bringing public and private sectors together. Such occasions also reinforce the feeling of 'eliteness' and solidarity of interest between MBAs across national boundaries, sectors and functions and strengthen the group in that way. The use of such gatherings is widely recognised, for as one respondent said,

I'm not a fanatical supporter of the [INSEAD] club but I think its existence is an excellent idea. What the INSEAD friends do there is of good quality, lunches with eminent people in many fields etc.

For its members, *la famille INSEAD*, as alumni often refer to themselves, is a second kinship network, conferring rights and providing services in exchange for mutual recognition and the acceptance of obligations to each other and to the mother institution, who equally relies much on her offspring to generate funds and ensure good quality students and an 'excellent reputation'.

Reinforcing the group: information and opinions

If there is an *esprit INSEAD*, and if that style is to endure beyond the first few years of graduation, it needs to be reinforced and applied to issues not immediately arising from the content of educational courses. Journals and newspapers are the main providers of information about and presenters of an image of the world in which managers operate and which they shape through their daily decisions. The range of sources used is both narrow and essentially internationalist and 'new-managerial' in focus.

Analysis of the sources of printed data used suggests a conservative group but one nevertheless open to the newer ideas contained within the business ideology in Europe in the 1970s which covers conceptions of the role of business, in both the economic sphere and in public matters. Many INSEADs read the business and current-affairs journals such as *L'Expansion* which have explicitly associated themselves with the 'new' managerial techniques and approaches and proselytised through 'Europeanising' them the use of American business techniques. Indeed, note the name, *L'Expansion*. Aimed at the new *cadres*, many such journals give advice on career choices, indicate the successful business managers of the moment, and provide a mixture of economic and political analysis of the major issues of the day. Most of these journals, at least until the 1980s, emphasised the need of the economy of Europe for 'good management' rather than a change of direction, emphasising again the concerns common to MBAs.

The three most widely read journals were all in English, *Time*, *Fortune* and the *Economist*, frequently read in combination, by members of all nationalities. In contrast to the three-quarters of the sample who read one or more of these three journals, a mere 1 % read such magazines as *Encounter* or the *New Statesman*.

The internationalism of respondents also showed in the proportions reading journals in languages other than their own. Eighty-five people in the non-French sample (28 % of the sample) read French journals. Of these, four-fifths read *L'Express* alone, a journal with a specifically Centrist political line, including a third who read it in combination with business journals such as *L'Expansion* or *La Vie Française*, while in contrast only 7 % read the more Left-wing *Le Nouvel Observateur*. The proportions among the French reading the same journals was, of course, much higher. Of the 1974 French sample, nearly two-thirds read *L'Expansion* and half *L'Express*. Two-fifths read *Les Informations* and a third the now-defunct *L'Entreprise*. A third, however, preferred *Le Canard Enchâiné* and a fifth the *Le Nouvel Observateur*.[2] The range of journals read by French nationals is, therefore, clearly much greater and includes more Left-wing and critical revues than does the reading matter of foreigners living and working in France or having an interest in French politico-economic life. This is likely to be true of other nationalities and it would seem that foreigners working in a country are only exposed to a small sample of possible views on issues of the day, whether economic or political.

In this way, Internationals receive only limited information, concentrating attention on only a few issues. This limited view of local events in most countries further contributes to a common store of knowledge and opinion for, as seen through journal-reading, it seems that the non-national reading of the respondents includes only one principal current of thought. Much of the information they receive is American in origin (*Time, Fortune*) or British (*Economist*) and much of the rest is mediated through journals with what European editors at least perceive as a 'modern', largely American, business-management focus.

Information obtained from daily newspapers shows the same pattern. The American orientation of the sources of information read on a daily basis but also its internationalisation was also predominant. That information is principally from one newspaper source, the *International Herald Tribune*, the leading American newspaper with a daily European edition, read by two-fifths of all respondents. Only tiny proportions read any other newspaper and many did not read it in conjunction with a newspaper of their host country.

Two-fifths of the sample regularly also read at least one British newspaper, usually only the *Financial Times*. *The Times* itself was not being published at the time of the study or it might have had more adherents. As it was, 8 % were waiting for it to reappear. In contrast, only 7 % read the *Daily Telegraph* and only 5 % *The Guardian*.

Exactly a third of the non-French sample claimed to read a French daily newspaper. Of these, nearly three quarters read *Le Monde* and only 10 % the more right-wing *Le Figaro*. Among the French, three quarters read *Le Monde* and 28 % *Le Figaro*. Nearly a third read the more business-oriented *Les Echos*. Reading what is often perceived as the relatively 'Leftist' *Le Monde* distinguishes again the 'younger', more 'modern' manager from the traditional bourgeois *patron*, more addicted, according to Bourdieu and others' studies, to *Le Figaro* and the Catholic *La Croix*.[3]

More than a third of the sample read German daily newspapers, more people than there were German respondents and doubtless including many foreigners living in Germany. The regional structure of Germany here, too, meant much greater dispersion in newspapers, although 6 % read *Die Welt* and 9 % the *Süddeutsche Zeitung*, with a few more reading them in combination with others. Few people read Spanish or Italian newspapers.

In majority, however, in their daily, weekly or monthly intake of information on politics, economy and society and especially on the international scene, the respondents everywhere had a principally American or at least Anglo-Saxon diet and received only a very limited range of facts and opinions, both about their countries of origin and the host nations.

Newspapers and journals are not, of course, the only printed sources either of information or of opinion-formation. Books, too, have a role to play. Almost all the respondents claimed to find time to read books on a variety of themes, including novels. Books as a source of additional information were therefore potentially important, in spite of respondents' busy lives.

Through careers, beliefs and ideologies, contacts, shared information and ideas, the 'esprit INSEAD' is maintained and strengthened over time, linking in to the mainstream public voices of the 'new management' and a forward-looking, international orientation. Just as members of the *famille INSEAD* are linked over space and time to others with similar lives and positions so the ideas of the *esprit INSEAD* are strengthened, developed and confirmed in the medium of print and through contacts with other decision-makers. In the translation of these ideas into daily professional decisions, an élite defined by position and background is turned into an active and self-conscious socio-economic force.

9. Reaching the top: origins, competence and connections

Careers in business have always owed much to the right mix of origins, competence and connections. The social description of the managers of the business world in Europe is far from complete but it is clear that business élites in every European country have long been drawn principally from a very restricted range of competitors. Studies everywhere show that while business as a whole may have a socially more open recruitment than professions such as medicine or law, the social origins of senior managers are limited indeed. Not only are most top businessmen, whether owners or the most senior executives, drawn from each society's most privileged strata but they are principally from families working within the business world. Over the greater part of the twentieth century little has changed.

In France, for example, a study of 2,000 senior business managers (*dirigeants d'entreprises*) by Delefortrie-Soubeyroux (1961) showed that in the 1950s a very large proportion, two-fifths of the sample providing information, were raised in families headed by business owners or top managers. A further 47% came from the upper class, including military, administrative, professional and management families, while in contrast only 9% came from shopkeeper backgrounds and 4% from those of farm, artisan or manual workers. The picture has changed little over time. Almost a decade after the Delefortrie-Soubeyroux study, Hall and de Bettignies (1968) found in the 1960s an identical recruitment among the *Présidents-Directeurs-Généraux* (PDG) of the 50 largest French companies. For a similar period, Monjardet (1972), taking only the 100 largest enterprises, including state-owned ones, found that three-fifths of the PDG were the sons of businessmen – business owners, merchants, brokers and bankers. Between a quarter and a third were from other bourgeois families, while only a tiny 0.03% were from farm or primary-school-teacher families and none at all were the sons of manual or white-collar workers. It would seem, then, that the larger the company, the higher the social origins of its controllers and the more exclusive the recruitment to top positions from the business world. Later still, in the mid 1970s, Birnbaum and his colleagues (1978) found that nearly half the PDG of large firms were the sons of business owners and managing directors.

In Britain, often thought to have a more 'democratic' managerial recruitment, a similar picture emerges in large companies. In the 1960s, Hall and de Bettignies found that of the chief executives studied, 69 % were from the 'upper class' (1969: 51). A few years later, Leggatt (1978) found that of his sample of directors just under a third were themselves the sons of managers and over half from other middle-class families. Students at British business schools were from even more restricted social origins than the average British manager or company director, for more than half their fathers were either owners of 'substantial' businesses, company directors, or senior managers (together 29%), senior administrators and independent or 'higher' professionals (Whitley, Thomas and Marceau, 1981: 83).

In Germany, too, not only are the social origins of the national business élite extremely narrow in range but, as in France, they become even more restricted as the size of the companies they control increases.

Cross-tabulating size of firm and social class background . . . [shows that] with increasing size, social background gains in importance: the percentage of the upper class rises from 26.8 % in firms with less than 50 employees to 40 % in those with 5,000 or more employees.

(Biermann and Benno, 1971, quoted May, 1974: 28)

Other studies conclude similarly. Thus, Hall, de Bettignies and Amado-Fischgrund (1969) in their study of German PDG found that not only were almost half (48%) from the upper classes but 28 % were the sons of businessmen and 15 % the sons *and* grandsons of top executives. These findings differed little from earlier ones by Zapf (1965a) of the *Vorstand* (executive board) of the 50 largest German firms and by Pross and Boetticher, both in the mid 1960s, of the thirteen largest joint-stock companies. In the latter, for instance, half the fathers had held senior industry-related posts and a great majority of grandfathers had been either business owners or in middle and upper-class professions.

The pattern does not differ greatly in Belgium, the Netherlands, and Italy. Beckers and Frère (1974), for example, found that two-fifths of the top managers of fifty-four Belgian firms employing more than 500 people were the sons of top managers or business owners (many of the firms seem indeed to be family firms). Hall, de Bettignies and Amado-Fischgrund (1969) found that 70 % of Belgian PDG had business-owner, senior-executive, liberal-profession and university-professor fathers, with only a tiny 2 % being from the 'lower' class. With the French, the Dutch and Italian PDG had the highest social origins in Europe; 83 % of the Dutch were from the 'upper class' as were 82 % of the Italians. Derossi (1974) studied several levels of managers in the 50 largest Italian companies and found that, even including the lower levels, 40 % were from the upper classes and 47 % from the middle ones.

Scandinavian top executives, although they did come from somewhat more diversified backgrounds than those in the other European countries considered, were also in considerable proportion from business families – half in Sweden and Norway, a quarter in Denmark (Hall, de Bettignies and Amado-Fischgrund, 1969). This was confirmed by Higley and his colleagues in Norway, where half the present business élite were themselves from élite families, mostly (84%) in its business fraction. The other half were drawn principally from other sections of the upper-middle class (Higley, Lowell-Field and Crholt, 1976).

In all these countries, the evidence suggests that marriage patterns mean an even greater restriction in recruitment than appears when the occupation of fathers alone is considered. Thus, in Scandinavia, Higley speaks of a 'strong strain of family capitalism' in the business élite, for many had inherited their positions from fathers or fathers-in-law and 12% had married the daughters of other members of the business élite (1976: 180). In the 1960s, de Bettignies and Evans found an even greater degree of marital social homogamy, with Denmark having the lowest proportion of managers married in the same social groups (30%). In Germany, three-quarters had married into the upper or middle class, and a very large proportion, 60%, of company presidents had married the daughters of businessmen (Hall, de Bettignies and Amado-Fischgrund, 1969). Hall and de Bettignies (1968) found that almost three quarters of French business leaders had moved into the upper and upper-middle classes, the majority of these into business-owning families. They also found that the great majority came from families whose grandfathers were also in the business world.

In the Europe of the 1990s and beyond, this study suggests, little will have changed: important enterprises will continue to be managed by people born into and raised within the business world. The young MBA holders who are potentially candidates for recruitment to leading positions in major companies in Europe over the next few decades are overwhelmingly from families with close attachments to the business world. These attachments are frequently of long standing (three generations) and considerable breadth, with a wide range of relatives involved in business enterprises. As we saw in chapter 6, *in every country in the sample, except in Scandinavia, the largest single proportion of students was from families where the father owned (partly or wholly) one or more businesses and usually had an important share in the management of them.* The proportions varied by nationality, from a maximum of 38% among the Germans to a minimum of 19% among the Scandinavians. In this sense, recruitment to top company positions will continue to be a family business in almost every European country, following a long-established tradition in which business leads to business.

Socially, as all the studies quoted show, the personnel controlling major companies have not changed, but their claims to their position are beginning to be legitimised differently and the organisational routes to the top are everywhere being modified. The structural modifications of enterprise organisation in the face of new market and production conditions spread, as we saw in chapter 2, at varying speeds across all the national economies of Europe. As observed by Bourdieu in France, these managerial changes encouraged companies to alter their recruitment patterns and to seek to employ young people with an education felt to be more in tune with new demands. Across Europe, there have been long-standing educational credentials which have marked members of élite professional groups and served to legitimate their position. Business, in continental Europe in particular, has been no exception. Indeed, the education credentials obtained by top managers in business closely resemble each other over most of Europe – Britain being the obvious exception – both in general education level reached and major subjects studied.

It is clear that a small range of prestigious institutions across Europe, teaching a few prestigious subjects, have long disproportionately been the training considered appropriate for senior managers and business owners. The prestige of the institutions was particuarly marked in France where, for example, Monjardet found in the 1960s that 38 % of the PDG of the 100 top companies had graduated from the apex of the French system, the Ecole Polytechnique, while, in stark contrast, only 13 % had ceased studying at the end of their secondary education. This finding was largely confirmed in studies by Hall and de Bettignies (1968) and by the *Union des Industries Métallurgiques et Minières* for a range of other companies. In countries with tertiary-education institutions, less minutely hierarchically arranged and without *grandes écoles* of the French kind, university education has played the crucial role. German business leaders have long been particularly likely (89 %) to hold a university degree (Zapf, 1965b), as have their Italian (87 %, Derossi, 1974) and Swedish colleagues (80 %). Over the same period they were followed by the Spanish, with 78 % (Makler, 1974) and the Belgians with 75 % (Beckers and Frère, 1974). Further down the list, but still remarkably high when compared to the proportion of each national population holding university degrees, came the Norwegians (63 %), the Dutch (53 %) and the Danes (51 %). The British came a clear last, with only 40 % of top executives in the 1960s (Hall and de Bettignies, 1969)[1] and 25 % of company directors in the 1970s holding university degrees (Leggatt, 1978). The British, where they do hold degrees, followed the French lead in preferring the most prestigious institutions: the universities of Oxford and Cambridge alone had educated between just over half of the top managers in some sectors (Copeman, 1955; Clements, 1958 and Heller, 1973) and three-quarters of another (Whitley, 1974), with banking showing the highest proportion. In Britain, of course, credentialling often took place earlier in the educational *cursus* and all studies of managers emphasise the importance of public-school attendance as a social and educational filter for a career in business. Whitley in 1973 even found that 35 % of the directors of the banks and insurance companies in his sample had been to one school alone, Eton College.

Over the same post-war period, the subjects studied by business controllers again followed a very similar pattern across Europe for every country except Britain, and interesting trends emerge in the relative usefulness for a business career of different subjects. Whereas there are some variations due to the structure of different countries' tertiary education systems – so that, for example, in Germany, members of the Executive Board (*Vorstand*) were more likely than other top managers to hold doctorates – overall an extraordinary homogeneity is apparent. Over the 1960s and 1970s, the holders of corporate power remained everywhere men trained in engineering and science – 41 % of élite businessmen in Norway (Higley), 57 % in Germany (Zapf), 60 % in Belgium (Beckers and Frère), 47 % in Holland (Hall and de Bettignies), 52 % in France (Monjardet), with even more (65 %) in Sweden (de Bettignies and Evans). Even in Britain Fidler found that as many business élite members had science or engineering degrees as had degrees in arts (1981: 84–5). Following engineers came executives trained in law. In Germany, the social élite has long considered law to be the most prestigious academic subject and a suitable avenue to top management, because it is seen as generalist. Dahrendorf (1964) has called law faculties the schools of the German élite, fulfilling a function similar to the 'public schools' in Britain and the *grandes écoles* in France. Lawyers in the 1960s in Germany still held the most senior positions on the *Aufsichtsraten* (the Supervisory Boards which assess the work of the *Vorstände*) of German industry and were especially important in banks, which still preferred 'apprenticeship' training. In Belgium, 20 % of the executives studied by Hall, de Bettignies and Amado-Fischgrund had degrees in law, as did 31 % of the Dutch (Hall, de Bettignies and Amado-Fischgrund, 1969) and 44 % of the Norwegians (Higley *et al.*, 1976). France favoured lawyers less, with only 11 % or so holding law degrees (Monjardet, 1972). Spain has long preferred engineers for top positions, their predominance and that of lawyers rising with the size of firm (Makler, 1974).

Such was the education of men at the top of national corporate trees in Europe in the post-war decades up to the 1970s. It seems, however, that their successors in the 1990s and beyond will have different educational credentials, in spite of the fact that their social origins will remain the same. An important European trend is emerging. While in some of the only recently industrialised countries of Europe such as Italy, economics and commerce have long held an important place in the credentials of top managers (Derossi, 1974), by the 1970s in almost every country these two subjects seemed gradually to be coming to match or even outstrip the importance of engineering and law, crucial in the earlier phase of 'heavy' industrialisation. Thus, in Germany, for example, Hartmann and Wienold (1967) and Kruk (1967 – listed under May,

1974) suggest that in the 1960s engineers were beginning to lose prestige while graduates in business and economics gained ground. Younger managers reaching towards the top in Germany were also increasingly less likely to be trained in law. Beckers and Frère reveal a similar trend in Belgium, away from science and engineering degrees and towards 'social science' (economics and commerce), although law was still most prominent. In Sweden, too, de Bettignies and Evans (1969) reported in the 1960s that 'a trend from engineering to business economics was to be expected in Sweden' among younger company presidents, and, further, speaking of lower echelons of the education system, that 'commercial upper-secondary schools have been gaining ground among the younger generations in Denmark and Norway', a trend also seen in the educational credentials obtained by Scandinavian INSEADs. In Britain, too, Fidler found that 46% of all chief executives studied who held a degree favoured a qualification more or less related to economics, such as accounting (1981: 85–6).

Many studies, then, suggest a Europe-wide trend over the last two decades away from the traditional disciplinary fields of recruitment to top management positions, away from engineering and law and towards the disciplines of business, commerce, and economics. It would thus seem that fields considered functional to the general management of large and medium enterprises in the past, in an earlier industrial age, have been giving way everywhere to subjects deemed more appropriate to a business environment characterised by mass consumer products and complex financial transactions. Explanations for this trend outside France mirror those of Bourdieu. Hartmann and Wienold's view, for example, as summarised by May, is that one should

attribute the expansion of this particular discipline [business economics] to the growing importance of such areas as sales, marketing, market research etc. and the increasing complexity of economic transactions which necessitate the application of scientific methods and techniques.

(1974: 57–8)

May also quotes Kruk:

Engineers and scientists constitute as yet a majority among the younger generation but their domination is challenged . . . This is further supported by changes in the salary structure: in 1964 production was at the top of the salary scales; by 1968, however, it had fallen back to a middle position with sales in leading place . . . closely followed by R and D.

(May, 1974: 68)[2]

For Belgium, Beckers and Frère also suggest that the change in recruitment credentials was related to change in the relative importance of intra-firm functions, and a new need for specialists, in the Belgian case suggesting the example of personnel management whose practitioners are perceived to need a social-science training. Derossi, analysing the situation in Italy, also records a change in the relative importance of different functions in enterprises. One of her respondents reported that:

There has been a change in trends. Once the production manager had power; but today, in Italy as elsewhere, the greatest power is in the hands of administrative or financial managers. Promotion is much slower and more difficult for technicians [i.e. engineers] now.

(Derossi, 1974: 177)

Others echoed that sentiment, linking the new trends to a change in the needs of the enterprise, so that respondents reported:

I think there is a great future for financial managers because they have one important advantage; they are involved in all the problems of the firm.

The modern trend means that commercial responsibility leads to the highest rungs of the ladder.

Many Presidents come from marketing departments.

Finally, the study by Higley and his colleagues (1976) of the business élite in Norway, echoing some of those in Germany, emphasises another increasingly important element in promotion. For a long time, business leaders have stated their preference for the 'generalist' over the specialist in the criteria of choice for their successors and have emphasised 'leadership' ability. However, it seems that the leadership traits seen as necessary changed somewhat in the 1960s. The leadership qualities mentioned to Higley include the more traditional 'forceful personality' and the 'courage to take responsibility for tough decisions', but also now the 'ability to work with others' and to be a 'good team member'. (Few executives, however, required 'innovativeness', 'originality' or 'creativeness', which may be one reason why Levinson (1974) advised that chief executives should not themselves choose their successor.) The emphasis remarked by Higley in Norway in the late 1960s on management through 'subtle, discreet manipulations', through 'cooperation and persuasion rather than coercion' accords strikingly well with the 'updated' vision of the role and methods of the good manager described by Bourdieu both as new and increasingly predominant in France and typical of the American influence spreading to European companies, partly through the teachings of business schools.

It seems, therefore, that through the 1970s there was a trend, strong enough to be perceptible in many studies, across almost all the countries of Europe towards a change in the formal and informal (attitudes and other skills) credentials considered appropriate for recruitment to controlling positions in Europe's largest enterprises. New skills, in finance (economics) and marketing (commerce), came to weigh more heavily in recruitment and promotion decisions than engineering and law, subjects 'functional' not only to an earlier form of enterprise but also to an earlier stage of the European economy, in which production decisions and methods were more important in the life of many firms than their success in marketing products and when the problems of financial control of enterprises of greatly increased size were still to come. In short, it seems that in response to similar changes in the environment of their activity, major firms all over Europe reorganised their structures and recruited and promoted new kinds of personnel. A kind of general renewal was in progress. The kinds of 'competence' recognised were changing.

Recruitment to INSEAD reflected these national trends. Many, trained in élite engineering schools, seized on the MBA as a mechanism for changing direction so as to join the stream most likely to rise fast in the corporate hierarchy. For those already endowed with legal, economic and commercial credentials, a degree in business management in the 1970s became the means of distinguishing themselves from the many competitors already trained in these fields. 'Business management' as an academic discipline in the 1970s came to be perceived by many as the key to promotion in Europe's major companies. Given the kind of organisation which many such companies were adopting, the growth of giant firms crossing national boundaries and the concomitant demand for training in financial control, the skills of the MBA seemed those best matched with hirers' requirements.

Chances of access to credentials useful in that labour market, however, remained and remain even more socially constrained than chances of access to the first degrees which in an earlier period were necessary for entry to the fast tracks towards corporate control. We have shown that to the extent that these still-young managers do indeed become the 'leading Europeans' which the Institute expects, the international business élite will come from even more restricted social origins than existing national élites. If, as the families concerned seem to believe, the way to maintain their sons' positions in the bourgeoisies of Europe is to invest in prestigious management education with an international focus, then the social and cultural gate to participation in the new élite is strait indeed. Not only are the new, multinationally oriented managers working in major businesses across Europe from socially far more restricted sections of the population than even their national counterparts, but the range of educational institutions through which they take the first steps towards the international stage is indeed narrow: in twelve European countries only forty university-level institutions of the hundreds potentially available, and within those only a couple of faculties each, provided all the initial training.

Even within this tiny fraction of potential competitors, however, this study also suggests that as careers develop one particular group will probably do better than its peers. This group is composed of the sons springing from Europe's existing top business stratum, the *patronat* of each national entity. Some *patronat* career choices will indeed be especially successful.

Some of these differences are linked to different choices of career pattern.

Most respondents see MBAs, and particularly INSEAD MBAs, as progressing faster than those without the magic letters after their name entering the same or similar initial positions in their companies. In part this is due to perceived competences, in part to networks of connections which lie behind the competences and in part to choices of career direction and strategy.

Five routes to the top

To reach senior business positions, it is not enough in the late twentieth century to possess the right credentials, even combining the best social and educational background. We have seen in chapter 5 the importance of track record established. Moreover, even within the range of possible paths, not all aspirants will use the same strategies. Some will want to play essentially on the international stage whereas others are content to achieve appropriate positions at home.

At the senior levels of multinational European business, one can distinguish five major types of career strategy, each covering a different field of competition. Two of these are pursued by a group called in an earlier chapter the 'true internationals', the people who play to a maximum on the international stage, living and working for at least most of their careers outside their countries of origin, in large companies with essentially multinational operations. These firms, operating as they do on the international stage, offering mass-market products or financial services, are perhaps the field of competition preferred by MBAs who are stifled by similarly large enterprises working in a purely national arena and unwilling to compete with the entrenched mafias from the most exclusive educational institutions of their countries. These mafias are often groups to which they either do not belong or whose closed and inward-looking nature offends the internationalist 'progressive' ideology felt by the MBA to be his particular strength and which leads him to despise such competitors as 'backward'.

Of the 'true internationals', one group essentially plays in the large multinationals of Europe. In many of these companies, the MBA is now a well-recognised credential and to some extent there are established career tracks within enterprises. In the first firms they joined, more than half (58 %) of the respondents here had colleagues also from INSEAD: this proportion remains high (34%) even in the third firms. Not only were there INSEAD colleagues already in the company but they were there in numbers which are strikingly large, given the small total number of INSEAD alumni on the European managerial labour market. In their first firms, half the alumni reported that the companies then employed at least five other INSEAD MBAs and a third employed eight or more, these proportions only dropping by half even by the third firm. In addition to the INSEADs, the same companies also employed other MBAs: at least five in two-thirds of the first firms (and in some, upwards of twenty) and half with eight or more, proportions only dropping slightly by the third firm.

The presence of so many MBAs means, of course, that companies recognise their particular skills and in almost all companies the great majority (80 %) of alumni were convinced that they would not have reached their current positions without their MBA. Many of these indeed felt not only that they had progressed faster than their non-MBA colleagues but had done so much faster.

While companies thus recognise their talents, however, the presence of a number of MBAs means that many are competing with the same credentials and skills. In this case, individuals must find ways to distinguish themselves from the ruck. This is notably the case in multinational banking and new manufacturing where young MBAs concentrate and where employers have a highly developed policy of sending non-MBA managers on short senior management courses, frequently at INSEAD itself, thus increasing the pool of competitors with similar credentials. In these companies, possession of the MBA is not a sufficient exclusion mechanism. Thus, while they reward INSEADs well, the companies' hiring policies also mean that an INSEAD who wishes to progress as fast as his ambitions suggest is appropriate must first find ways of persuading others to single him out.

Finding a way to be singled out, however, is often difficult, for the companies' policies also have the effect of creating an environment in which it is hard to make an impact. Employing MBAs mostly in staff positions, precisely those where 'capacity' and 'achievement' are hardest to measure, large firms are frequently hierarchical, bureaucratised and inflexible, unable or unwilling, in one respondent's phrase, to 'bend the rules' to fit individual needs or felt desserts. At the more junior levels, too, differential use of MBA skills also means that many large companies reward the man with marketing and product development skills rather than the financial controller or corporate strategist who ultimately will probably rise highest. In firms with these practices, time must be allowed for the necessary transitions to be made and appropriate experience gained.

In such companies, *loyalty* may be a good career strategy, as we saw in chapter 5, but it is one which demands patience, for the firms offer a relatively 'slow-burn' (Bailyn, 1978) route towards the top. This loyalty strategy, which might be called *bureaucratic internationalist*, is favoured by many MBAs from management and especially non-business family origins, perhaps because 'bureaucratised' careers seem most secure, directed as they are by company policies and structures which demand little risk-taking by the individual manager.

Such 'slow-burn' careers, even on the international stage, however, are uncongenial to many of the *patronat* sons, raised by their families to value above all independence and leadership and to believe that exceptional rewards should go to hard work and enterprise. While large multinationals pay better, offer their managers high status and a prestigious lifestyle, they appeal less, it seems, to the sons of top businessmen than to others.

These, in contrast, prefer high risk, 'challenge–success' career trajectories, using the whole of Europe in their search for the most golden if risky career opportunities. Members of this second group of true internationals take all of Europe – and beyond – as their field for play in the search for power, a high salary and fun. At home anywhere and everywhere, frequently with a wife of a different nationality, moving where the stakes are high but the rewards even higher, these are the trouble-shooters of European business, the very model of the 'young Turks' of the business magazines. Specialising in finance and in reviving ailing companies, these young men use the skills of the MBA, their knowledge of the business world of Europe and their many international connections to correct the mistakes of companies expanding too fast, merging unwisely or finding themselves in difficulty with unwieldy multinational decision-making structures in subsidiaries or divisions. The task is important, for, like economic development as a whole, the transnationalisation of production does not always proceed smoothly; there are setbacks as well as progressions. Successfully correcting strategic or organisational errors gives the ambitious manager maximum visibility and a distinguished track record so that after some years he writes his own ticket, choosing company, sector and country in such a way as to maximise returns.

Of this group, few at the time of the study were yet at the peak of their careers. Their skills of financial control are not wholly the 'negative' ones involved in tightening company belts: the interviews suggest that they are also entrepreneurs, developers, concerned with product innovation, whether in commodities or services, and with penetration of new markets. This combination makes them general managers *par excellence* and they are likely to be as much in demand in an expansionary phase of the economy as in the recession. These are the true international high-flyers, the *entrepreneurial internationalists.*

A third route is followed by some of their colleagues from similar backgrounds who have also been following a 'challenge–success' entrepreneurial career. Some, competing initially in the international arena, eventually leave and return to 'home' base. They seem to decide that smaller enterprises, operating from their home country but oriented to the international business world, offer the best milieu in which to use their talents and, for their age, to receive the greatest rewards. They are very well represented both in the group of forty-five in the sample reaching nearest to the top, and the smaller group of twenty-one on the boards of subsidiaries or on the main boards of the companies they worked for in 1979. These 'international nationalists' include many sons of the *patronat*, especially in consulting, who return to their home arena after gaining international experience. This move allows them to maximise the rewards to their proven professional competence by also maximising the return on a privileged position of origin, for it is at home that the network of contacts and connections provided through school and family is most dense and hence most valuable. In these enterprises, too, very variable in size and in product, they are likely to be the only MBA and it is here that they can use to best advantage both MBA skills and prestige and established track record. They are *domestic internationalists*. The move 'home' is likely to be a professional success while at the same time it may also satisfy private needs, especially those of wives tired of being international domestic managers and movers, and of children who need to complete their secondary education in one place. The companies this group returns to run are not always the largest but they are firms where there is plenty of scope for the initiative, independence and rewards to enterprise valued highly by so many. Some are family firms, either inherited from relatives or created by respondents, using family economic capital and often family connections. It is frequently through this kind of professional activity that the 'modernising' and 'internationalist progressive' orientations of the MBAs have most impact on their home society. It is here that ownership and control probably re-merge first.

A fourth career strategy can also be seen. Not all INSEADs leave their country to work. In spite of their interest in and commitment to 'internationalism', many prefer to limit their venture into the international arena to that offered by a foreign multinational with branches in their home country, or a national company with foreign operations or markets. To those *marginal internationalists*, this strategy offers status, prestige and frequently early financial reward without the need to change cultures or languages. The French are particularly likely to follow this route, using the INSEAD diploma as a mechanism for increasing opportunities within their own milieu, reconverting into the international milieu but not relocating on to the international stage. Even though they first enter large multinational companies, they are unlikely to reach the top there, even by the slow-burn route, for their commitment to internationalism is too low. The ambitious among them, then, will probably eventually be obliged to move back further on to the purely national stage, probably to smaller companies in which, like their colleagues, they are the only MBA. They will thus eventually rejoin the final group who were never international at all, except during their year of INSEAD. This group, operating a fifth strategy, never left either home country or national companies, using INSEAD not at all as a passport to the international arena but only as a means of acquiring a piece of cultural capital useful to distinguish them in the national field of managerial competition or to revitalise an ailing family firm, for many of these expect to return to their heritage. It is probably these who use their INSEAD credential least and whose careers least approximate to those typical of the 'new manager', while most resembling those of their more traditional peers, often relying most heavily for their success on the economic capital inherited through family position in the possessory bourgeoisie. These *entrepreneurial nationalists* have little in common with the true internationalists.

Competence and connections

Acquisition of the MBA, then, can be seen to work as an intra-class exclusion and reconversion mechanism which can be used in diverse ways. Most holders of this prestigious credential can use it to develop a variety of strategies to maintain themselves in positions socially equivalent in terms of income, prestige and influence to those occupied by senior members of their families of origin by playing in a different arena. Their position is socially equivalent even though most move, at least initially, to salaried posts, rather than remaining independent businessmen living off a direct return to economic capital invested. In this move, they are continuing, through their own career trajectories, the transformation of the business fractions of the upper classes of Europe and participating in the creation of a European salaried but still wealthy bourgeoisie, a process begun a century or so ago with the first major changes in business structures.

As time goes on, however, within this general re-conversion process careers across Europe develop in different ways. Within the framework of the five major strategies, there appear many variations and a complicated structure of rewards to background, competence and connections which underpin the paths chosen and the success of any particular series of tactics. In principle, all opportunities are open at graduation from the Institute. In practice, not only is much determined already by earlier educational paths followed, as was seen in chapters 5 and 6 above, but some decisions once taken effectively preclude others. Few can move out from the national to high posts in the international arena; for those posts there is an international apprenticeship to follow. Few can move from marketing to finance without adopting the risk-taking strategies described, or change from manufacturing to banking. Few can move from small to large firms. Some combinations of these moves are even harder. Several strategies, several combinations are good but no single one can be seen to be optimal at every point: escalators sometimes turn into roller-coasters and people on them go down as well as up. Thus, for instance, a *patronat* son with an engineering degree entering manufacturing will do less well than the same person with a commercial degree; holding more common skills in this field, engineers have to distinguish themselves from the rest. Those from *non-patronat* backgrounds who have engineering qualifications do better, although the advantages of engineering are cancelled out in a multinational. The relationship between social origins, education and salary is particularly clear in banking where *patronat* sons with economics and commerce degrees, those most 'vocational' in the field, consistently did better than those similarly qualified but from other social backgrounds. Similar relationships are clear in consulting, which seems across Europe to value particularly the social skills and contacts acquired from a business-owning background, especially when combined with a scientific training.

The reasons for these differences are complex – some apparent advantages cancel each other out, while others combine and accumulate but do so in different ways in different circumstances and probably at different stages of a career. Particular attributes have greater or lesser value in different markets and vary as a function of hirers' expectations and requirements at a given time. Some of the differences in career outcomes as between this social group and others and between different sections of the group result from the complex nature of the evaluation of jobs and performance which companies must engage in when hiring and promoting, especially at the highest levels.

Some of the success of those chosen for the top is clearly a function of their competence recognised by their employers. In this population, however, competence is often in good part a matter of connections, seen, for example, in the responses in the survey to questions about getting jobs and moving on, reported in chapter 5. A Swede making a reputation in an American bank through connections made at a party in New York by an invitation received as a result of having a diplomatic uncle in Paris may be an extreme case, but it is surely not unique. Contacts and connections are made through school, INSEAD and family, categories which in this population frequently overlap, even on the international stage. The right 'background', both private and professional, plays a pervasive role in 'slow-burn' but particularly in 'challenge–success' careers.

The first reason for this is that, except in 'high-risk' positions, competence is not always easy to measure. In staff positions, except perhaps in merchant banking, it is rare for people early in their career to be able to make visible contributions to the profitability of an enterprise as a whole, or even to that of one of its sub-units (see Pfeffer, 1977). In some functions, notably perhaps in production or marketing, it is sometimes possible to judge performance by results and in some companies management by objectives (MBO) has been introduced with that specifically in mind. But such management techniques, widespread in the United States, have been slow to gain acceptance in Europe (Trépo, early 1970s). This means that in both staff and many functional line jobs there are frequently few easy ways to assess performance.

In many junior line positions, those occupied in the crucial early years of a career, the situation may be even more complex. As Claus Offe has pointed out (1976), once a certain level of productive complexity has been achieved in a company it becomes almost impossible for any individual to demonstrate his or her capacity in the performance of tasks. Even though companies frequently make formal efforts at job description, even for high-level managers, these usually only indicate roughly the boundaries of action and essential duties of the post. Moreover, formalised assessment procedures are in practice much more geared to detecting deficiencies in performance, to indicate who is falling down on the job, than they are towards demonstrating success and even less are they able to indicate 'capacity' in a more general sense. Thus, in many managerial positions in a company it is often impossible to measure a good performance, only a disastrous one. Moreover, there is, of course, no necessary correlation between performance at any one level in any one role and potential capacity to perform well in any other (hence the well-known *boutade* about promotion to the level of incompetence).

Speaking of 'workers' in a general way, Offe states:

In many cases technological working conditions . . . [mean that] productivity cannot any longer be ascribed to specific individuals. Other types of performance certainly are still subjectively experienced and understood in terms of the model of 'producing' yet because of organisational changes it is no longer possible socially to demonstrate them as such: they cannot therefore any longer be used in any intelligible justification of claims for social status. When both these changes occur together, then they create a conflict with the still firmly institutionalised principle that status is legitimated by performance. Given the ideologically maintained fiction that there is a functionally necessary link between status and performance, both the technological restriction of productive work ascribable to specific individuals and equally the organisational limits on the supervision of performance create a legitimacy vacuum . . . This vacuum is filled partly by *performance substitutes* such as occupational symbols and ideologies: [we thus hypothesise that] if the individual labour ability used in productive and administrative organisations is 'socially invisible' then this leaves the authorities who judge performance with no alternative but to judge the individual's performance capacity symbolically, in other words, to use indicators of performance which more and more diverge from the core of task-adequate performance. One could take as examples of such indicators symbols of performance which are acquired externally to the organisation, institutional loyalties, criteria of origin and other ascriptive criteria. Without exception, these are criteria which are only loosely (if at all) connected with the productive aims of the organisation, but which serve instead to stabilise relationships of economic and cultural domination. Since individuals remain forced to acquire differential status in terms of their individual performance ability, and since equally organisations have to explain differential status in these same terms, *both individual strategies of social mobility and organisational criteria for promotion are based on the category of extra-functional orientations and symbols.*

(1976: 56–7, my emphasis)

The major exceptions to this rule about the difficulty of measuring managerial performance are found in the directly profit-earning centres, favoured by the 'risk-takers'. For those in positions without such obviously visible results, positive or negative, the lack of decisive objective criteria for promotion if not for recruitment has a number of consequences and the social position in its widest sense of the individual manager is likely to be of considerable importance in the development of a career.

The most important element in that social position will probably remain, in the late 1980s and beyond, that of the immediately family background of the managers concerned. High social origins endow aspiring executives with symbolic capital of a very important order, a 'name'. As earlier chapters have suggested, family background indicates general 'suitability' for command posts and adherence to appropriate values, for families provide the opportunity for their sons to acquire both the right *éducation* (at home) and the right education (at school), together 'guaranteeing' the appropriate mixture of technical competences and attitudinal orientations. In ensuring this mix, families reinforce their sons' symbolic capital (name) and begin the transformation of 'potential' into concrete achievements and hence into assets ready to be utilised and transformed into further achievements. Finally, families situate the person at the centre of an important network which itself will contribute both to achievement and to making that achievement visible in a way that is known to hirers and promoters. If performance is hard to measure, 'recommendation' becomes important, especially to the high-level and sensitive business positions whose incumbents represent the company to the outside world.

The specific ways in which springing from exclusive social origins assists rapid career progression are not always easy to see but have on occasions been studied indirectly. An American study, which compared the careers of MBA managers with others, tested three hypotheses about the relations between social origins, education and career success as measured by salary and position held and the mediation of these through certain organisation structures (Pfeffer, 1977). The hypotheses were, first, that socio-economic origins would have more of an effect on career progress in staff rather than line positions; second, that socio-economic origins would have more of an effect on career progress in small rather than large organisations; and third, that socio-economic origins would have more effect on career progress in finance, banking, insurance and real estate than in manufacturing.

These hypotheses were based on the growing evidence that, holding education constant, family background may have an impact on career in two principal ways. First, socio-economic origins affect language, self-confidence, social skills, attitudes and beliefs and interaction style. These elements can be assessed over a period of time in a job, and probably even from the beginning, in the interview situation, a view confirmed by Suleiman's study of admission to the Ecole Nationale d'Administration (1974). As Pfeffer says, similarity in beliefs and attitudes as well as experience and self-presentation may be important in building a favourable response among those making hiring and promotion decisions, particularly in circumstances in which more objective bases of evaluation are absent.

The second reason for the importance of the right background lies in the ways socio-economic origins affect access to social networks useful first in obtaining a desirable job and then in succeeding in it. Thus:

High social class may provide more than just access to prestigious universities. It may provide integration into a network through which higher paying managerial positions are allocated. It may also provide similar social attributes which are important in earning favourable recognition from those in organisations who have the power to promote and hire.

(Pfeffer, 1977: 556)

As Bourdieu has summarised the situation:

those who possess the most prestigious qualifications also have at their disposal an inherited capital of relationships and skills . . . made up of such things as the practice of the games and sports of high society or the manners and tastes resulting from good breeding, which, in certain careers (not to mention matrimonial exchanges which are opportunities for increasing the social capital of honourability and relationships) constitute the condition, if not the principal factor, of success. The *habitus* inculcated by upper-class families gives rise to practices . . . which are extremely profitable to the extent that they make possible the acquisition of the maximum yield from academic qualifications whenever recruitment or advancement is based upon cooptation or on such diffuse and total criteria as the 'right presentation', 'general culture', etc.

(Bourdieu, 1971: 69–70)

The families in the INSEAD study constituted this kind of valuable network. Chapter 7 showed the considerable breadth of contacts possible at any one time but only showed a photograph of the network at one point of time. It is important to remember that many of these relatives are likely to advance further in their careers while the older ones have already made significant moves along their own career paths. Any given individual in the group must be seen not only as the central point of a 'horizontal' network but also of a 'vertical' network composed of the positions held in the past, during the course of a long professional life, and the contacts made then. As each individual helps others, so the network's links take on a multiplier quality, for as each individual moves up he becomes more valuable as he and his contacts hold more important positions. Every member of a family thus at any given time possesses a 'tail' of contacts, expanding over time. As Luc Boltanski (1972) has suggested, interpreted correctly, the contours of the 'position' of any person are also a function of all the positions he has held, and the effect of cumulative position-holding means that linkages are potentially far more widespread than appears at a given moment. The 'social surfaces' each can command become more extensive as each member of the 'surface' rises. The wider the dispersion of posts occupied successively, the greater the social power of any individual, because the broader are the fields which he can dominate, directly and indirectly. The number of positions held by respondents' relatives analysed by Boltanski rose according to social origin. Respondents whose fathers were *patrons* of industry (as were those of many INSEADs) each held 6.7 positions, as against a tiny 1.7 for those with fathers who were manual or white-collar workers, or the 4.4 of those with private-sector executive fathers. The importance of possessing such a wide social surface is underlined by Boltanski himself when he says that:

by the intermediary of the network of contacts . . . an important number of transactions are carried out, transactions which are objectively political or economic but which, not being carried out with money, are not perceived as such . . . for example, recommendations, exchanges of information, etc. Moreover, the occupation of a given position itself implies the possession of a certain capital of social relations, of prestige, of symbolic credit, legitimacy, and power. It follows that the social capital that an individual can mobilise depends not only on his family origins but also on the social surface that he can himself dominate (which is itself, at least in most cases, social capital accumulated by the family), which depends in its turn on the breadth of one's network of contacts, multiplied by the social surface controlled by each member of one's extended family, and, to a lesser extent, that of each of the members of the network of contacts. One could not explain the omnipresence of certain names, certain lineages, and certain individuals, able to control indirectly, at a distance, a far greater number of positions than that which they are able to occupy directly, nor the breadth of their power, without bringing into [the analysis] a multiplier of this kind.

(Boltanski, 1972: 10–11)

We begin to see, therefore, why young people from business families embarking on careers in business will usually have an advantageous start, especially when armed with the appropriate formal credentials. That starting advantage may be multiplied as the career progresses by a mixture of subjective and objective factors. Upper-class families, in particular, maintain extensive and intense relationships with a wide network of relatives who reinforce in their members both general orientations and particular ambitions. The position of many of these relatives at crucial points in the socio-economic system surrounding, more or less closely, the enterprise or series of enterprises in which any one family member is involved enables them to be of concrete assistance. As sources of information and introduction, they may provide contacts leading directly to new jobs or they may provide information that leads to actions whose results are registered as objective career performance; for instance, when they provide privileged financial information or legal advice, suggest approaches to make about new inventions or products, indicate new or cheaper suppliers, propose deals that might be done, indicate market opportunities at home or overseas, or advise on possible changes in government policies or regulations. Much success in business careers, on the admission of several respondents interviewed, is due to 'flair'. That 'flair' is not always the result of chance or the specific talents which the word suggests but the structural position in which its possessor finds himself. The famous *pifomètre*, the 'nose', works better when supplied with information. Possession of that information increases the obvious organisational value of its holder and thus makes him appear a more likely candidate for more senior positions at an early age. Holding those positions, then, itself multiplies opportunities for indicating the potential or demonstrating the capacity of the holder and may push him onwards in an accelerating manner, ensuring that he is caught in 'an upward spiral of success'.

For their individual members, families are thus very important sources of information on and contacts with the outside world: they may also be useful the other way round, in the transmission of information 'out' by an individual. In that way, they may be directly important in the effective labour market in which a manager operates. Very many, perhaps most, management positions are never formally advertised. This tends to mean that management labour markets are internal to the company, but it does not necessarily do so. Even where they are internal, transmission of privileged information on a candidate may help. Companies usually prefer to recruit senior people discreetly, away from the scrutiny both of other internal candidates and from other competing companies: hence their frequent preference for 'headhunter' consultants and for direct approaches to external candidates.

Such factors may come into play for the filling of existing jobs but equally may be decisive in the creation of new ones. Should an apparently appropriate candidate from outside be drawn to the attention of a company or indicate his interest in a position, that may be enough to open up the market for the position. Company structures are frequently flexible at senior levels and where a person and certain skills are particularly sought posts are often created for specific individuals where no position existed before and whose potential existence was not known to internal candidates for promotion. At the top, posts are frequently modified to suit candidates available (Glickman, Hahn, Heishman and Baxter, 1968: 27). In one of the very few studies of personal contacts as a factor in the white-collar labour market, Granovetter (1974) gives numerous examples of the importance of personal contacts, not only in applications for existing vacant jobs but also in the creation by companies of new jobs tailored specifically to the characteristics of the chosen incumbents, a situation especially important for managers.

In both cases, recruitment to existing posts and the creation of new ones, emphasis on 'personal suitability' frequently disguises demand for 'social suitability'. In some cases, or at higher levels in more 'delicate' functions, social acceptibility may be more explicitly demanded. Once the first tests are passed and management potential established, conversations and discreet inquiry explore the more delicate question of lifestyle and network of *relations*. As a young Swede working in a French bank rapidly became aware:

The French are socially very bourgeois . . . if one doesn't have one's house in Cannes, one's chalet in the Alps or one's hunting stretch in the Sologne one is not *quelqu'un de bien*. Before taking you on, people check on how you correspond to these criteria.

Hence one reason for the importance of the access to family properties described in chapter 7. Another banker interviewed also confirmed the importance of this, for he recounted how a thorough investigation of his social background and family connections had been conducted before he was asked to apply for a job. As this was a Swede, working in an American bank in London but approached through the Paris office of the bank, it is clear that these investigations can be and are carried out on an international scale.

In the banks in particular, it would seem, confirming Pfeffer's suggestion, that the social persona, including the network of relationships implied, is particularly important, both to recruitment and to promotion:

the banking world has very archaic structures (like the insurance business) especially in France because banking is an old sector and there's no longer any competition (indeed there is often a need for holding back rather than fighting to get hold of a market). In this kind of situation it's more important to have contacts (*relations*) than competences . . . This is beginning to change. Where banks are having to establish themselves abroad they have to have more aggressive policies which mean a different promotion strategy, but at home . . .

(French, 1975, French bank)

In banking, the importance of characteristics other than possession of the MBA is also confirmed by Whitley and Thomas' study of British MBAs' careers in financial institutions in the City of London (Whitley, Thomas and Marceau, 1981: 193–4).[3]

Inheritance of access to such attributes enables the young, even while on low salaries, to live in the appropriate way and, above all, to interact with the appropriate people, as was confirmed in the present study. Possession of the 'external signs of wealth' seen in lifestyle is important, first, because it is taken as an indication of adherence to a system of values that is supportive of those of established business and society and, second, because it indicates not only possession of a network of potentially useful relationships, but also the material possibility of maintaining the villas and chalets in suitable places which permit strategic invitations, both extended and received. The perceived importance of business entertaining at home, undertaken by three-quarters of all respondents, was clear in the present study. Wives and other female kin, as we saw, have a primordial place in the upkeep and organisation of the activities implicit in the playing of a full bourgeois social role, for the material symbols of the network are nothing without occupants.

Kin groups, of course, are not the only source of contacts, or, rather, 'families' may be created in other ways. Contacts made or available through the more exclusive schools and universities are formalised into address books and *annuaires* such as those of the Ecole Polytechnique, HEC and Sciences Po, and of Oxford and Cambridge, whose alumni clubs operate in the major cities of Europe and beyond. INSEAD itself is, as we saw above, a major source of contacts useful in the labour market. Not only does the year spent there provide the occasion for making contacts with peers of many nationalities but the teaching methods used, involving close-knit groups in the work done, foster the creation of long-lasting relationships at the same time as the acquisition of an INSEAD MBA develops a set of attitudes and expectations that create claims on people from different generations of alumni and a sense of its holders as an important élite peer group. That 'fellowship' is concretised in the form of an annually updated address book and regular monthly meetings for alumni working in many European cities, including London, Geneva, Frankfurt, Basle and Brussels. It is further encouraged by the international INSEAD alumni association and the constant involvement of many alumni in recruitment interviews with candidates for the MBA at the Institute, in recruitment of graduates to companies and in the many fund-raising activities the Institute organises all over Europe. Indeed, those fund-raising activities bring participants into regular contact both with significant business leaders and representatives of the public sector, both politicians and senior public administrators. In these ways, too, important networks of contacts are formed. A fund-raising dinner for INSEAD held in London in the mid-1970s was hosted by Lord Aldington[4] and the Hon. David Montague. Guests of honour included Edward Heath and Roy Jenkins. The guest list included Lord Hankey, Lord Farnham, Sir Donald Barron, Sir Robert Clark, Sir Jasper Hollam, Sir Kenneth Keith and Sir Arthur Knight (*The Daily Telegraph*, 5 November 1976). An élite institution thus forms the basis on which further élite contacts are formed and maintained. That INSEAD graduates are beginning to form an effective 'mafia' to help each other in a concrete manner was suggested by several interviewees in the present study. Already in 1976, a German newspaper commented on the degree to which younger INSEADs were helped to find jobs by older alumni. Companies recognise them as a group and even in recession they were given a chance:

Auch in der Rezession gibt . . . den INSEAD-Absolventen ein chance. Wenn ein guter Mann gebraucht wird, hat ein 'Inseadien' grosserer Aussichten als Manch ein anderer – voransgesetzt, *man weiss was INSEAD ist.*

(*Handelsblatt*, June 1976, emphasis added)

There are, of course, also many other ways of ensuring the right social and professional interaction, such as membership of exclusive local clubs, notably in London and Paris (Bourdieu and de Saint Martin, 1978). In the present sample, 28 % of respondents said that they belonged to a club and a further 13 %, recognising their importance, said they intended to join one later on.

In a study largely conducted by questionnaire it is impossible to estimate exactly the ways in which individual respondents acquired their jobs, either when they moved into a company or when they changed positions within it. Not only can one not know exactly how the person and the position were 'known' to each other but one cannot estimate the motivations of the company for appropriating that person rather than any other. It does seem, however, that, for the variety of reasons suggested, what is perceived and rewarded as 'competence' remains closely linked to connections and, through that link in particular, social origins continue to count for career success, not just on the national but on the international stage, in the closing decades of the twentieth century. Even if it is true that 'le caractère ne suffit plus', formal credentials do not suffice either. The picture is a highly complex one, mediated by company structures, education, nationality and ambitions, but 'family' in many senses of the word remains of great importance in the rise to the top on the European business stage.

10. A family affair

By the investigation of the operation of micro-processes of conservation and change, seen in the experience of a small but significant group of young Europeans, this study has attempted to contribute to a discussion of macro-level social processes and developments taking place over quite long periods of time. It arose from a feeling that the broad-brush analyses of social reproduction developed by certain sociologists in the 1960s and early 1970s in Europe missed some crucial aspects of the process and needed to be complemented by finer detail for, while these approaches indicated trends and likely links between the social phenomena observed, much fell through their net. Moreover, they emphasised social reproduction over change when it was clear that some changes, at least in the economic sphere, were taking place. In part, too, the explanations offered seemed unduly mechanistic, leaving too little room for the interplay of individual elements composing together the institutions whose functioning they describe and for the 'mistakes' of direction inevitably made in a complex world. Further investigation of micro-level activities in the light of the broader theories seemed appropriate. Choosing as the crucible an educational institution whose existence symbolised many changes and who produced both people and ideas for major areas of the economies of Europe allowed the selection of a sample of people whose experience could be taken as a microcosm of many factors: the operation each of family, education system and élite labour market and their interactions, which shape individual careers while contributing to the well-known overall result.

The study has been constantly concerned with the operation of opposite forces – those producing changes and those ensuring much social, political and economic conservation. The people at the centre of the study are decision-makers. Their professional lives lead them across much of Europe and beyond. Many occupy positions which affect the ideas and life chances of others. 'Who' in social terms these people are is of considerable significance. So, equally, are the processes and mechanisms through which they came to acquire their positions and disseminate their ideas.

The processes of change and conservation considered here are both economic and social. On the one hand, during the last twenty to forty years major firms everywhere across Europe seem to have been reacting in structurally similar ways to the internationalisation of the economies in which they were embedded, their exact reactions being a function of their degree of participation in new products and markets and of the characteristics of their controllers. Change at a macro level, translated into altered productive structures, seemed to be the order of the day. In particular, major and expanding enterprises came to demand new skills of the incumbents of senior managerial positions. On the other hand, and in contrast, it became clear as the study proceeded that the processes of decision making by families, individuals and companies about choices for the labour market had scarcely been modified. These micro-processes, which together produce the familiar macro-statistical results in terms of 'who gets what' in any country are extremely stable. While some changes of direction have taken place in contemporary Europe, the essential influences on decisions have remained much the same.

It seems from the study that the most important reason for this continuity lies in the operation of families, both true kin groups and their surrogates. Although frequently invisible, in the business world families and their resources are vital at every stage of many highly successful managerial careers. They first ensure the production of suitable candidates for office. During the crucial periods of child-raising, bourgeois families seldom leave anything to chance. While still in their early years, business sons receive such intensive lessons in the values, ambitions and experiences of their milieu that, as we saw in the early part of this book, few career options are effectively open. By the time sons reach young adulthood, their families have made sure that they are appropriately ambitious – as seen in the constant declaration by candidates to INSEAD that they wished to 'reach the top' and to do so fast. As success is defined in terms of power, influence, status, independence and a high salary, few professional choices are left. Family members – fathers, brothers, uncles, cousins – join the chorus of advice to follow an 'appropriate' path, mostly that furnished by their own example and hence overwhelmingly in business. Architecture, music, medical, legal and the learned professions are considered only briefly if at all. In these circumstances, the pool of candidates for posts in business is largely determined early on. In view of the weight of family pressure experienced by respondents, the wonder is not the degree of professional inheritance: rather it is that anyone leaves the business world at all.

Families with such ambitions for their children are also unlikely to leave the ultimate verdicts of the education system on their scions to the hazards of public examinations or teacher assessments or assume the inevitable triumph of the innate capacities of their sons. By investing their economic capital in private education almost everywhere in Europe, business families maximise their control both of what is learned, moral and intellectual alike, and of chances of a favourable outcome in the mechanisms which stamp the child an educational success. On occasion, and in some places, state educational institutions may be trusted either because there are no suitable alternatives or because parental place of residence, an exclusive catchment area for the school of their choice and a selective entry system thought to ensure high intellectual and social standards, render the public as close to the private system as possible. Where any of these elements prove unsatisfactory, the child is moved to another school, given private lessons or forced to repeat grades until the desired result is obtained (see articles in *Le Monde de L'Education*, 1983). Given the social homogeneity of the population of the schools selected, élite education does little to widen the professional horizons of its pupils. 'Ruling-class' schools operate in a market finely tuned to parental social and economic positions and the expectations which these engender, as Connell and his colleagues have shown (1982, *passim*).

By the end of secondary education, choices of career sector have largely been finalised. Doctors, lawyers, engineers, and economists set off on different routes, although they stay together in the same tertiary institutions in many countries. While a few will have 'failed' despite their families' efforts, most will acquire after a few years of study a credential seen as the passport to entry to a prestigious career. These credentials, however, are only the beginning. They have to be 'cashed' in the labour market where different rules apply and where the skills imparted by the education system must prove their worth in an environment dominated by other concerns (Hussain, 1976). It is during the first few years of the interaction inside companies between skills offered and hirers' requirements that the first problems arise for many ambitious young men who have chosen careers in business but who have had to compete on the salaried management labour market rather than enter a family business.

We have seen that early choices of business sector, size of company and post frequently prove less satisfactory than expected in the salary, job interest and promotion prospects which they offer. In some companies, notably those most 'modern' and reliant on the education system as an initial sifting mechanism, many aspirants have the same qualifications, rendering competition intense at the same time as it makes distinguishing oneself difficult, especially in the staff positions which most people occupy early in their careers. In other firms, the stratification of credentials in the education system is translated into differential chances of making one's mark and particularly of making it early. While only forty élite institutions in Europe provided those credentials for the populations studied here and did so in a narrow and focused range of subjects, some formal qualifications will nevertheless have the 'wrong' value on the changing managerial labour market developing as major firms everywhere across Europe reorganise, closing off some avenues for promotion as they open up others. The very independence of the education system from the economy causes gaps to develop between expectations and openings in a labour market subject to changing economic circumstances, seen in particular in the Europe of the 1950s, 1960s and 1970s in the internationalisation of production and distribution and the opportunities and constraints of international financial markets. The traditional value of some credentials is everywhere downgraded when new skills are in demand. It is into these gaps that some people fall. It is, moreover, precisely in these important early years of a career that the power of another credential, that of the family, is most attenuated and young men are most vulnerable. Away from the certainties of the educational world in which they mostly did so well, they are not yet in a position to maximise their family connections. Because of the relative disengagement from family which everywhere accompanies young adulthood, following the student years in which peers play the most influential role, they find themselves less supported than before and in an unfamiliar market.

For these reasons, during the years of the early twenties much has to be rethought. In the search for the best ways to fulfil early ambitions a new educational credential, one whose value is made clear in the business journals of Europe and increasingly discussed in the enterprises in which they work, is likely to seem a promising investment to the young manager.

Disengagement from families, however, even during these years, is only relative. While individuals take the decision to make the business-education investment, families none the less still remain important for, while their direct power and influence may be at a minimum, they continue to provide resources which can be capitalised on, notably information and economic assets. Business-owner, *patronat*, sons, for example, hear of the Institute earlier, frequently from family members, acquire the MBA younger, thereby maximising their early career chances and thus the return on their investment, and more frequently than others use family money both to pay the fees and compensate for the year of earnings foregone through full-time study at a time when many are married and some have children of their own. In this, of course, wives also help, both by increasing the range of relatives with a vested interest in the success of an individual's career and by providing assistance, either financial through the income they provide, or, more generally, through the support they offer. Having much to offer even during these years, families in the upper classes never completely lose contact with their offspring: they are only waiting, their influence in abeyance, their power not broken and not replaced by any lasting force so strong. Apparently reduced in this milieu to a provider of holiday homes by the sea and in the mountains and to a regular series of dinners and beds for the night during the years of student and early professional life, by that very provision the family retains its value, its contacts and its influence. Marriage provides the occasion for the 're-entry' of the young to a place closer to the family bosom. At marriage, to the families of origin are added the affinal links which broaden networks and the rights and obligations of kinship. Presents received and hospitality extended on the occasion of the wedding draw the relatives together and establish the new couple in an appropriate manner. Elaborate weddings symbolise acceptance of the alliance by both sides and ensure appropriate access to the property and connections of each group. The transfer of capital on the creation of the alliance and the birth of the next generation of heirs bind the family more closely. Marriage also provides a young man with a domestic manager and partner in a career which is an enterprise in which both spouses have a stake. In this joint venture, wives maintain the contacts, the cultivated lifestyle and the hospitality needed to maximise through family solidarity the yield from investments in family capital of all kinds.

Important in the early years as a weapon in the battle to distinguish oneself from competitors in the chosen field, family capital also ensures that maximum value can be obtained from the educational credentials possessed. Expressed at its simplest, to his employer an engineer is always useful; an engineer with an MBA is still more valuable; an engineer with an MBA and a range of relatives in high places in the public sector or private business is a resource much to be sought after. An engineer who uses both his skills and his contacts to minimise the risks involved in a company's national development or international expansion, to return a division or a subsidiary to profitability, correcting mistakes of product or direction, or to scan the environment for essential information, is an asset for which an enterprise will pay handsomely and may reward with the top positions these high-flyers seek. Even managerial aspirants choosing the slow-burn route seem at times to use their capital of connections to make the crucial leaps from staff to line positions and for moving sideways to new jobs, new sectors or new companies. While perhaps of greatest value on the national stage, these networks of relationships, allied to an exclusive MBA, can both encourage people to play on and minimise the risks of the game in the international, trans-European business arena.

It is thus the *accumulation* of credentials of different kinds that seems to be the key to a high-level career in the businesses of Europe. The prestige of traditional diplomas prepared in élite educational institutions, added to the values, ambitions and contacts nurtured in upper-class families in Europe, combines with possession of the 'best' management skills certified by an international and internationally recognised MBA to allow those who so wish to enlarge the arenas in which they play out their professional lives. The combination enables them to seek out and be sought for the best opportunities on the international stage, those provided through the new organisational structures of expanding European multinational enterprises. It is thus also this combination which is likely to be the winning one for Europeans developing their careers in a wide variety of firms and in diverse national economic circumstances. Finally, it is this combination which will ultimately secure their admission to the business 'inner circle', whether at home or elsewhere in Europe.

Within this generally winning game, however, there are still some strategies which pay better returns than others and these must be constantly sought out in order to maximise individual advantages. The paths that lead to international finance, to risk-taking and a willingness constantly to reconsider directions, to re-convert as necessary, are for most the most profitable, although losses along the way can be considerable. These are possibly the best routes to the top in every business career. In the 1960s and 1970s in Europe, those most likely to take these routes and to succeed were *patronat* sons, armed with commercial education and some banking experience, working in an international company or a national firm with multinational operations, willing to relocate frequently, using the whole European arena as a professional stage, and assisted by a skilled and patient domestic manager. In the group of forty-five people identified in the study as then holding the most senior positions, *patronat* sons are notably well represented, much better than their proportion in the sample as a whole would suggest; constituting a third of the sample, they form more than half of both the forty-five in the senior positions and the twenty-one at the top.

They compete, however, with 'young Turks' of other élite social backgrounds and no single individual from a business-owning family can expect to do better in all respects. Nor, it should be re-emphasised, is the path smooth even on 'slow-burn' tracks. Trade-offs have to be made along the line between high positions in small firms and lesser positions in large companies, between staying at home where rewards may ultimately be surer and foregoing the excitements of working in other countries' market places or taking off across Europe, uprooting the family but taking the risks that lead to rapid advancement, choosing between salary and interest, status and independence in the great majority of cases where even these golden boys cannot claim everything, at least not all at once. The way is also strewn with pitfalls – mergers, bankruptcies, reorganisations, retrenchments, all close off possibilities and are not unknown in every company, least of all those in highly competitive if ultimately promising markets. Personnel movements, we have seen, sometimes have devastating effects on those left behind and often lead them to change company or direction. All these changes, in times of recession especially, are potential disasters: once again, their direct effects may be mitigated by kin or by members of the INSEAD family and access to both combined makes the necessary re-conversions easier and ultimately more profitable.

In the matching of the ambitions of the young to the opportunities in the labour market, of the skills they possess and their hirers' requirements, there is much room for friction, for mistakes of direction, for failure to read the signs correctly, even for missing the most profitable career opportunities. Given the streamlined nature of the passage of most upper-class sons through the secondary education system and their considerable chances of access to suitable tertiary institutions, it is in the early years in a career that the danger of mishap and thus downward social mobility is greatest. These years of choice are years of considerable 'milling about' and uncertainty about directions for many. The credential gained at INSEAD promises for its holders an asset particularly valuable in these years of search, allowing them to offer skills in demand, international connections and public legitimacy in the fastest-expanding labour market, that of the European multinational company. Through acquisition of the MBA, at a stroke the competition from others for desirable positions is severely restricted and a class of ineligibles is created, while the frontiers of the job market are pushed further afield. While some will remain 'at home' in the companies they enter, many will make tracks across Europe, bringing with them family connections and through their own career success returning interest to the investment of the family of origin in the form of expanded opportunities for other members.

In these ways, then, while not guaranteeing entrée to the top echelons of businesses in Europe, old and new, formal and informal credentials mix, merge and multiply to reconstruct, renovate and expand the opportunities open to young people from the upper classes of Europe, to open international doors and forge new avenues as older ones are closed. It is essentially these processes which lie behind the overall statistics on the social reproduction of each national society.

In the light of this, it would seem a mistake to view the debate about whether managers are 'born' or 'made' and about the effects of the professionalisation of management as one in which educational credentials *replace* other criteria. Business careers, it is quite clear, will always be open to people possessing economic capital even if they have few formal educational credentials. Moreover, given the need to make profits and in doing so to adapt constantly to changing environments, calling thus for a variety of skills, firms will always be resistant to closing off opportunities to the educationally less well endowed. At the most, the more bureaucratised firms, those most dependent on the use of modern management techniques in personnel as well as financial control and marketing, may develop fast tracks for entrants with particularly valuable educational qualifications. But it is performance on those tracks which counts, at least to the extent to which it can be measured. Possession of the skills implied by the MBA probably encourages firms to trust the judgements of MBA holders when they are younger than others, thus giving them real responsibility and tasks. Hence, aping the effects of the magic 'X' diploma described by one respondent, the MBA may mean, in short, that 'to him who hath shall more be given', the fast tracks ultimately being those that include more varied experience, gathered while young. The MBA will almost always be especially valuable when changes are occurring and companies are reorganising or entering new fields, demanding thus the special skills of the domain of the MBA – corporate strategy, financial management and marketing. In these domains, few others are so well trained at entry.

Business graduates will also contribute to change in the business sections of their societies. To the extent that business schools crystallise 'best' business practices and teach them as the disciplines of modern management and to the degree that, in business organisational changes, product and technological developments and management techniques such as forward or strategic planning are becoming more and more the order of the day, so business-school graduates are likely to obtain employment in a wide range of companies to which many would not otherwise have gained early admission in senior positions. In that way business-school education and MBAs' practices do indeed contribute to the faster transformation and 'modernisation' of business enterprises of Europe. To the extent to which they gain controlling positions they may indeed also help to transform the business fractions of Europe's bourgeois classes. It seems likely that they will do so in a manner in keeping with the progressive image which business organisations and spokesmen claimed as their own through the years of expansion and which large firms in particular still wish to present to their public-section interlocutors, who are able to do so much to affect the environment of the corporation and hence its chance of profits. In turn, they will also influence the public sector. From the 1960s and 1970s onwards, in many countries of Europe, public administrators, watching the success of these very corporations, themselves took over many of the management doctrines developed in the private sector and taught by business schools, transformed for the occasion into schools of *management*. Proclaiming thus the essential similarity of private profit-making and public management, they began the portrayal of the state and its institutions as the equivalent for the public sector of the conglomerate in the private, faciliating thus, through this common language and set of concerns, an interaction so much more intimate than the old, where each failed to understand the other, except in the realm of political decision-making.

Such management ideas, however, are not value neutral. Underlying the rhetoric are the kinds of values which respondents here espoused – free enterprise in a free economy as the basis of a free society. In this view, the role of the public sector is one in which government protects but does not restrict entrepreneurial activity. The rhetoric of the large enterprise which recognised government's economic obligations in late capitalist society in most of Western Europe replaced in the years of economic boom the public individualism of an earlier generation of smaller entrepreneurs. By the later years of the 1970s and into the decade of the 1980s, however, both big government and big business seemed to have in some senses failed. The latter failed to produce jobs, to grow, to protect citizens and governments from the distribution and legitimation problems caused by low economic growth, while governments were accused of wasting resources and of draining labour from productive to unproductive pursuits. In that climate, anti-interventionism, anti-planning, anti-'big-government' rhetoric exploded on the political scene, its power on the voter changing the colour of several European governments. The forces behind this rhetoric produced a swing away from proper 'management' of the economy as the centrepiece of government's legitimate activities, replacing it with an ideology aiming to 'roll back' the activities of the public sector and the resurgence of the older reliance on private economic organisations to create enough social benefits and on the family for social welfare. A new *laissez-faire* doctrine, a twentieth-century version of the market resembling the nineteenth century's 'invisible hand', swept many countries of Europe. The 'visible hand' of managerially reorganised capital had received a slap from another limb.

In response to these new conditions, over several years a further change in the demand for some managers became increasingly apparent. The recession years of the 1970s caused many leaders of the business world to reassess priorities. By the end of the decade, executive search companies in Europe were suggesting in interviews that demand for marketing skills had peaked, that the long-despised production function was returning to the fore. Indeed, the dominant idea of a 'good manager' seemed itself to be undergoing rapid change, with 'headhunters' receiving requests not for men with subtle manners and the team spirit but for those with the more traditional characteristics of the *patron*: an 'ability to command', to 'be firm', to 'say no when necessary'. The rhetoric of the dominant discourse became less neutral, more overtly political, closer to the older language which applied to industry the expressions of the military, the language of 'combat' and 'victory', signalling a return to older values of entrepreneurship and individualism. The future came to seem more problematic, less 'inevitable' than the technocratic managers had suggested.

The change in the business outlook can be seen from press comment. In 1981, an article in *Time* magazine, a journal read by many senior managers, was entitled 'The money chase: business school solutions may be part of the problem' (*Time*, 4 May 1981: 36–42). It emphasised the vogue for hiring MBAs that swept across the USA in the 1970s, but also suggested the beginning of a backlash. A New York financial consultant was quoted as saying:

A lot of what is preached in business schools today is absolute rot. It is paper management. It is not the management of hard resources and people. Business schools teach that business is nothing but the numbers – and the numbers only for the next quarter.

(*Time*, 4 May 1981: 36)

Moreover, says the article, MBAs now working their way up the ranks feel themselves to be a professional managerial caste, destined to take command of the nation's corporate life. Were they to do so,

This might prove a misfortune of some magnitude. For although the MBAs generally see themselves as the best and the brightest, and the most energetic and ambitious as well, a growing number of corporate managers look on them as arrogant amateurs, *training only in figures and lacking experience in both the manufacture of goods and the handling of people.* Worse, the flaws in the polished surface of the MBA now appear to reflect flaws in the whole system of American business management, in its concepts, techniques, it values and priorities.

(*Time*, 4 May 1981, emphasis added)

and

Critics say that there has been too much emphasis on short-term profit, not enough on long-range planning; *too much on financial manoeuvering, not enough on the technology of producing goods;* too much on reaching available markets, not enough on international development.

(*Time*, 4 May 1981: 38, emphasis added)

American technology is now, it seems, looking old, since the brightest recruits to business have gone not to research and development or production but to finance and marketing. That is what they have been taught to do and that is what companies have rewarded, as can be seen in Europe from the present study.

Virtually none of the INSEAD high-flyers worked in production and never had done, at least not after acquiring the MBA: ambitious engineers had read the writing then on the wall and used their new credential to move to other sectors and functions, to enter 'new' industries and financially or marketing-oriented activities in pursuing their goal of early access to senior posts in general management.

The values and circumstances that led to those opportunities do seem indeed to be changing. While exaggerating both the influence of MBAs (although the *Time* article says that Harvard boasts that 3,500 of its MBAs head US corporations and they include 19% of the top three officers of the *Fortune* 500) and the one-sided 'ideology' developed in business schools on the economy, the quotations cited in the article indicate clearly the close relationship between definitions of good management and the state of the economy to be managed. Indeed, business schools themselves are aware of this and adjust their emphasis accordingly; in recent years INSEAD proposed the creation of a Chair in Entrepreneurship and Innovation, feeling perhaps that large corporations are

now increasingly faced with the challenge of attracting and developing young managers capable of providing *a new type of leadership where the spirit of entrepreneur-*

ship coupled with innovation skills can be channelled towards *helping organisations to meet new societal demands.*

(Fund-raising publicity for the proposed Chair, emphasis added)

Some MBAs themselves see business schools as having channelled managers into increasingly bureaucratic careers and in so doing as having deprived the business world of the essential ethic that keeps it going. One banker interviewed in the present study, for example, pointed, in the context of a discussion of his own career, to differences in outlook which oppose the rewards accruing to and satisfactions gained from different career structures and linked these differences with important differences in values:

I hate big companies. They're full of politics, of hierarchy. I always wanted to work in small firms . . . That depends on what you call 'professional success'. If it's a big salary, responsibility for big investments . . . etc., then one has to work in a large American bank. If one is seeking true contact with clients, the opportunity to 'get ones hands dirty', then small firms are better. *All that depends on one's idea of capitalism. I myself, I am a true capitalist, an entrepreneur.* For me that means owning a significant share of a company. *Most INSEADs are neither more nor less than employees* . . . INSEAD produces only for big companies . . . 'big company men'. The most typical example is INSEAD MBAs who go to M. (a big consulting firm) . . . and claim to be doing interesting things. In fact they don't do much at all . . . What do they mean by 'having responsibilities'? It's an illusion. Their responsibilities are only on paper. *The worst thing that can happen to a consultant is to lose his job. The worst thing that can happen to me is to go bankrupt.*

(English, own bank, 1972, emphasis added)

In this interview, the tensions which continue to exist within the economic and productive structure as a whole are apparent, tensions between the big companies and their 'big-company men', who have little or no contact with the 'real' world of individual risk-taking and individual responsibility for the livelihood of others, and the entrepreneur, the 'smaller' man, the 'true capitalist', making a come-back now in a real way, at least at the level of public policy and public discourse, and perceived as the repository of the original and 'pure' capitalist values. In this latter ideology, 'big-company men' are almost in the same camp as the public-sector bureaucrats, to whose education and 'reform' business schools everywhere are increasingly turning their attention.

In this general return to an older tradition, those most associated with the softer managerialist ethic of the boom years may lose influence and position. The credentials of the MBA may lose their power. To the extent, however, that MBA holders are recruited from the most high status and politically 'reliable' sections of the societies of Europe they may still hold a winning combination of advantages. They may be seen to combine efficient management knowledge with 'correct' social values, the latter overlaid in the 1970s but not suppressed by the rhetoric of teamwork and a 'soft' management style. The risk-taking high-flyers in particular have shown their appreciation of the need to make profits as well as the ability to make socially acceptable the difficult decisions associated with restructuring, retrenching and rethinking directions. They will undoubtedly continue to do well. In the new climate, however, their colleagues in marketing may be less well placed, with their skills seen as those appropriate to periods of rapid expansion rather than contraction and their ability to say 'no' as yet unproven. They may find that they must yet again undertake re-conversion strategies or resign themselves to having the salary but not the influence they once aspired to. Their predicament illustrates once again how fast élite labour markets can change and how consistently alert to new circumstances and the closing off of apparently certain opportunities, how willing constantly to adapt and take risks the ambitious high-flyer must be. Some careers will suffer more than others from this business volatility. Indeed, the many INSEADs working in banking may find that economic crisis means new opportunities, since in such times banks may become more central to the economy because in times of crisis 'capital accumulation on a given technological base has to be abandoned, and capital has to be amassed in liquid form to enable its organised reinsertion into at least partially renewed productive processes. The mobility of banking capital . . . entitles it to prominence in periods of restructuring' (Van der Pijl, n.d., quoted Fennema, 1982: 199). Be that as it may, many MBAs may find in this new time of altered directions that once again their 'family' assets yield good value. Where this does not happen, the changing economic environment will increase and make more apparent the differences in opportunity open to those endowed less handsomely with capital of all kinds.

What, then, are the chances of INSEAD MBAs forming the new international business élite? And, perhaps even more important for the future development of capitalist societies in Europe, of gaining membership of the international 'inner circle' now beginning to emerge? It is, of course, impossible to predict in individual cases, but analysis of business organis-ational practices revealed in a variety of studies suggests that for some at least the chances must be good. The exceptional fit between both social background and training of INSEAD graduates, their 'character' and their competence, their connections and belief systems, and what we know of hirers' require-ments for top jobs indicates that, of all candidates in Europe, these must be very well placed. The trump cards INSEAD graduates hold are manifold.

First, the international evidence surveyed in the last chapter shows that most existing top executives and company directors across Europe are from high social origins. Most are from the upper classes of Europe, notably from the business fractions. Useem (1984) has shown that the scions of the upper classes when they enter business rise both further and faster, entering the 'inner circle' both more frequently and at a younger age. Promoting INSEADs with their impeccable bourgeois, and especially business-bourgeois, origins would involve no change in practice and, on the contrary would reinforce representation of people originating from the highest levels of the business world. Second, the same international evidence indicates the change in recruiting practices, away from engineering and law and towards a greater demand for the commercially and managerially trained. INSEAD graduates score well on both counts. They can offer the traditionally rewarded technical qualifications which may well be increasing in importance again in the 1980s as the developed world returns to a more productivist ethos, organised around new technology, than prevailed a decade before. To this they add the high-level managerial training implicit in an MBA degree from INSEAD, thus more than adequately responding to the altered demand.

The competence of the MBA, moreover, will take on greater salience in the face of increased evidence that the professional worker is the critical resource in the kind of professionalised activity which enterprise management has become (Shapero, 1985). As Shapero says, the most important management decision faced by a company is hiring. If the firm hires well, the chances are that the organisational output will be more than satisfactory. The importance of hiring the right person is underlined by evidence that the quality of performance – high or low – persists over time and that a small proportion of those hired are responsible for a disproportionate amount of performance (Shapero, 1985: 1). INSEADs once again stand out. They are exceptionally well trained and data on their careers, during even the first years after graduation, indicate their success in the professional field, a success recognised in the remuneration companies offer them. This high performance overall, especially by the risk-takers, seems likely to continue.

The types of career decision taken by INSEAD MBAs, the choices of function and sector, in both 'slow-burn' and 'challenge–success' career paths, also seem likely to favour their advance to senior and top executive positions. As a study by Glickman and his colleagues carried out in 1968 for the influential American Committee for Economic Development (CED) showed, in order for a man to come up through the ranks to become a top executive of a large corporation, he must move up fast within a relatively short period of time. This, says the study, is 'essential if he is to "arrive" equipped with a sufficient range of experience at an age when he has the time and vitality to do the job' (Glickman, Hahn, Heishman and Baxter, 1968: 10). This places a premium on early discovery and a minimum delay *en route* to the top. To ensure early discovery it is essential to be 'visible'. One must not stay too long in staff positions because the 'hew to the line' principle works in favour of operating executives whose results can be seen. It is essential to establish a reputation as a good line manager and not become known first as 'a good staff man'. The data on INSEAD careers shown in chapters 5 and 6 of this book demonstrate that INSEADs follow exactly such career paths. They give preference to visible jobs with visible results, notably in marketing and finance. They seek as soon as possible to make the switch to line positions and establish the generalist nature of their competences. They take the first step by going to INSEAD itself and later ones by their subsequent career choices. They further follow the CED study's advice to 'hitch your wagon to a rising star' and follow someone moving up, as several interviews indicated. After the first few years they also often prefer jobs where they are 'big fish in small pools' such as subsidiary companies or divisions, thereby increasing their visibility. The risk-takers in particular seek out such positions. In the risks they take they benefit again from the 'enhancement by contrast' and success in crisis which they achieve. As managers studied by Shapero pointed out, 'people involved in problem situations tend to be better known' and 'crises create heroes' (1985: 43).

INSEADs clearly appreciate this and act upon it. They are rewarded by seeing MBAs, particularly INSEAD graduates, progress faster than competitors without the magic letters after their name, as many respondents to the present study perceived. Thus, while possession of a particular educational credential is never a prerequisite for top management positions, the training inculcated in the MBA holder allows the young both to succeed in visible positions and to succeed faster. They succeed because they have learned the techniques and because both their families of origin and the outlook developed at the Institute indicate the appropriate career decisions. To advance, of course, a majority of good judgements is essential, but so too is the ability to make judgements at all for it is *not* taking decisions which employers see as the fatal flaw (Shapero, 1985: 44). INSEADs are both specifically trained to make decisions under conditions of uncertainty and given the skills to ensure that the majority are good judgements. They are, in the words of one of the CED interviewees, taught 'to hit a long ball early in the game'. While being in the right place at the right time is still vital to final selection, the route to that place is in good part socially and educationally determined. This combination of skills and flair for taking risks across national frontiers clearly marks them out as both unusual and valuable in the international business arena.

The likelihood of success in their strategies is reinforced further by the considerable extent of movement to particular companies which occurs through 'self-recruitment'. Several studies, including those of Granovetter (1974) and Shapero (1985), show that those who come to company positions through friends and acquaintances are the best performers on the job. We saw above (chapter 6) how frequently INSEADs are recruited this way. To the extent that such recruitment does indeed mean best performance once in post, this too will push the INSEAD well ahead in the race towards the top.

One final but major development in company policies may also considerably advantage the technically trained and risk-taking INSEAD graduate. This is the new and fast-developing trend in many major corpor-

stages, as well as earlier. Not only do many owe to their origins the personality and manners which make conducting external relations easy but also they know many of their interlocutors through the family, education and wider professional contacts in which they are so rich. They also are peculiarly well placed to develop class-wide organisations and policy positions on an international scale. Even while young enough to be included in the present study, most have developed a clear sense of the politics and policies affecting the business world, both as it operates inside different national boundaries and across national frontiers, while a third already belong to business clubs and associations and others plan to join 'later on'. They are well informed on international trends and developments and well connected to the political world. They are excellently – and most unusually – well placed to give advice where company activities involve interaction not only with governments across Europe but also with the supreme European bodies, the Commission in Brussels, a city where many *anciens* work or have worked, and the Parliament in Strasburg. They have a strong sense of the European ideal and their everyday professional lives show them both its strengths and limitations. Multilingual and multicultural, at home anywhere in Europe, as the interviews persistently showed, conscious of themselves as a special inter-national group, most are true Europeans both in ideology and practice.

Finally, once at the top they can be relied on to be fully committed to the values of business and to the continued achievement of profits. Raised in a business world composed of families in the process of diversifying their investments, they early absorbed the spirit of *libre entreprise*. In a world of restructured capital, they know that to safeguard their families' portfolios of investment they must safeguard the performance of many non-family-owned enterprises. Their own shareholdings, both economic and symbolic, in the range of businesses which they have inherited from families of origin, acquired through families of marriage and built up in the course of their own professional lives, ensure a particular interest in the profits of the firms which in many cases now control their families' economic destinies. Given these assets and their structural position in the productive world of Europe, these managers are particularly likely to wish for further involvement in the development of an *international* class-wide logic of accumulation and the promotion of public policies to that effect. The companies they join, financial and industrial, are already central to the development of international links in Europe. Companies such as Paribas, the Deutschebank, Philips or Monsanto are professional home to many of them. As their companies' networks develop, so too will those of our respondents. They are thus placed in the centre of the groups transforming the structure and operations of European capital and with it inaugurating a new phase of European politico-economic organisation to be formalised in the union planned for 1992.

The establishment of business schools in Europe, and the successful careers of many of their graduates on the European stage, must thus be seen as part of an ongoing process in which economic changes and the value orientations of the business community which contribute to, legitimate and attempt to influence these changes, interact to maintain over time both the capitalist economic order of Western societies and the privileged positions of the strata controlling them. One can at the same time see both the establishment of the 'new' bourgeoisie in opposition to the 'old' and the beginning of the transformations which in their turn will soon make the creation and presentation of an even 'newer' one (or, more probably, a 'purer' version of an older one) necessary to the public legitimation of business activities. Business schools by their operation have in recent decades in Europe contributed both people and ideas to the process of continuity in change. Some of their people will be approaching the control positions in major European enterprises in the year 2000, using some of the ideas generated and passed on. To the extent that such enterprises are powerful (as, for instance, are many of the banks in which MBAs work) then their controllers will exercise influence on the business world well beyond that which their numbers would suggest.

The resurgence of an older tradition in business rhetoric and orientation is unlikely to be complete. International managers, used in the daily practice of their profession to treating Europe as one market, one professional arena, informing themselves from international business journals and leading multinational personal and professional lives, are not likely to return to viewing problems through the lenses of national politics and national business concerns. The extension of the Common Market from six to nine, to ten and then twelve members enhances their opportunities and further widens their field of action. Less constrained than their local counterparts by government regulation of enterprise, since their field for investment and production decisions covers all of Europe, they are conscious of public-sector decisions rather as opportunities than restrictions. Too used to dealing with a multitude of national policies and points of view, too committed to the idea of 'Europe', economic and political, too wedded in their personal lives to multinationalism, as a group they are not likely to become locally protectionist nor to espouse the inward-looking individualism of the 'new conservatism' trumpeted by the right wings of the national *patronats* of Europe. To the extent that they control the major enterprises of Europe and that they influence the politicians, public servants and fellow businessmen with whom they interact, it seems likely that they will remain a moderating and progressive force in the business worlds of Europe in the last and difficult decades of the twentieth century. To this extent, at least, the avant-garde of the 'new' bourgeoisie of Europe will have been altered by its experiences. 'Europe', despite its fragilities, is probably too entrenched to be easily demolished or abandoned. To the degree, however, that economic development within that framework creates polarised economies in which the smaller national firms diverge

further from their internationalist counterparts and national policies encourage a resurgence of family enterprise, the followers of the avant-garde
may diminish in number and some choose other models, returning rather to
the narrower vision of their grandfathers than emulation of their fathers. Such
a return is feasible, since they still hold many of their older ancestors'
fundamental values and attitudes, and, again through their families, have
access to these other economic reins, but seems unlikely on a large scale.

Economies, in short, are never static. The circumstances of the post-war
period in Europe encouraged change in productive systems of a kind that
provided new outlets and encouraged new enterprise, through corporations
which in conjunction with social and political changes contributed to the
creation on the continent of an international business élite. In their efforts to
maintain their families' positions, members of the business fraction of each
national bourgeoisie contributed their sons to a new style of life and thinking
just as they inculcated a traditional set of values and aspirations. The
international élite managerial labour market has undoubtedly provided
opportunities for the sons of the national bourgeoisies to maintain through
their own careers the social position of their families of origin and to earn the
high salaries which enable them to live in a manner at least equivalent to that
to which their upbringing had accustomed them. The stock of capital,
economic, social and cultural, which they inherited from families of origin,
acquired on marriage ('inherited' through their wives) and augmented
through the education system helps both to guarantee the success of many in
these new and less-tested waters and ensure that their own children will have
similar chances in the labour markets of Europe in the opening decades of the
twenty-first century. In the daily management of the economic system of late
capitalism, central processes of social and cultural reproduction mean that,
while individuals change, groups retain power. That system, however, over
time, also modifies and redistributes the chances of individual group members
and will always provide opportunities for gifted outsiders. In countering this
tendency to dispersion, family solidarity, the laws of inheritance and the
mechanisms of competition in seeking for profits by business enterprises will
continue to yield to the privileged the rewards which, as risk-takers and the
self-proclaimed generators of the wealth on which others depend, they
consider to be their due and to ensure that their investments are successful in
what remains ultimately and essentially a family business.

Appendix A. Methods of study

The data used as the basis of the analysis in this book were gathered using archival research, questionnaires and interviews extending over the period 1973 to 1980. There were two studies. The first was financed by the British Social Science Research Council and focused exclusively on the French students and alumni of INSEAD. The second, financed by the research arm of the French Plan, the CORDES, covered eleven other national groups and was carried out on a part-time basis between 1977 and 1980.

Together, the two studies covered 2,110 students and alumni of INSEAD. The archival studies covered the first nineteen *promotions* of the Institute's students, entering between the first year, 1959, and 1977. The 2,110 were divided by nationality as follows:

French	661
British	354
German	375
Scandinavian (Swedish, Norwegian, Danish)	185
Belgian	129
Swiss	147
Dutch	94
Italian	73
Austrian	69
Spanish	23

Data on careers after INSEAD were gathered on 504 alumni, of whom the majority were French. Data were gathered by three main methods – analysis of admission files at the Institute, questionnaires to alumni and their spouses, interviews with students on campus, with alumni in selected European cities, with 'head-hunters' in Europe and the USA and with staff of INSEAD.

Background data were gathered from Institute files on students entering between 1959 and 1977. Constraints of time and resources meant the use of samples with varying coverage. The biggest national group, the French, had itself to be sampled. The first study, 1973–5, included all French students

217

entering INSEAD in three groups of three years: 1959–62, 1964–6, 1970–3. The second study added all the French between 1974 and 1977. The next biggest groups, the British and the Germans, included all entering students from 1959 to 1977, while other national groups included all members entering between 1959 and 1976. The totals of each here may differ slightly from Institute figures, because they exclude some individuals who had dual nationality or who had lived all their lives outside their country of nationality. For comparative purposes, analysis of admission files was supplemented by that of 263 files of rejected candidates and of 414 French, Dutch and German candidates who withdrew after admission.

The files yielded data on social and educational backgrounds, on pre-INSEAD professional experience, on motivation for entry to the Institute and on career aspirations. The questionnaires sought to explore in much greater detail influences on choices of education and career, on career paths followed after graduation, on career, political and social attitudes and on expectations and assessments of the usefulness of the MBA as a credential. Each questionnaire represented a complete career path to date. The questionnaires also provided data on the occupations and education of a wide range of extended family members.

In the first study 485 questionnaires were sent to French alumni, of which 200 were returned. In the second study, 800 questionnaires were sent to alumni chosen on the basis of nationality and country of work, of which 304 were returned. As the two sets were not exactly identical, the data are sometimes analysed separately in the text of the book. While the response rates were around 45 %, comparisons with file data suggest no serious biases in education or background and comparisons with data in the Address Book suggest none in terms of sector of work, while studies carried out by INSEAD itself suggest the reliability of the salary and other career data.

Questionnaires were also returned by 134 wives of the French (in 1975) and 169 other wives (1980), making a total of 303. These recorded data on backgrounds, careers if any, attitudes to, and expectations about their husbands' career, on weddings and dowries and cultural and social activities, as well as the education and occupation of a range of other family members.

Interviews were also an important part of the study. Sixty were conducted with French students on campus in 1973–4 and with twenty of their wives. In 1980, 120 interviews were carried out with alumni of all the nationalities in the study. The interviewees were chosen on the basis of the kind of company they worked in and their place of work, balancing those at home and those abroad. All those selected had graduated from INSEAD at least five years before. Interviews were conducted in London, Paris, Brussels, Geneva, Basle, Zurich, Frankfurt and Munich. Some of the French interviewed in 1973–4 were re-interviewed. The interviews supplemented the questionnaires by emphasising effective choices in career paths, ways of obtaining jobs, plans and expectations for the future, and contacts with other alumni, and included an exploration of attitudes such as 'internationalism' and the creation of the INSEAD 'mafia'.

Finally, interviews were conducted with major executive search companies in London, Brussels, Boston and New York, so as to investigate trends in employers' preferences in recruiting MBAs.

Appendix B. Coding of social origins

From the brief descriptions recorded in the files, judgement about what constitutes a business owner is not always simple, especially where twelve nationalities are concerned. Where possible, local knowledge of the interpretation of terms used (*industriel, Kaufmann, Fabrikant,* etc.) was used, and accorded with usual census usage where appropriate. Titles and their significance, however, frequently vary. Some distinctions in classification of positions within the top levels of the business world have been made and the rules of classification applied across the nationalities. A category for *Présidents-Directeurs-Généraux* (PDG), *Administrateurs de Sociétés*, chairmen of the board and directors general was created, because of the difficulty of equivalences. In some cases, it is clear that the PDG is running a non-family business, but not always – many of them and many *administrateurs* will in fact be running their own or their families' companies, but tax advantages and other legal requirements require them to take that or an equivalent salaried title. Many of those in this group, especially perhaps among the Belgians, are therefore in reality business owners. In any event such people are the major controllers of enterprises and probably hold considerable quantities of the economic capital invested in them. In all cases they seem likely to be members of the board. It seemed more appropriate in the analysis, therefore, to put these two groups together and describe them, following usage by Bourdieu and others, as the *patronat*.

A harder classification task is posed by titles such as managing director, general manager or simply *directeurs* (director, *Direktor*). Some managing directors are members of the board, others are not. Some, and apparently increasing numbers, of companies have chief executive officers who are senior to the MD. With *directeurs*, we do not know if the person concerned is the 'boss' or not. After discussion, it was decided to form a separate category and to consider such people as managerial or executive staff rather than important capital holders or ultimate policy-makers, although they mostly hold responsibility for the daily running of their enterprises. Together, however, they fulfil the functions of capital and, in the analysis of Poulantzas, for example, form an integral part of the bourgeoisie.

The next category included such people as company secretaries, *directeurs de finance* or *marketing*, *Prokurist*, and bank managers, managers holding responsible important line-management posts. 'Other management' includes all who have a 'managerial' title but who are somewhat lower in the hierarchy, or who have less crucial responsibilities. These include purchasing managers, training managers and plant managers. It proved difficult to follow Carchedi's schema and separate those fulfilling the functions of capital and those controlling labour. More information would have been needed. Hence, some in this category are 'bourgeois' while others are not.

'Professionals in business' include all those described simply as 'engineers' or 'economists', *chimiste* or accountant, as it is impossible to tell whether their role is managerial or essentially staff. The 'independent service business' includes such people as stockbrokers, real-estate agents, *ingénieurs-conseils* and consultants.

Together, all these groups represent the senior levels of business.

Appendix C. Basis of regrouping of sector categories

The INSEAD sectoral classification includes 25 categories. These are: (1) metals and mining; (2) chemicals, plastics and rubber; (3) petroleum; (4) pharmaceuticals; (5) energy: electricity, gas, coal, etc.; (6) mechanical engineering products; (7) motor vehicles and accessories; (8) aeronautics and shipbuilding; (9) electrical engineering and electronics; (10) textiles and clothing; (11) food and drink; (12) cosmetics and toiletries; (13) timber, paper and packaging; (14) other products (glass, cameras, scientific instruments, etc.); (15) building and construction; (16) travel, transport and tourism; (17) commerce, trade and retailing; (18) banking, finance and insurance; (19) printing and publishing, radio and television; (20) advertising and public relations; (21) consulting; (22) public services, government etc.; (23) teaching and education; (24) conglomerates, holding companies and venture capital; (25) other services (including real estate, law, executive development programmes, etc.).

In the scheme used in this book these are re-grouped in various ways, but principally as follows:

1. Traditional industries – INSEAD categories 1, 5, 7, 8, 10, 11, 13, 14, 15
2. New manufacturing – INSEAD categories 2, 3, 4, 6, 9, 12
3. Banking, insurance and finance – INSEAD category 18
4. Consulting – INSEAD category 21
5. Service – INSEAD categories 16, 20, 24, 25
6. Public sector – INSEAD categories 22, 23

Notes

1. Introduction

1 A much more complete ethnography is, of course, long overdue but far beyond the scope of the research reported here.

2. The creation of a new business Europe: the rise of the multinational firm and its managers

1 See, for example, analyses of the situation of the French textiles firms made in the journals *L'Expansion* and *Entreprise*, especially B. Brizay, 'Les grandes dynasties du Nord', *Entreprise*, no. 1020 (1975), 75–81.
2 The orientations given through the French plan were especially important in this process in that country. See, for example, the description of the policy of 'national champions' operating in France during the 1960s by C. Michalet in Vernon (1974). Most governments initiated merger policies and institutions such as the Industrial Reorganisation Corporation in the UK to encourage this.
3 This company symbolises events of the period. Saint-Gobain, founded in 1665, was one of the world's oldest companies. Pont-à-Mousson, founded in the mid nineteenth century, was still controlled by members of the two founding families until one sold out in 1966. The two companies merged in 1968 (*Cahiers Français*, 1979: Notice 3).
4 The following sections are based on the analysis in Franko, 1976 and Dyas and Thanheiser, 1976.
5 An *undergraduate* school, Nijenrode, was founded early in 1946 by a group of Dutch businessmen.
6 The quotation has been translated by the author from the French in which it is cited in Le More (1976: 99).

3. The routes to internationalism: family backgrounds, and educational experience

1 For a description of the sample population see the Introduction above and Appendix A at the end of the book. In this chapter, unless otherwise stated, the data are derived from analysis of the admission files to the Institute.
2 For an explanation of the classification of the titles see Appendix B.

3 A preliminary analysis of the backgrounds from selected nationalities of candidates to INSEAD who were rejected or resigned after acceptance was also made and showed no great differences in social origins. There were greater differences, as could be expected, in educational attainments.

4 The 'Clarendon Nine' are Eton, Harrow, Winchester, Rugby, Merchant Taylors', St Paul's, Shrewsbury, Westminster and Charterhouse. The 'well-known' are those classed as such by Boyd in *Elites and their Education* (1973: 41–7).

5 The greater links in France between institutions and career possibilities also mean a lesser need for supplementary training for those from the most prestigious schools.

6 See, for example, Bourdieu, Boltanski and de Saint Martin, 1973 and Boltanski, 1981.

4. Choosing a career: family edicts and school verdicts

1 The Arts-et-Métiers is a school that offers a very practical engineering training, less prestigious because less abstract and 'generalist' than the other engineering *grandes écoles*.

2 Unless otherwise stated, all emphases in the quotations in this and subsequent chapters have been added.

5. Careers across Europe

1 See Appendix C.

2 The groupings used in the INSEAD list of sectors has been modified here, for fewer categories are needed to establish patterns. The revised list included traditional manufacturing, new manufacturing, banking and finance, consulting, other services and miscellaneous. The basis of the regrouping is described in Appendix C.

3 Because of the small number of respondents from certain nationalities, only six major groups are discussed – the British, Germans, Scandinavians, Swiss, Belgians and Dutch. In the discussion, unless otherwise stated, the figures do not apply to changes made by individuals, only to overall movements such as sectional gains and losses; but they largely overlap.

4 Figures are usually only analysed for three firms, because of the very small numbers of respondents working in fourth or fifth firms.

5 Some of these links may be due to different proportions of each nationality in the sample in each of the periods of years considered.

6 The conclusion that mobility between firms *per se* may not pay in salary terms is reflected in advice given by Beaudeux in *L'Expansion* in 1981, in which he said: 'Restez où vous êtes' and 'Négociez une augmentation' (1981: 107–12).

7 The Austrians were not represented in the forty-five and the numbers of Italians and Spanish were too small to be significant.

6. Escalator or roller-coaster? Moving on and flying high in the businesses of Europe

1 The data in this chapter are from the 120 interviews with alumni of more than five years' standing carried out in 1980 in France, the UK, Belgium, Switzerland and Germany.

2 The date inside the brackets indicates the year of graduation from INSEAD in this and all subsequent quotations.

3. The respondent was confirmed in his view by the consulting firm Egon Zehnder, whose representative, interviewed in Brussels in 1977, said that by the age of 38 one should be a general manager of a subsidiary, with all one's functional experience behind one.

7. Invisible resources: families of origin and marriage

1 The data in this chapter are drawn from the questionnaire surveys of 1973 (French) and 1979 (other nationalities).

8. A family of beliefs and character

1 The less successful may drop out: 'I used to have a lot of contacts with alumni . . . but I've let it drop. As time passes after leaving INSEAD, the alumni have different degrees of professional success. Those who have succeeded are not modest about it. My own success has been less than average. One doesn't like to be brought up against one's failure.'

2 For an analysis of the 'public' of *Le Nouvel Observateur*, see Pinto, 1981. The INSEAD population is remarkably similar in this to younger managers who, although not MBAs, were from similar *grandes écoles* and social backgrounds to those of our sample. Fontaine (1977: 65) showed that of the *cadres* aged thirty years, 23% read *Le Monde*, 14% each *L'Express*, *Le Nouvel Observateur*, *Le Point* and *L'Expansion*.

3 See, for example, Bourdieu and de Saint Martin, 1976.

9. Reaching the top: origins, competence and connections

1 The figures above of course vary somewhat according to the range of companies and managerial levels studied, but the overall trends remain clear.

2 May reports Kruk as concluding that 'in Germany, an arts graduate has little chance of becoming a top manager' (quoted May, 1974: 65).

3 In the late 1980s banking may, however, be changing to reward 'competence' as well as connections, as world finance capitalism develops, and may thus become the province *par excellence* of the risk-taker.

4 The centrality of the figures present to both politics and business is clear. Lord Aldington, for example, is a former minister, deputy chairman of the Conservative Party, chairman of Grindlay's Bank and Sun Alliance, deputy chairman of GEC, and a director of Lloyd's Bank – a man who links politics, the City and industry (Fidler, 1981: 244).

References

Acton Society Trust, 1956. *Management Succession*. London: Acton Society Trust
1962. *The Arts Graduate in Industry*. London: Acton Society Trust
Ahlström, G., 1981. *Engineers and Industrial Growth*. London and Canberra: Croom Helm
Allard, P., M. Beaud, B. Bellon, A.-M. Lévy and S. Liénart, 1978. *Dictionnaire des groupes industriels et financiers en France*. Paris: Le Seuil
Allen, V., 1961. 'Management and the universities', *The Listener*, 13 July
Althusser, L., 1969. *For Marx*, Harmondsworth: Penguin Books
1970. 'Idéologie et appareils idéologiques d'état', *La Pensée*, 157: 3–38
Andreff, W., 1976. *Profils et structures du capitalisme mondial*. Paris: Calman-Lévy
Anglo-American Council on Productivity, 1951. *Education for Management*. London: AACP
Bachy, J-P., 1971. *Les Cadres en France*. Paris: A. Colin
Bailyn, L., 1978. 'The slow-burn way to the top: implications of changes in the relation between work and family for models of organisational careers', Paper presented to an Industrial Liaison Program Symposium on Women in the Workplace: Management of Human Resources: Massachusetts Institute of Technology, 26 January 1978
Baldwin, A., 1978. The changing nature of managerial positions and their incumbents. Unpublished paper, Manchester Business School
Ball, R.J., 1967. 'British business schools', *Electricity*, May–June: 3–8
Barjonet, C., 1981. 'Les 1000 premières entreprises françaises', *L'Expansion*, 180, November: 105–87
Bassan, J., 1969, *Les Nouveaux Patrons*. Paris: A. Fayard
Baudelot, C. and R. Establet, 1971. *L'Ecole capitaliste en France*. Paris: Maspéro
Bauer, M. and E. Cohen, 1981. *Qui gouverne les groupes industriels?* Paris: Le Seuil
1980. 'The skills of engineers and managers in large French firms', *International Studies of Management and Organisation*, 10 (1–2): 21–45
Baumier, J., 1967. *Les Grandes Affaires françaises: des 200 familles aux 200 managers*. Paris: Julliard
Baumol, W., 1959. *Business Behaviour, Value and Growth*. London: Macmillan
Beaud, M., 1977. 'Note sur la connaissance des groupes capitalistes', *Recherches Economiques et Sociales*, 7–8: 91–7
Beaudeux, P., 1972. 'Les cent qui font l'économie', *L'Expansion*, 55: 119–32
1974. 'Le prix des cadres, 1974', *L'Expansion*, 75: 105–27

226

1977. 'Le prix des cadres', *L'Expansion*, 99: 125–56, and June every year

1981. 'Sept conseils pour mieux gérer votre carrière', *L'Expansion*, 172: 107–12.

Beckers, M. and J.P. Frère, 1974. 'Individual characteristics of Belgian top managers and their career path in the firm', *International Studies of Management and Organisation*, 4 (1–2): 41–67

Bell, C., 1968. *Middle Class Families*. London: Routledge and Kegan Paul

Bell, D., 1961. *The End of Ideology*. New York: Collier Books

1976. *The Coming of Post-Industrial Society*. New York: Basic Books

Bellon, P., 1980. *Le Pouvoir financier et l'industrie en France*. Paris: Le Seuil

Benguigui, G., 1967. 'La professionalisation des cadres dans l'industrie', *Sociologie du Travail*, 9 (2): 134–43

Benguigui, G. and D. Monjardet, 1970. *Etre un cadre en France?* Paris: Dunod

Berle, A. and G. Means, 1932. *Modern Corporation and Private Property*. New York: Macmillan

Bernoux, P., 1974. *Les Nouveaux Patrons*. Paris: Editions Ouvrières

Berridge, T., 1978. Work experience and career paths of accountants. Unpublished paper, Manchester Business School

Berry, D., 1976. 'L'Europe des "business schools" à la croisée des chemins', *Informations*, 79 (June)

Bertaux, D., 1977. *Destins personnels et destins de classe*. Paris: Presses Universitaires de France

Bettignies, H.-C. de and P. Evans, 1971. 'Europe looks north at the Scandinavian business élite', *European Business*, 26

Birnbaum, P., C. Barucq, M. Bellaiche, and A. Marie, 1978. *La Classe dirigeante française*. Paris: Presses Universitaires de France

Board of Trade, 1946. *A Central Institute of Management*. London: HMSO

Bodinat, H. de, 1973. 'Les écoles de gestion au banc d'essai', *L'Expansion*, 63: 169–77

Boissevain, J., 1974. *Friends of Friends*. Oxford: Blackwell

Boltanski, L., 1972. L'espace positionnel: les professeurs des écoles du pouvoir et le pouvoir. Unpublished paper, Paris: Centre de Sociologie Européenne

1981. 'America, America . . . le plan Marshall et l'importation du "management"', *Actes de la Recherche en Sciences Sociales*, 38: 19–41

Boltho, A., ed., 1982. *The European Economy: Growth and Crisis*. Oxford: Oxford University Press

Bonzon, P., 1968. 'Le défi des business schools: l'opinion des employeurs', *Hommes et Commerce*, 101 and 103: 187–93

Bouchet, J-L., 1976. 'Diversification, composition of the top management team and performance of the firm'. Paper presented to the EGOS Conference on the Sociology of the Enterprise, December, Oxford

Boudet, J., 1952. *Le Monde des affaires en France de 1830 à nos jours*. Paris: Société d'Edition de Dictionnaires et d'Encyclopédies

Boudon, R., 1973. *L'Inégalité des chances*. Paris: Armand Colin. Translated 1974 as *Education, Opportunity and Social Inequality*. London: John Wiley

Bourdieu, P., 1970. Le Marché des biens symboliques. Unpublished paper, Centre de Sociologie, Paris

1971. 'Reproduction culturelle et reproduction sociale', *Informations sur les Sciences Sociales*, 10 (2): 45–79

1978. 'Classement, déclassement, reclassement', *Actes de la Recherche en Sciences Sociales*, 24: 2–22

1979. 'Les trois états du capital culturel', *Actes de la Recherche en Sciences Sociales*, 30: 3–6

1980. 'Le capital social', *Actes de la Recherche en Sciences Sociales*, 31: 2–3

Bourdieu, P. and L. Boltanski, 1976. 'La production de l'idéologie dominante; encyclopédie des idées reçues', *Actes de la Recherche en Sciences Sociales*, 2 (2–3): 4–74

Bourdieu, P., L. Boltanski, and M. de Saint Martin, 1973. 'Les stratégies de reconversion', *Social Science Information*, 12: 61–113

Bourdieu, P. and Y. Delsaut, 1975. 'Le couturier et sa griffe: contribution à une théorie de la magie', *Actes de la Recherche en Sciences Sociales*, 1: 7–36

Bourdieu, P. and J.-C. Passeron, 1964. *Les Héritiers*. Paris: Editions de Minuit

1970. *La Reproduction*. Paris: Editions de Minuit

Bourdieu, P. and M. de Saint Martin, 1976. 'L'anatomie du goût', *Actes de la Recherche en Sciences Sociales*, 5: 5–81

1978. 'Le patronat', *Actes de la Recherche en Sciences Sociales*, 20–1: 3–82

Bouvier, J., 1974. 'Capital bancaire, capital industriel, et capital financier dans la croissance française au XIXe siècle', *La Pensée*, 178 (December): 3–17

Bowles, S. and H. Gintis, 1976. *Schooling in Capitalist America*. London: Routledge and Kegan Paul

Boyd, D., 1973. *Elites and their Education*. Slough: National Foundation for Education Research

British Industry Week, 1967. 'Business Schools in Business – but still a long way to go', 20 September

British Institute of Management, 1968. *The Employment of Graduates*. London: British Institute of Management

1971. *Business School Programmes: The Requirements of British Manufacturing Industry*. London: British Institute of Management

1977. *National Management Salary Survey*. London: British Institute of Management

Brizay, B., 1976. *Le Patronat*. Paris: Le Seuil

Bunel, J. and J. Saglio, 1976. *La Société des patrons. Contribution à l'analyse du système français des relations professionnelles: le Cas Rhône-Alpes-Lyon*. Paris: Economie et Humanisme

Bunel, P., 1974. *Les Nouveaux Patrons*. Paris: Editions Ouvrières

Burch, P., 1972. *The Managerial Revolution Reassessed*. Lexington, Mass.: Heath

Burger, N., 1968. *The Executive's Wife*. New York: Macmillan

Burnham, J., 1941, republished 1968. *The Managerial Revolution*. Harmondsworth: Penguin Books

Business Graduates' Association, 1971. *British Industry's Attitudes to Business Graduates and Business Schools*. London: British Graduates' Association

1971. 'The rate for the job', *Business Graduate*, 1: 3–6

1973. *The Business Graduate in Britain, 1973*. London: British Graduates' Association

Cahiers Français, 1979. 'Les multinationales', *Cahiers Français*, 190 (March–April): 5 and 23

Carré, B., 1978. *Le Pouvoir de l'elite familiale*. Paris: Presses Universitaires de France

Carré, J.-J., P. Dubois, and E. Malinvaud, 1973. *Abrégé de la croissance française*. Paris: Le Seuil

Cézard, M., 1973. 'Les cadres et leurs diplômes', *Economie et Statistique*, 42: 25–41

Chandler, A., 1962. *Strategy and Structure*. Cambridge, Mass.: Massachusetts Institute of Technology

1976. 'The development of modern management structure in the US and the UK', in L. Hannah, ed., *Management Strategy and Business Development*. London: Macmillan

1977. *The Visible Hand*. London: Macmillan

Chandler, A. and H. Daems, 1980. *Managerial Hierarchies*. Cambridge, Mass. and London: Harvard University Press

Channon, D., 1973. *The Strategy and Structure of British Enterprise*. London: Macmillan

1976. 'Corporate evolution in the service industries', in L. Hannah, (ed.), *Management Strategy and Business Development*. London: Macmillan

1977. *British Banking Strategy and the International Challenge*. London: Macmillan

Chester, T., 1965. 'Industry, management and the universities: trends and problems of a changing relationship', *District Bank Review*, 156: 3–27

Chevalier, J., 1970. *La Structure financière de l'industrie américane*. Paris: Cujas

Child, J., 1969. *British Management Thought*. London: Allen and Unwin

1972, 'Organisation structure, environment, and performance – the role of strategic choice', *Sociology*, 6: 1–22

Clark, D., 1966. *The Industrial Manager*. London: Business Publications

Claude, H., 1966. 'Les groupes financiers', *Economie et Politique*, 139: 112–20

Clement, W., 1977. *Continental Corporate Power: Economic Elite Linkages between Canada and the United States*. Toronto: McClelland and Stewart

Clements, R., 1958. *Managers: a Study of their Careers in Industry*. London: Allen and Unwin

Cleverley, G., 1971. *Managers and Magic*. Harmondsworth, Penguin Books

Coleman, D., 1973. 'Gentlemen and players', *Economic History Review*, 26: 92–116

Connell, W., D. Ashenden, S. Kessler, and G. Dowsett, 1982. *Making the Difference*. Sydney: Allen and Unwin

Contesse, J., 1961. 'Le marché des dirigeants d'entreprise', *Entreprise*, 315: 58–9

Copeman, G., 1955. *Leaders of British Industry*. London: Gee and Co.

Coston, H., 1975. *Dictionnaire des dynasties bourgeoises et du monde des affaires*. Paris: Editions Alain Moreau

Council of Engineering Institutions, 1977. *The 1977 Survey of Professional Engineers*. London: Council of Engineering Institutions

Crooks, L. and J. Campbell, 1974. *Career Progress of MBAs: an Exploratory Study Six Years after Graduation*. Princeton: Education Testing Service

Curzon, G. and W. Curzon, 1976. *The Multinational Enterprise in a Hostile World*. London: Macmillan

Daems, H., 1977. *The Holding Company and Corporate Control*. Leiden and Boston: Martinus Nijhoff

1980. 'The rise of the modern industrial enterprise', in A. Chandler and H. Daems, *Managerial Hierarchies*. Cambridge, Mass.: Harvard University Press, pp. 203–24

Daems, H., and H. van der Wee, 1974. *The Rise of Managerial Capitalism*. Louvain and the Hague: Leuven University Press and Martinus Nijhoff

Dahrendorf, R., 1964. 'Recent changes in the class structure in European societies', *Daedalus*, 92 (1): 225–70

Daily Telegraph, 1968. 'Companies facing snags over "blue chip" graduates'. 14 October

Dalle, F. and J. Bounnine-Cabale, 1971. *L'Entreprise du futur*. Paris: Calman-Lévy

Daris, S., 1977. *Managing and Organising Multinational Corporations*. New York: Pergamon Press

Degot, V., 1980. 'Types of French engineers and the implementation of company policies: a case study', *International Studies of Management and Organisation*, 10 (1–2): 165–84

Delefortrie-Soubeyroux, N., 1961. *Les Dirigeants de l'industrie française*. Paris: A. Colin

Department of Industry, 1977. *Industry, Education and Management*. London: Department of Industry

Derivry, D., 1975. 'The managers of public enterprise in France', in M. Dogan, ed., *The Mandarins of Western Europe*, Berkeley: Sage Publications

Derossi, F., 1974. 'A profile of Italian managers in large firms', *International Studies of Management and Organisation*, 4 (1–2): 138–202

Devillelongue, R., 1977. *Péchiney-Ugine-Kuhlmann, pourquoi?* Paris: Stock

Domhoff, G., 1978. *The Powers That Be*. New York: Random House
1980. *Power Structure Research*. Beverly Hills: Sage

Dougier, H., 1970. 'Diriger: un métier qui s'apprend jeune', *Le Management* (April): 63–7

Dougier, H. and T. Houston, 1968. 'Europe's business schools: overshadowed or creative?', *European Business*, 19: 5–13

Drancourt, M., 1973. 'Les trois profils du manager', *Entreprise*, 912: 72–3

Dunkerley, D., 1975. *Occupations and Society*. London: Routledge and Kegan Paul

Dyas, G., 1972. The strategy and structure of French industrial enterprises. Unpublished PhD thesis, Harvard Business School

Dyas, G. and H. Thanheiser, 1976. *The Emerging European Enterprise*. London: Macmillan

Eales, R., 1985. 'Multinationals and business schools', *Multinational Business*, 1: 10–17

Eggens, J., 1970. 'Le prix des cadres 1970', *L'Expansion*, 31: 125–37

Eglin, R., 1977. 'Business schools come under fire from action man', *Industrial Management*, May: 25–7

Elliott, R., 1977. 'Fontainebleau – still a centre of elitism', *Training*, September: 8–11

Entreprise, 1962. 'Chef d'entreprise, est-ce un métier qui s'apprend?' 26 May: 51–7
1966. 'Comment détecter les cadres internationaux', no. 558: 75–81

Entreprise et Progrès, 1974. 'L'évolution de carrière des cadres.' Paris.

Eulau, H. and M. Czudnowski, 1976. *Elite Recruitment in Democratic Polities*. New York: Sage Publications

Eurosurvey, 1979. 'Evolution du statut des cadres supérieurs. Tendance des rémunérations', Brussels

Fayol, H., 1974. *Administration industrielle et générale*. Paris: Dunod

Fennema, M., 1982. *International Networks of Banks and Industry*. The Hague: Martinus Nijhoff

Fennema, M. and H. Schiff, 1985. 'The transnational network', in F. Stokman, R. Ziegler and J. Scott, eds., *Networks of Corporate Power*. Cambridge: Polity Press, pp. 250–66

Ferris, P., 1960. *The City*. Harmondsworth: Penguin Books

Fidler, J., 1977. *The British Business Elite: Recruitment and Attitudes to Social Stratification*. University of Aston Management Centre, Working Paper Series No. 64

　　1981. *The British Business Elite: Its Attitude to Class, Status and Power*. London: Routledge and Kegan Paul

Finniston, Sir M., 1978. 'Creative management', *Journal of the Royal Society of Arts*, 5263: 407–201

Fontaine, J., 1977. 'Les grandes entreprises jugent les grandes écoles', *L'Expansion*, 100: 64–71

　　1980. 'Douze portraits de chefs', *L'Expansion*, 21 March–3 April: 99–109

Francis, A., 1980. 'Families, firms and finance capital: the development of UK industrial firms with particular reference to their ownership and control', *Sociology*, 14 (1): 1–27

Franko, L., 1976. *The European Multinationals*. New York: Harper and Row

Freyssenet, M., 1977. *Le Division capitaliste du travail*. Paris: Savelli

Furstenburg, F., 1961. 'Aspects sociologiques de la promotion dans l'entreprise', *Sociologie du Travail*, 3 (1): 18–29

Galbraith, K., 1971. 2nd edn. *The New Industrial State*. New York: Mentor

George, K. and T. Ward, 1975. *The Structure of Industry in the EEC: An International Comparison*. London: Cambridge University Press

Gerstl, J. and S. Hutton, 1966. *Engineers: The Anatomy of a Profession*. London: Tavistock

Giddens, A., 1974. 'Elites in the British class structure', in P. Stanworth and A. Giddens, eds., *Elites and Power in the British Society*. London: Cambridge University Press

Giddens, A. and G. Mackensie, 1982. *Social Class and the Division of Labour*. Cambridge: Cambridge University Press

Giddens, A. and P. Stanworth, 1978. 'Elites and privilege', in P. Abrams (ed.), *Work, Urbanism, and Inequality*. London: Weidenfeld and Nicholson

Girard, A., 1961. *La Réssite sociale en France*. Paris: Presses Universitaires de France

Girard, A., G. Bastide, and G. Pourchier, 1963. 'Enquête nationale sur l'entrée en sixième . . .', *Population*, 18: 9–48

Glickman, A., C. Hahn, E. Heishman, and B. Baxter, 1968. *Top Management Development and Succession*. New York: Committee for Economic Development

Glover, I., 1976. 'Executive career patterns: Britain, France, Germany and Sweden', *Energy World*, December: 3–12

Goggin, W., 1974. 'How the multidimensional structure works at Dow-Corning', *Harvard Business Review*, 52 (1): 54–65

Granovetter, M., 1974. *Getting the Job: a Study of Contacts and Careers*. Cambridge, Mass.: Harvard University Press

Granwick, D., 1972. *Managerial Comparisons of Four Developed Countries*. Cambridge, Mass.: Massachusetts Institute of Technology Press

Guerrier, Y. and N. Philpot, 1978. *The British Manager: Careers and Mobility*. London: British Institute of Management

Gunz, H., 1980. 'Generalists, specialists and the reproduction of managerial structures', *International Studies of Management and Organisation*, October: 137–64

Gutteridge, T., 1973. 'The hardest job of all: career planning', *MBA*, October: 19–20

Habermas, J., 1976. *Legitimation Crisis*. London: Heinemann

Hahlo, H., J. Graham Smith, and R. Wright (eds.), 1973. *Nationalism and the Multinational Enterprise*. Dobbs Ferry and Leiden: Oceania Publications and Sijthoff

Hall, D. and G. Amado-Fischgrund, 1969. 'Chief Executives in Britain', *European Business*, January: 23–9

Hall, D. and H.-C. de Bettignies, 1968. 'The French business elite', *European Business*, 3: 1–10

Hall, D., H.-C. de Bettignies, and G. Amado-Fischgrund, 1969. 'The European business elite', *European Business*, October: 45–55

Handy, C., 1977a. 'Business schools – missionaries or mercenaries?' *International Management Development*, 4: 3–5

1977b. *Understanding Organisations*. Harmondsworth: Penguin Books

Hannah, L., 1976. *The Rise of the Corporate Economy*. London: Macmillan

Hannah, L. and J. Kay, 1977. *Concentration in Modern Industry*. London: Macmillan

Harmon, F., 1977. 'European top managers' struggle for survival', *European Business*, 28 (1): 4–19

Harris, A. and A. de Sédouy, 1977. *Les Patrons*. Paris: Le Seuil

Heath, A., J. Ridge, and A. Halsey, 1980. *Origins and Destinations: Family, Class and Education in Modern Britain*. Oxford: Clarendon Press

Heidrick and Struggles Inc. Many reports through the 1970s on profiles of chief executives, boards of directors, directors of functions (e.g. personnel), in both manufacturing and banking, in the USA and Europe

Heller, R., 1973. 'The state of British boardrooms', *Management Today*, May

1977. 'Smart Lads wanted', *British Airways High Life Magazine* (November): 31–5

Herblay, J., 1972. 'Les Gadzarts: un ingénieur qu'on s'arrache', *La Vie des Cadres*, 2: 25–9

Herman, E., 1981, p.b. 1982. *Corporate Control, Corporate Power*. New York: Cambridge University Press

Herzog, D., 1978. 'The study of elites in West Germany', in M. Kaase, and K. von Beyme, eds., *Elections and Parties*. London: Sage Publications

Higley, J., G. Lowell-Field, and K. Crholt, 1976. *Elite Structure and Ideology. A Theory with Applications to Norway*. Oslo and New York: Universitetsforrlaget and Columbia University Press

Hiljerding, R., 1910. *Das Finanzkapital*, translated 1981 and published as *Finance Capitalism*. London: Routledge and Kegan Paul

Hill, R., 1974. 'Exxon plays Global Chess with its Managers', *International Management*, September: 14–20

Hirschman, A., 1970. *Exit, Voice and Loyalty*. Cambridge, Mass.: Harvard University Press

Hofstede, G., 1978. 'Businessmen and business school faculty: A comparison of value systems', *Journal of Management Studies*, 15 (1)

Holden, P., C. Pederson and G. Germaine, 1968. *Top Management*. New York: McGraw-Hill

Hornyold-Strickland, H. and W. Weskamp, 1977. 'INSEAD and Germany: a survey of career and salary prospects for INSEAD alumni working in Germany'. Unpublished document

Horovitz, J., 1980. *Top Management Control in Europe*. London: Macmillan

Hughes, B., 1977. 'The Graduate', *The Financial Post Magazine*, September: 11–18

Humblet, J., 1966. *Les Cadres d'entreprise*. Paris: Editions Universitaires

Hussain, A., 1976. 'The economy and the educational system in capitalistic societies', *Economy and Society*, 5 (4): 413–34

Industrial Management, 1971. 'A lesson for business schools', July

International Labour Office, 1973. *Multinational Enterprises and Social Policy*. Geneva: International Labour Office

1976. *Career Planning and Development*. Management Development Series No. 12. Geneva: International Labour Office

International Management Development, 1977. Management Education in France 2: 10–14

Jacquemin, A. and H. de Jong, 1976. *Markets, Corporate Behaviour and the State*. The Hague: Martinus Nijhoff

1977. *European Industrial Organisation*. London: Macmillan

Jacquin, F., 1955. *Le Cadres de l'industrie et du commerce*. Paris: A. Colin

James, D., and M. Soref, 1981. 'Profit constraints on managerial-autonomy: managerial theory and the unmaking of the corporation president', *American Sociology Review*, 46 (February): 1–18

Jamison, K., 1974. 'Exxon plays global chess with its managers', *International Management*, September: 14–20

Jemain, A., 1974. 'La Lainière n'est plus la même', *Enterprise*, 967: 21–7

Johnson, T., 1972. *Professions and Power*. London: Macmillan

Kapoor, A., and P. Grub, 1973. *The Multinational Enterprise in Transition*. Princeton: Darwin Press

Karpik, L., 1977. 'Technological capitalism', in S. Clegg, and D. Dunkerley, eds., *Critical Issues in Organisations*. London: Routledge and Kegan Paul, pp. 41–71

Katz, R., 1974. 'Skills of an effective administrator', *Harvard Business Review*, 52 (5): 90–102

Kelsall, R.K., A. Poole, and A. Kuhn, 1974. *Graduates: the Sociology of an Elite*. London: Tavistock

Kosciusko-Morizet, J., 1973. '*La Mafia' polytechnicienne*. Paris: Le Seuil

Kumar, K., 1978. *Prophecy and Progress*. Harmondsworth: Penguin Books

Lawrence, P., 1984. *Management in Action*. London: Routledge and Kegan Paul

Lefranc, G., 1976. *Les Organisations patronales en France*. Paris: Payot

Leggatt, T., 1972. *The Training of British Managers*. London: HMSO

1978. 'Managers in Industry: their backgrounds and education', *Sociological Review*, 26: 807–25

Legge, K., 1978. *Power, Innovation and Problem-Solving in Personnel Management*. London and New York: McGraw-Hill

Le More, H., 1976. 'Classes possédantes et classes dirigeantes'. Thèse de troisième cycle. Paris

Le Point, 1978. 'Les salaires des cadres 1978', *Le Point*, 277 (January): 73–82

Levinson, H., 1974. 'Don't choose your own successor', *Harvard Business Review*, 52 (6): 53–62

Levitt, T., 1974. 'The managerial merry-go-round', *Harvard Business Review*, 52 (4): 120–8

Lévy-Leboyer, M., 1979. *Le Patronat de la seconde industrialisation*. Paris: Editions Ouvrières

Lewellen, W., 1971. *The Ownership Income of Management*. New York: National Bureau of Economic Research and Columbia University Press

Lewis, R. and R. Stewart, 1958 and 1961 (2nd edn.). *The Managers*. New York: Mentor

L'Expansion almost every month has articles on career prospects, on examples of successful managers and on the characteristics of managers in different functions

Linz, J. and A. de Miguel, 1974. 'Founders, heirs and managers of Spanish firms', *International Studies of Management and Organisation*, 4 (1–2): 7–40

Livingston, J.S., 1971. 'The myth of the well-educated manager', *Harvard Business Review*, January–February

Lupton, T. and S. Wilson, 1959. 'The social background and connections of top decision makers', *Manchester School*, 27

Luzatto-Fegis, P., 1971. *Formazione Scolastica, Carriera e Affermazione dei 'Dirigenti' in Italia*. Milan: Doxa

McEwan, A., 1977. 'Britons excel at Europe's school for go-getters', *Johannesburg Star*, January 13

McGivering, I., D. Matthews, and W. Scott, 1960. *Management in Britain: a General Characterisation*. Liverpool: Liverpool University Press

Makler, H., 1974. 'Educational levels of the Portuguese industrial elite', *International Studies of Management and Organisation*, 4 (1–2): 41–67

Mann, R., ed. 1970. *The Arts of Top Management*. London: McGraw-Hill.

Mansell, C., 1972. 'Fontainebleau's keen cadets', *Management Today*, July: 73–5 and 118–20

Marceau, J., 1976a. *The Social Origins, Educational Experience and Career Paths of a Young Business Elite*. INSEAD Monograph 1/76: Fontainebleau

1976b, 'Role division and social cohesion: the case of some young French upper-class families', in S. Allen and D. Barker, eds., *Dependence and Exploration in Work and Marriage*. Harlow: Longman

1977. *Class and Status in France*. Oxford: Oxford University Press

1978, 'Le rôle des femmes dans les familles du monde des affaires', in A. Michel (ed.), *Les Femmes dans la Société Marchande*. Paris: Presses Universitaires de France, 13–24

1979. 'Business policies, business élites and business schools: a conference overview', *Social Science Information* 18 (3): 473–86. Reprinted in *International Studies of Management and Organisation*, 19 (1–2): 6–20

1981a. 'Plus ça change, plus c'est la même chose? Access to elite careers in French business', in A. Cerny, ed., *Elites in France: Origins, Reproduction and Power*. London and New York: Frances Pinter

1981b. 'The management of the international economy: multinationals in the service of multinationals.' Paper presented to a conference on *Organisation, Economy and Society*, Brisbane, July 17–19

Marceau, J., A. Thomas and R. Whitley, 1978. 'Business and the state: management education and business elites in France and Great Britain', in G. Littlejohn *et al.*, eds., *Power and the State*. London: Croom Helm

Marcus, G., 1980. 'Law in the development of dynastic families among American business elites: the domestication of capital and the capitalisation of family', *Law and Society Review*, 14 (4)

Margerison, C., 1978. 'Making tomorrow's managers', *Management Today*, May, 87–8: 152

Marris, R. and A. Wood, eds. 1971. *The Corporate Economy*. London: Macmillan.

Mason, R., R. Miller and D. Weigel, 1981 (2nd edn). *International Business*. New York: John Wiley

Mathewson, W., 1976. 'The French penchant for hiring MBAs from American schools seems to fade', *The Wall Street Journal*, 24 (August)

Maurice, M., R. Monteil, J. Guillon, and J. Gaulon, 1967. *Les Cadres et l'Enterprise*. Paris: Université de Paris, Institut des Sciences Sociales du Travail

May, B., 1974. 'The background of German managers: a review of the evidence.' Report prepared for the Department of Trade and Industry, London. In this, May reviews a number of articles and books, of which the most important to concern us here are (NB. No further details on publishers or place of publication are available from May's report)

ASU/JU Umfrage, 1966. *Selbständige Unternehmer*

Biermann, B. and O. Benno, 1971. *Die Soziale Struktur de Undernehmenschaft*, Stuttgart

Brinkmann, G., 1967. *Die Ausbildung von Führungskraften fur die Wirtschaft*. Koln: Universitatsverlag Wienand

Hartmann, H., 1956. 'Die Zahlenmassige Beitrage des Deutschen Hochschulen zur Gruppe der Industriellen Führungskrafte', in *Zeitschrift fur die Gesamte Staatswissenschaft*, 112: 144–63

Kruk, M., 1967. *Die Oberen 30,000*. Wiesbaden
1972. *Die Grossen Unternehmer*. Frankfurt: Societatas

Pross, H. and K. Boetticher, 1971. *Manager der Kapitalismus*. Frankfurt: Suhrkamp

Zapf, W., 1965. 'Die Deutschen Manager – sozial profil und karriereweg', in *Beitrage zur Analyse der Deutschen Oberschicht*, 136–49

Zeidler, K., 1971. *Rollenanalyse von Fuhrungskraften der Wirtschaft*. Erlanger

Melrose-Woodman, J., 1978. *Profile of the British Manager*. London: British Institute of Management

Melucci, A., 1974. *Idéologies et pratiques patronales pendant l'industrialisation capitaliste: le cas de la France*. Paris: Ecole des Hautes Etudes en Sciences Sociales

Meynaud, J., 1960. *Technocratie et Politique*. Etudes de Science Politique No. 2. Paris: Fondation des Sciences Politiques

Michalet, C., 1976. *Le Capitalisme Mondial*. Paris: Presses Universitaires de France

Midley, S., 1978. 'British engineers fall behind Germans in status and salary', *The Times Higher Education Supplement*, 10 February: 10

Mokken, R. and F. Stokman, 1978–9. 'Corporate-governmental networks in the Netherlands', *Social Networks*, 1: 333–58

Monjardet, D., 1972. 'Carrière des dirigeants et contrôle de l'entreprise', *Sociologie du Travail*, 13 (2): 131–44

Morin, F., 1974. *La Structure financière du capitalisme français*. Paris: Calmann-Lévy

Morin, F. with A. and C. Alcouffe, X. Freixas and M. Moreaux, 1977. *La Banque et les groupes industriels à l'heure des nationalisations*. Paris: Calmann-Lévy

Mosson, T.M., 1965. *Management Education in Five European Countries*. London: Business Publications

1972. 'And now a word from our sponsors . . .' *Management Education and Development*, 3: 74–8

Nakagawa, K., ed., n.d. *Strategy and Structure of Big Business*. Tokyo: University of Tokyo Press

Negroni, F. de, 1974. *La France noble*. Paris: Le Seuil

Nelson, Lord, 1964. *Management Education and the British Business Schools: Report on the 1964 Appeal and Statement on Future Policy*. London: Foundation for Management Education

Neuschwander, C., 1974. *Patron, mais . . .* Paris: Le Seuil

Newcomer, M., 1955. *The Big Business Executive*. New York: Columbia University Press

Nichols, T., 1969. *Ownership, Control and Ideology*. London: Allen and Unwin

Normanbrook, Rt Hon. Lord, 1964. *British Business Schools: The Cost*. London: British Institute of Management

Nyman, S. and A. Silberston, 1978. 'The ownership and control of industry', *Oxford Economic Papers*, new series, 30: 74–103

OECD, 1972. *Management Education*. Paris: OECD

1979. *Concentration and Competition Policy*. Paris: OECD

Offe, C., 1976. *Industry and Inequality*. London: Edward Arnold

Pahl, J. and R. Pahl, 1971. *Managers and Their Wives*. Harmondsworth: Penguin Books

Pahl, R. and J. Winkler, 1974. 'The economic elite: theory and practice', in P. Stanworth and A. Giddens, eds., *Elites and Power in British Society*. London: Cambridge University Press

Papanek, H., 1973. 'Men, women and work: reflections on the two-person career', *American Journal of Sociology*, 78 (4): 852–72

Parker, H., 1970. 'Introduction' to R. Mann, ed., *The Arts of Top Management*. London: McGraw-Hill

Parkin, F., 1974. *Class Inequality and Political Order*. London: Macgibbon and Kee

Partridge, Sir J., 1970. 'What's wrong with business education?', *Economist*, 21 November

Patronat Français, 1968. 'La Commission "Entreprise-Ecole de Guerre" dégage les principes de base d'un système efficace de perfectionnement des cadres supérieurs' *Patronat Français*, 287: 4–10

Perceron, R. and G. Nay, 1974. 'Le bon usage de l'université: première école de gestion française', *Le Management* (June–July): 55–61

Perlmutter, H. and D. Heenan, 1974. 'How multinational should your managers be?', *Harvard Business Review*, 52 (6): 121–32

Peyrenet, M., 1978. *La Dynastie des Gillet: les maîtres de Rhône-Poulenc*. Paris: Le Sycomore

Pfeffer, J., 1977. 'Toward an examination of stratification in organisations', *Administrative Science Quarterly*, 22: 553–68

Pinchot, G. III, 1985. *Intrapreneuring*. New York: Harper and Row

Pinto, L., 1981. 'Les affinités électives. Les amis du *Nouvel Observateur* comme "groupe ouvert"', *Actes de la Recherche en Sciences Sociales*, 36–7: 105–24

Poulantzas, N., 1974. *Les Classes sociales dans le capitalisme aujourd'hui*. Paris: Le Seuil

Prais, S., 1976. *The Evolution of Giant Firms in Britain*. London: Cambridge University Press

Priouret, R., 1963. *Les Origines du patronat français*. Paris: Grasset
　　1968. *La France et le Management*. Paris: Denoël et Hommes et Techniques

Pugh, D.S. and D. Hickson, 1976. *Organisational Structure in its Context*. Farnborough: Saxon House

Punch, M., 1978. 'The sixth column: elite socialisation at a Dutch business school'. Paper presented to an EGOS Conference, 'Business Policies Business Elites and Business Schools'. Paris: November 2–4

Radice, H., 1971. 'Control type, profitability and growth in large firms', *Economic Journal*, 81: 547–62

Raw, S., 1977. *Slater Walker*. London: Deutsch

Reboul, O., 1980. *Langage et idéologie*. Paris: Presses Universitaires de France

Renwick, N., 1985. 'Forty years of multi-nationals: the robber barons revisited', in C. Bell, ed., *Forty Years On: Studies in World Change in the Four Decades after 1945*. Canberra: Australian National University, Research School of Pacific Studies, Department of International Relations, pp. 89–110.

Reynaud, J.-D., 1963. *Les Syndicats en France*. Paris: A. Colin

Richardson, G.B., 1972. 'The organisation of industry', *Economic Journal*, 82: 883–96

Rivière, C., 1970. 'Les maréchaux d'industrie qui arrivent par les salons . . .', *Entreprise*, 785: 81–5

Robertson, A., 1965. 'Management education in Britain: the recent history', in R. Malik, ed., *Penguin Survey of Business and Industry 1965*. Harmondsworth: Penguin Books
　　1970. 'Business schools – is the backlash justified?', *Management Decision*, 4: 12–15

Roulleau, J.P., 1969. *Les Champions de l'expansion: une nouvelle race de dirigeants*. Paris: Cercle du livre économique

Rowley, A., 1974. *The Barons of European Industry*. London: Croom Helm

Saglio, J., 1977. 'Qui sont les patrons?', *Economie et Humanisme*, 236: 6–11

Saint Martin, M. de, 1980. 'Une grande famille', *Actes de la Recherche en Sciences Sociales*, 31: 4–21

Salais, R., 1970. 'Les niveaux de diplômes dans chaque catégorie professionelle', *Economie et Statistique*, 9: 49–57

Sales, A., and E. Savage, 1974. 'Introduction: studies of industrial elites in western Europe', *International Studies of Management and Organisation*, 4 (1–2): 3–6

Sarton, A., 1968. 'Les "business school graduates" dans l'économie européenne', *Direction*, 150 (May): 459–60

Schein, E., 1967. Organisational socialisation and the profession of management. Third Douglas Murray McGregor Memorial Lecture, Sloan School of Management, Massachusetts Institute of Technology, Cambridge, Mass

Scott, J., 1979. *Corporations, Classes and Capitalism*. London: Hutchinson
1982. *The Upper Classes*. London: Macmillan

Scott, J., and M. Hughes, 1980. 'Capital and communication in Scottish business', *Sociology*, 14 (1): 29–48

Sédillot, R., 1976. 'Les affaires s'enseignment à Fontainebleau', *La Vie Française*, 49, 6 December

Séréville, E. de and F. de Saint-Simon, 1975. *Dictionnaire de la noblesse française*. Paris: La Société Française du XXe Siècle

Servan-Schreiber, J.J., 1969. *The American Challenge*. Harmondsworth: Penguin Books. Originally published (1967) as *Le Défi américain*. Paris: De noël

Shanks, M., 1963. 'Britain's "Harvard" begins to take shape', *Financial Times*, 17 June

Shapero, A., 1985. *Managing Professional People*. New York: Free Press

Shepherd, G.F., Duchêne, and C. Saunders, 1983. *Europe's Industries*. London: Frances Pinter

Sibbald, A., 1978. 'A case of education', *Management Today*, July: 19–22

Silk, L. and D. Vogel, 1976. *Ethics and Profits: The Crisis of Confidence in American Business*. New York: Simon and Schuster

Sorrell, M., 1966. 'Finding tomorrow's managers', *Management Today*, 112: 60–3

Spiegelberg, R., 1973. *The City*. London: Quartet Books

Stanworth, P. and A. Giddens, eds., 1974. *Elites and Power in British Society*. London: Cambridge University Press
1975. 'The modern corporate economy: interlocking directorships in Britain 1906–70', *Sociological Review*, 23: 5–28

Steele, J. and L. Ward, 1974. 'MBAs: mobile, well-situated, well-paid', *Harvard Business Review*, January–February: 99–100

Steuber, U., 1976. *International Banking*. Leiden: A.W. Sijthoff

Stokman, F., R. Ziegler, and J. Scott, eds., 1985. *Networks of Corporate Power*. Cambridge: Polity Press

Stoléru, L., 1969. *L'Impératif industriel*. Paris: Le Seuil

Story, J. and M. Parrott, 1977. 'An essay on management in France – Does it work?', *International Herald Tribune*, 5 May

Suleiman, E., 1974. *Politics, Power and Bureaucracy in France*. Princeton, NJ: Princeton University Press
1978. *Elites in French Society*. New Jersey: Princeton University Press

Supple, B., ed., 1977. *Essays in British Business History*. Oxford: Clarendon Press

Table Ronde, 1978. 'Cadres: l'avenir est aux "Généralistes"', *Le Point*, 277 (January): 74–5

Tendron, R., 1977. 'Establishment: les intouchables', *Le Nouvel Economiste*, 102: 66–72

Thoenig, J.-C., 1973. *L'Ere des technocrates: le cas des Ponts-et-Chaussées*. Paris: Editions d'Organisation

Thomas, A., 1978. 'The British business elite: the case of the retail sector', *Sociological Review*, 26: 305–26

Tindall, R., 1975. *Multinational Enterprises*. Dobbs Ferry and Leiden: Oceana Publications and Sijthoff

Tugendhat, C., 1971. *The Multinationals*. London: Eyre and Spottiswoode

Turner, G., 1969. *Business in Britain*. London: Eyre and Spottiswoode

Twigger, T., 1978. 'The managerial career', *Management Today* (December), 55–7: 114

Union des Industries Métallurgiques et Minières 1970. *Ingénieurs et Cadres*. Paris

Useem, M., 1984. *The Inner Circle*. New York: Oxford University Press

Useem, M. and A. McCormack, 1981. 'The dominant segment of the British Business elite', *Sociology*, 15 (3): 381–406

Utton, M., 1970. *Industrial Concentration*. Harmondsworth: Penguin Books

van den Berg, J., 1969. 'Can Europe close the "Management Gap"?', *McKinsey Quarterly*, Fall: 24–34

van der Merwe, S. and A., 1980. 'The man who manages multinationals: a comparative study of the profiles, backgrounds, and attitudes of Chief Executives of American, European and Japanese MNCs', in A. Negandhi, ed., *The Functioning of the Multinational Corporation: a Global Comparative Study*, pp. 209–24. New York: Pergamon

Vernon, R., ed., 1974. *Big Business and the State*. London: Macmillan

Veyret, G., 1968. 'La France cherche ses business schools', *L'Expansion* (April): 113–16

Vogüé, R. de, 1974. *Alerte aux patrons: il faut changer l'entreprise*. Paris: Grasset

Ward, L. and A. Athos, 1972. *Student Expectations of Corporate Life*. Boston: Harvard Graduate School of Business Administration, Division of Research

Watling, T., 1970. *Plan for Promotion: Advancement and the Manager*. London: Business Books

Weinshall, T., ed., 1977. *Culture and Management*. Harmondsworth: Pengiun Books

Weiss, H., 1974. 'Why business and government exchange executives', *Harvard Business Review*, 52 (4): 129–40

Whitley, R., 1974. 'The city and industry: the directors of large companies, their characteristics and connections', in P. Stanworth and A. Giddens, eds., *Elites and Power in British Society*. London: Cambridge University Press

Whitley, R.D., 1973. 'Commonalities and connections among directors of large financial institutions', *Sociological Review*, 21: 613–32

Whitley, R., A. Thomas and J. Marceau, 1981. *Masters of Business?* London: Tavistock

Willig, J-C., 1970a. 'La nouvelle mafia', *L'Expansion*, October: 116–18
1970b. 'Organisation man or entrepreneur? Europe's business school managers', *European Business*, 27: 21–30

Xardel, D., 1978. *Les Managers*. Paris: Grasset

Zapf, W., 1965a. *Beitrage zur Analyse der Deutschen Oberschicht*. Munich: Piper
1965b. *Wandlungen der Deutschen Elite*. Munich: Piper

Zehnder, E., 1975a. *The INSEAD Graduate in Europe*. London: Egon Zehnder International

1975b. *Survey of Business School Graduates in Europe.* London: Egon Zehnder International

Zeitlin, M., 1974. 'Corporate ownership and control: the large corporation and the capitalist class', *American Journal of Sociology,* 79: 1073–119

1980. *Classes, Class Conflict and the State: Empirical Studies in class analysis.* Cambridge, Mass.: Winthrop

Index